INTERNATIONAL GUIDE TO MUSIC FESTIVALS

EDITED BY DOUGLAS SMITH & NANCY BARTON
FOREWORD BY SIR RUDOLF BING

In Great Britain: Book Sales Ltd., 78 Newman Street,
London W1P 3LA.
In Canada: Gage Trade Publishing, P.O. Box 5000,
164 Commander Blvd., Agincourt, Ontatio M1S 3C7.
In Japan: Music Sales Corp./Quick Fox, 2-13-19
Akasaka, Tamondo Bldg., Minato-ku, Tokyo 107.

Book and cover design: Barry L. S. Mirenburg
Cover illustration: Sanford Hoffman

CONTENTS

FOREWORD

There are so many festivals nowadays. Everyone tries to be different from the other. A guide telling the public what to hear and see is a most valuable help to festival visitors.

How would one characterize a festival? Having been deeply involved with two of the most successful festivals of Europe—Glyndebourne and Edinburgh—I have, of course, my own ideas. First of all, the location of the festival site sets the tone. The location must be beautiful. No money on earth would turn Liverpool or Manchester into a festival city; nobody could possibly enjoy strolling between performances through the streets. The beauty of Edinburgh and Salzberg, on the other hand, puts everybody in a festival mood.

Glyndebourne is a special case. It is right in the middle of the Sussex Downs and is really a country place. Also, it has only one building and is, therefore, limited in its scope.

When I thought up the idea of a festival in Edinburgh, I knew that in addition to its old-world charm and beauty, the city had four excellent theatrical facilities. So on one evening we could perform opera in the King's Theatre, drama in the Lyceum, concerts in Usher Hall, and chamber music in a nice smaller hall. That is an almost unique situation. Other festivals may have to confine themselves to one art form if they have only one theater.

Usually one finds festival performances are on a much higher level than the average performance in a regular season. There are many reasons for that. Any festival manager will engage the artists—be they singers, dancers, actors, or musicians—for a good length of time before the opening, and during this time, the artists will work and concentrate on one work only. Also, just like the visitors, the artists will enjoy the beauty of their location during their spare time and the spirit of the festival will stimulate them to greater efforts. I cannot emphasize enough that it is the "spirit" that builds a festival. The same artists may perform the same part in Salzberg better than in

New York. They are less harassed, less driven from one part to another, and they face an audience that is equally relaxed.

Glyndebourne was originally built for Mozart operas. Mr. John Christie, who planned and built Glyndebourne, was—more than anything else—a Mozart lover. He also loved pugs and always had one with him. I remember one evening we went for a short walk outside Glyndebourne and met some soldiers along the way. Christie stopped them and pointed to Glyndebourne, saying: "This is Mozart's home." He then pointed to the dog and stated: "This is Mozart's dog." The soldiers greeted the dog politely, though they appeared a little bewildered.

However, in later years—long after my time—the repertoire changed somewhat and one year even a contemporary opera was introduced. During intermission, Mr. Christie, with a few guests, strolled on the lawn. He asked if they saw the cows in the distance. When his guests said indeed they did, Christie retorted: "Whenever we play Mozart they are always right here."

Obviously running a festival differs from running a regular season. For nothing helps art more than relaxed concentration.

I have to confess I know very little about festivals in the United States. When the Metropolitan Opera season in New York ended, I usually went on tour with the company. By the time the tour ended, I really had had enough of music for awhile. My wife and I would go to Europe to relax. Oh, we may have dropped in for a short stay at Glyndebourne or Edinburgh. But these two festivals were so closely associated with me that in effect it was like coming home.

The International Guide to Music Festivals serves an important purpose for anyone who truly cares for the performing arts and who also needs a well-deserved rest. I for one will keep a copy at hand. There are the many distinguished American festivals I have yet to visit and enjoy.
—Sir Rudolf Bing

ACKNOWLEDGMENTS

In addition to the many festivals around the world which supplied detailed information, a few individuals have made special contributions and we thank them for their assistance; Peter Arnold, Sir Rudolph Bing, Richard Boehm, Michael Bristol, Wendy Caplin, Jim Charlton, Ruth Flaxman, Barbara Hoffman, Mary Larsen, Jeanette Mall, Kim Dramer-Pannell, Eugene Weintraub, Veronica Windholz.

We especially want to acknowledge the cooperation over the years of the Philadelphia Folk Festival. By far one of the largest and most organized festivals, it still manages to maintain the casual and friendly spirit of the folks who perform there annually.

INTRODUCTION

The International Guide to Music Festivals is the most complete and informative book of its kind and the first that we know of to include all the important festivals in the United States and the rest of the world. We have reviewed every major jazz, classical, folk, country and bluegrass festival, as well as a great number of interesting lesser-known ones. Many people helped us with this effort, including researchers, performers, festival directors, and music lovers.

To make this guide as easy to use as possible, we've organized the book into two major sections: (1) the United States and Canada, and (2) International, which contains all the other countries hosting festivals. Within each of these two major divisions, all the festivals are divided into the four categories of classical, jazz, folk (including bluegrass and country), and miscellaneous (covering festivals outside the above categories or offering more than one of the above kinds of music). Within each category of music, all the festivals are listed alphabetically by states or by countries. If you are interested in jazz, for example, and planning a trip to France, Germany, and Spain, you would turn to the latter part of the book for the International section, then within that section, to jazz. You would then look up France, Germany, and Spain, and find all the jazz festivals listed under the name of the country. The index lists all festivals in the book in alphabetical order.

We've also included a currency conversion table, which you can use as a general guide to ticket prices in dollars. Since the dollar fluctuates against foreign currencies, check your newspaper for up-to-the-minute rates.

We have visited as many of the festivals as we could and have tried to include as much useful information as possible. This includes information about camping and recreational vehicle facilities and motel/hotel accommodations, time of year, ticket information, people who have performed at the festival in the past, whether there are other events or attractions of interest in the area. Addresses and phone numbers are included, and it is very important that you call or write before planning your trip. Even though the book is as up-to-date as possible, we found a number of changes in time of year, price, and performers. We tried to exclude any fly-by-night or transient festivals, but even so we found, in several cases, that festivals had been canceled. So, once again, please contact the festival before making definite plans.

One last note: The International Guide to Music Festivals will be updated and revised on a regular basis and we would love to have your help. Please let us know how you like the book. Did we miss any of your favorite festivals and did you enjoy the ones you attended? How were the accommodations? The location? Were there any problems? Please let us know; it will help make the next edition an even better and more valuable book. If we use any of your tips we will send you a copy of the next edition for your efforts. Just write: Editors, International Guide to Music Festivals, Quick Fox, 33 West 60th Street, New York, NY 10023.

Douglas Smith and Nancy Barton
New York City, May 1980

UNITED STATES AND CANADA

CLASSICAL

ALASKA

Sitka Summer Music Festival

P.O. Box 907, Sitka, Alaska 99835
Classical (chamber)
June
Chamber music of the finest quality is
presented on Tuesdays and Fridays.
Artists such as Gregor Piatigorsky,
Nathanial Rosen, Jerome Lowenthal, and
many others too numerous to list per-
form at the Festival.
Concerts are held in the Centennial
Building whose hall seats 500. Patrons
should come to Sitka prepared for the
possibility of foul weather.
Directors: James Atchison, Festival
Director; Paul Rosenthal, Music Director
Sponsors: Sitka Concert Association,
Sitka Community College, and Sheldon
Jackson College.
Accommodations/other items of interest
in area: Hotel-motel accommodations
are available near the Centennial Building, as are restaurants, shopping and entertainment. For information on camping, write to the forest service.
Sitka is renowned for its scenic beauty,
and has the unique flavor of three cul-
tures: Tlingit Indian, Russian, and
American.
Ticket information: Single concerts are
$5; a season ticket is $30.

ARIZONA

Flagstaff Festival of the Arts

211 N. Leroux, BNA Plaza, Flagstaff,
Ariz. (P.O. Box 1607)
Classical, dance, theater
Late June through early August
This 7-week summer festival is the
most comprehensive summer arts
program in the Southwest. It presents
classical symphonic concerts, other
classical music, dance, theater, film
classics and visual arts. First-rate guest
conductors and artists are among the
performers.
Concerts are held in Ardreu Auditorium
which seats 1,503, Creative Arts Theater
which seats 357, and University Auditorium seating 900. Patrons should be
advised that August is the rainy season,
and afternoon rains are to be expected.
Director: John Cunningham
Accommodations/other items of interest
in area: For information on motel and
hotel accommodations, restaurants,
camping and other facilities and attractions in and around Flagstaff write to
Flagstaff Chamber of Commerce, 101 W.
Sante Fe (on US-66) Flagstaff Ariz.
86001.
Flagstaff is 7,000 feet high amid the
world's largest Ponderosa pine forest in
the Coconino National Forest. It is 26
miles Northwest of Oak Creek Canyon
and 78 miles South of the Grand Canyon.
Ticket information: Admission ranges
from $5 to $7.
How to get there: The Festival is on the
campus of Northern Arizona University.

ARKANSAS

Inspiration Point Fine Arts Colony
Route 2, Box 348 AA
Eureka Springs, Ark. 72632
Opera and dance
Late July
This fine arts camp ends its summer
season with performances of opera and
dance during 10 evenings, as well as on
Sunday afternoons, in late July.
Performances are by students and take
place in a covered outdoor amphithea-
ter that seats approximately 100.
Executive Director: Jean Trusty
Sponsor: Federation of Music Clubs in
Arkansas, Illinois, Kansas, Missouri, and
Oklahoma
Accommodations: Crescent Hotel and
Inn of the Ozarks provide accommoda-
tions in Eureka Springs. Many picnick-
ing spots are located nearby.
Ticket information: Tickets are $2
How to get there: The Colony is located
6 miles W. of Eureka Springs on U.S. 62

CALIFORNIA

Beethoven Festival
San Francisco Symphony, 107 War
Memorial Veterans Building, San
Francisco, Calif. 94102
Classical
End of May through mid-June
Concerts with full symphony orchestra
and chamber music concerts. The opera
house seats 3,252; Herbst Theatre seats
900.
Directors: Edo de Waart, Music Director;
Peter Pastreich, Executive Director
Ticket information: For tickets write to
San Francisco Symphony Box Office,
Opera House, San Francisco, Calif. 94102

Cabrillo Music Festival
6500 Soquel Drive, Aptos, Calif. 95003
Classical and avant garde
Last weekend in August and Labor Day
weekend
Unfamiliar works of the master composers are performed along with contemporary music at this festival, by the
Cabrillo Festival Orchestra, founded in
1963, resulting in such juxtapositions as
the performance of Beethoven's works
in the same year that avant-garde composer John Cage was in residence. Other
featured artists who have appeared for
the Festival's 2 weekends of performances
include Aaron Copland, Lou Harrison,
Keith Jarrett, Paul Sperry, N.Y. Saxo-
phone Quartet, and the San Francisco
Trio.
Performances take place at the 540-seat
Cabrillo College Theatre, at Mission
San Juan Bautista, and at other locations
in Santa Cruz County.
Director: Dennis Russell Davies
Sponsor: Cabrillo Guild of Music
Accommodations: Reservations are
recommended for Santa Cruz-area motels
during the summer season
Ticket information: Ticket prices range
from $4 to $7 per concert
How to get there: Aptos is S. of Santa
Cruz on Highway 1

California Music Center Festival
College of Notre Dame, Belmont, Calif.
Classical
Late June to early August
The Festival provides a weekly concert
series for 6 weeks by artists-in-residence

as well as a summer study session in chamber music for high school and college students. One feature is presentation of works by composer-in-residence Meyer Kupferman. Daniel Kobialka, violin; Marc Gottlieb, violin; Irving Klein, cello; and Lambert Orkin, piano, are some who have performed since the Festival's inception in 1972.
Concerts take place in a covered concert hall (seating capacity 600) at the College of Notre Dame.
Director: Irving Klein
Sponsor: California Music Center
Accommodations: Holiday Inn on Ralston Ave. in Belmont can provide accommodation. No camping available.
Ticket information: Tickets for adults cost $5; their cost for students and senior citizens is $2.
How to get there: Belmont is 24 miles S. of San Francisco

Carmel Classic Guitar Festival
P.O. Box 7437, Carmel, Calif. 93921
Classical
First weekend in November
The Festival was organized in 1974 by guitar performers and educators to promote and develop the classical guitar as an important means of artistic expression. It is the first major event of its kind to take place in the United States and provides an annual meeting ground for the guitarist, composer, luthier, music scholar, student, and interested listener. Besides concerts and recitals, there are special events such as a competition for guitarists ($1,750 in awards), a guitar giveaway, a luthier (guitar craftsman) exhibition, an antique instrument display, lectures, and a composer's showcase.
Performances are in the Main Hall of the Sunset Cultural Center in Carmel which seats 850. There are also recital rooms and exhibit halls.
Director: Guy Horn
Accommodations/other items of interest in area: Accommodation in Carmel is available at La Plaza Hotel, Pine Inn Hotel, and Jade Tree Inn. Camping is available at a nearby beach. Trailer parks are located 6 or 7 miles from Carmel. The Big Sur area is a nearby scenic attraction.
Ticket information: Ticket prices range from $6 to $35 (for the entire 3-day series).
How to get there: The Festival site at the

Sunset Cultural Center is on Main St. in Carmel

Hollywood Bowl Summer Festival
P.O. Box 1951, Hollywood, Calif. 90028
Classical
Early July through mid-September
For over 50 years Hollywood Bowl has been the summer home of the Los Angeles Philharmonic. About 50 concerts are presented over the summer, with renowned guest artists and conductors. There are some pop and jazz programs in addition to the fine classical concerts.
The Bowl is essentially a park. Contained within its 116-acre grounds are numerous shady picnic spots, fountains, several performing areas, and a statue of Euterpe, the Muse of Music.
Director: Ernest Fleischmann
Sponsor: Los Angeles Philharmonic Assn.
Accommodations/other items of interest in area: Lodging is readily available in Hollywood and L.A. There is no camping. Of interest in the area are Disneyland, the Zoo, Planetarium, and many museums, theme parks, theaters, and beaches.
Ticket information: Admission ranges from $1 to $16.50. Tickets can be obtained from the Los Angeles Philharmonic Assn., 135 N. Grand Ave., Los Angeles, Calif. 90012.

Music Academy of the West
1070 Fairway Road, Santa Barbara, Calif. 93108
Classical
July through August
The Music Academy of the West trains professionally oriented students for positions with leading musical groups, the concert stage, and so forth. Now in its 33rd season, the summer series features 8 events—recitals, concerts, and the festival opera. Performers in past seasons have included Jerome Lowenthal, Reginald Stewart, Zvi Zeitlin, Gabor Rejto, Milton Thomas, and Judith Blegan. All events take place indoors.
Director: Maurice Abravanel
Accommodations: There are numerous hotels and motels in Santa Barbara
Ticket information: Tickets range from $7 to $11. For ticket information, write to Lobero Box Office, 33 E. Canon Perdido, Santa Barbara, Calif. 93101. tel. (805)963-0761.

Music at the Vineyards

Paul Masson Mountain Winery, Pierce Road, Saratoga, Calif.
Classical
June through August
Music at the Vineyards is a popular classical music series held outdoors during summer weekends at the historic Paul Masson Winery in the hills above Saratoga for audiences of up to 1,000. For over 20 years the concert series has stressed masterworks and compositions of musical worth outside of what is called "the standard repertory." The musical fare ranges from the baroque through the classical, and the romantic through the modern—tastefully chosen music and expert artists in the gracious ambience of the hilltop winery. Said Ralph Waldo Emerson, "Music and wine are one."
Director: Sandor Salgo
Sponsor: Paul Masson Vineyards
Accommodations: For information on lodging in the area, tickets, and directions to the Winery, write to Music at the Vineyards, P.O. Box 97, Saratoga, Calif. 95070
There is no camping or picnicking at the Vineyards.
Ticket information: Admission is about $6, only in advance

Ojai Music Festival

P.O. Box 185, Ojai, Calif. 93203
Classical and jazz
Mid-May to early June
Ojai's 3-day festival has been called "a little jewel in a lush nest." Since its start in 1947 the Festival has presented a repertoire ranging from 13th century works to avant-garde, with emphasis on rare works, works by great composers of the past, and new music, often premiered at the Festival. A great many distinguished artists and well-known orchestras and chamber groups have performed.
The 5 or 6 concerts are held outdoors in a tree-shaded bowl with seating for 1,000. Guests are advised to bring warm wraps for evening concerts.
Director: William Malloch
Accommodations: For information on lodging write to the Festival at the above address
Ticket information: Tickets range from $3 to $9.50
How to get there: Take Route 101 to Ventura, then Route 33 to Ojai

Redlands Bowl Summer Music Festival

P.O. Box 466, Redlands, Calif. 92373
Classical, semi-classical, opera, light opera, ballet
July through August
The Redlands Bowl Summer Music Festival presents free concerts every Tuesday and Friday evening. The balanced programs included classical and semi-classical concerts by the Redlands Bowl Symphony Orchestra, ballet and folk dancing, opera and light opera, and concerts by instrumental and vocal soloists and groups. Established in 1924, the Festival prides itself on offering fine music at no admission charge. The Festival is completely supported by donations. "Music for the People . . . Fully Supported by the People" is its motto.
Director: Conant K. Halsey
Sponsor: Community Music Association, Inc.
Ticket information: All concerts are free
How to get there: To reach Redlands Bowl, take Redlands Freeway to Orange Street (Downtown turnoff), then go S. on Eureka St.

San Diego Opera Verdi Festival

San Diego Opera, P.O. Box 988, San Diego, Calif. 92112
Classical
June to July
The San Diego Opera Verdi Festival was inaugurated in 1978 with the purpose of establishing a learning and performing center where "innovative ways of producing Verdi's works could be explored." The Festival provides seminars for young composers, singers and conductors. A goal of the Festival is to present in its first decade Verdi's entire body of operatic work. Participants have included Martina Arroyo, Carlo Bergonzi, Cristina Deutekom, Paul Pliskha, and Pablo Elvira.
Director: Tito Capobianco
Other items of interest in area: Of special interest is the Old Globe Shakespeare Festival which runs concurrently with the Verdi Festival, in Balboa Park
Ticket information: Tickets cost from $7.50 to $21.50. They can be obtained by mail, or telephone (714)232-7636.

San Luis Obispo Mozart Festival
P.O. Box 311, San Luis Obispo, Calif.
93406
Classical
First week in August
Since it began in 1971 with 3 concerts, this festival has grown to include 14, with emphasis on Mozart along with classical music from many composers and periods. In addition to performances by the Festival Orchestra, the Festival Singers and featured guests like the Pocket Opera, the Puppet Opera, and the Lumière String Quartet may appear. Concerts take place in the Cal Poly Theatre (seats 500) and at two historic missions, Mission San Luis Obispo (600) and Mission San Miguel (300).
Director: Clifton Swanson
Sponsors: City of San Luis Obispo and private individuals
Other items of interest in area: Hearst Castle, 40 miles to the N., is one of the attractions in the area.
Ticket information: Tickets cost from $4 to $10.

CANADA

Festival Ottawa
P.O. Box 1534, Station "B," Ottawa, Ontario, Canada
Chamber music and opera
July
Festival Ottawa presents operatic performances of world-class standard, equally distinguished concerts of chamber and orchestral music, and exhibitions of both Canadian and international art. Every summer, guest artists and groups from around the world perform at the Festival. The 46-member National Arts Centre Orchestra is led by Mario Bernardi. The National Arts Centre, located on a 6½-acre site in downtown Ottawa, was completed in 1969. It is largely underground with hexagonal components rising through multi-level terraces and promenades.
Performances are in the 4-tiered Opera House which seats 2,300 and the Theatre which seats 808.
Director: Mario Bernardi
Sponsor: The National Arts Centre
Accommodations: Hotel and motel accommodations are available in and around Ottawa
Ticket information: Opera tickets range from $6.50 to $17.50; tickets for the chamber music concerts are from $4.75 to $7.25. They can be obtained by writing to Box Office, National Arts Centre (at the above address). Patrons are advised to write early, as many concerts are sold out.

Guelph Spring Festival
Box 1718, Guelph, Ontario, Canada
N1H 6Z9
Classical and opera
Two weeks in early May
This festival begun in the late 1960s was founded in memory of Edward Johnson, Guelph-born tenor who became General Manager of the Metropolitan Opera in New York City. Canadian choirs, ensembles, and soloists perform operatic and classical pieces. Additional events include art exhibits and a bagpipe competition.
Performances take place in several halls and churches in Guelph with capacities ranging from 700 to 850.
Director: Nicholas Goldschmidt

Sponsor: Edward Johnson Music Foundation
Accommodations: There are many hotels and motels in Guelph
Ticket information: Tickets range from $3 to $10
How to get there: Guelph is 60 miles W. of Toronto in southern Ontario

Victoria International Festival
3737 Oak Street, Vancouver, B.C. V6H 2M4
Classical and opera
July through August
Victoria International Festival offers over 25 mid-summer concerts of great music performed by world-renowned soloists and ensembles. The program emphasizes great classical composers, keyboard works, and Canadian contemporary music. Concerts are held at two locations: McPherson Playhouse and St. Michaels University School. The Festival began over 8 years ago with the Shawnigan Summer School of the Arts, and grew to become an independent entity.
Director: J.J. Johanneson
Sponsor: Shawnigan Summer School of the Arts
Accommodations/other items of interest in area: Lodging is available in Victoria, and camping is allowed in appropriate areas outside the city.
Victoria is a city geared to tourists; there are many sights to see.
Ticket information: Admission ranges from $3.50 to $5. Write to the Festival office at the address above, or, in Victoria, contact the McPherson Playhouse box office.

COLORADO

Central City Opera Festival
Central City Opera House
Central City, Colo.
Opera and other
July through August
Opera high in the Rockies! Central City is an old mining town whose festival includes 7 weeks of opera and 1 week each of theater, dance, and jazz. There are 22 performances of 3 different operas, and 55 performances of 1-act operas, opera scenes, and Victorian salon recitals; also, 2 apprentice productions.
Many renowned opera singers have performed in Central City Opera House, an 1878 restored Victorian structure which seats 800. Other events are held at Williams Stables and Teller House Bar.
Directors: Peter M. Kellogg, Managing Director; Robert Edward Darling, Artistic Director
Sponsor: Central City Opera House Association
Accommodations/other items of interest in area: Hotel accommodations are available at Chain O'Mines Hotel, corner Eureka and Main Sts., Central City; Gold Dust Inn, Highway 119, 2 miles before Blackhawk; or in Idaho Springs and Denver. Camping facilities are located 2 miles from Central City at Columbine Camp; there is a $2 charge. There are picnicking areas near Central City.
Central City, 9,000 feet above sea level in the Colorado Rockies, is a restored mid-Victorian mining camp.
Ticket information: Ticket prices are about $11 to $14; write to Central City Opera House Association, Suite 636, 910 16th St., Denver, Colo. 80202
How to get there: Central City is a 40-mile drive on an excellent highway from Denver. Take Highway 6 going W. to the turnoff on 119.

Colorado Opera Festival
711 North Cascade Ave., Colorado Springs, Colo. 80903
Opera
Late June through early August
Established in 1971 as a resident professional company, the Colorado Opera Festival has produced more than 26 fully-staged, inventive new productions of important and sometimes rarely per-

formed works. Repertoire has included the world premiere revival of Traetta's *Il Cavaliere Errante,* the Western states premiere of the original version of Mussorgsky's *Boris Godunov,* and the American stage premiere of Handel's *Xeres,* presented in a commissioned English translation. The Festival has provided opportunites to explore the full range of operatic literature, from Mozart to Britten, with, among others, new productions of *Don Giovanni, Otello, The Tales of Hoffman, Carmen, Aida, The Love for Three Oranges,* and *The Turn of the Screw.* The Festival draws much of its vocal, orchestral, and production staff from the resources of the Colorado area. Guest vocal artists, designers, and directors join the Festival from opera houses throughout the country. Performances are held in Armstrong Theater, which seats 800.

Director: Donald P. Jenkins

Accommodations/other items of interest in area: A list of accommodations is available from the Chamber of Commerce, P.O. Drawer B, Colorado Springs, Colo. 80901. Of additional interest is the summer series of performing arts at Colorado College. Nearby are Monument Valley Park, the Fine Arts Center, and the Cheyenne Mountain Zoo.

Ticket information: Tickets range from $7.50 to $17. For information, call (303)473-0073

Colorado Philharmonic Orchestra

P.O. Box 975, Evergreen, Colo. 80439

Classical

Late June to mid-August

The Colorado Philharmonic is a national repertoire orchestra made up of 74 young musicians selected from over 900 who competed in nationwide auditions. Its summer season is comprised of 23 concerts—7 on Wednesday evenings, 9 on Friday evenings, and 7 on Sunday afternoons. The Central City Singers and the Evergreen Chorale also participate in some of these performances.

All performances take place in the Evergreen Junior High School (seating capacity 500).

Director: Carl Topilow

Sponsors: Various foundations, corporations, and levels of government

Accommodations: Bauer's Spruce Island Chalets, Davidson Lodge, Highland Haven, and Sunny Brook Lodge—all in Evergreen—can provide accommodations. Camping and picnicking is available in nearby parks.

Ticket information: Tickets are $4 for adults, $2 for students and senior citizens.

How to get there: Take I-70 to El Rancho exit, then take Highway 74 through Bergen Park to Evergreen.

CONNECTICUT

Music Mountain

Falls Village, Conn. 06031
Classical
End of June through the end of August
Music Mountain, founded by Jacques
Gordon in 1929, celebrated its 50th
anniversary season in 1979 as the oldest
continuous summer chamber music
series in the U.S.
Director: Urico Rossi, Music Director
Ticket information: Tickets are $5; $2
for students and children. Available at
the box office or by mail in advance.
Telephone reservations at (203)482-
8505.

DISTRICT OF COLUMBIA

American Music Festival

National Gallery of Art, 6th St. & Con-
stitution Ave., N.W., Washington, D.C.
20565
Classical
April and May
The Festival provides performances of
classical music by American composers
on 8 Sunday evenings in the spring. The
National Gallery Orchestra- plus many
artists since the Festival's inception in
1944–each year performs in the indoor
East Garden Court (450 seats) at the
National Gallery of Art
Director: Richard Bales
Sponsor: F. Lammot Belin Concerts
Ticket information: Free
How to get there: The Festival is within
walking distance of the U.S. Capitol

Pan American Week

Technical Unit on Music, Organization
of American States, Washington, D.C.
20006
Classical
April
A series of classical concerts featuring
artists from North and South American
nations is sponsored by the Organization
of American States during Pan American
Week in April. These concerts are held
in the Hall of the Americas on 17th and
Constitution Avenues in Washington,
D.C.
The hall seats 800.
Director: Efrain Paesky
Sponsor: Organization of American
States
Accommodations: Lodging is readily
available in Washington, D.C.
Ticket information: Admission is free.
Invitations are required, and are avail-
able on request by mail.

FLORIDA

The Bach Festival of Winter Park
P.O. Box 2731, Rollins College, Winter
Park, Fla. 32789
Classical
Late February
Four concerts of works by Bach, oc-
casionally interspersed with music of
another great composer, such as Handel,
Palestrina or Vivaldi, are performed
from morning to evening on the 2 days of
this festival. The program also includes a
lecture. The Bach Festival has presented
fine music at its winter festival since it
began in 1935.
Concerts are held in Knowles Memorial
Chapel, which seats about 600.
Director: Dr. Ward Woodbury, Music
Director and Conductor
Sponsor: Mr. John Tiedtke, President,
Bach Festival Society
Accommodations/other items of interest
in area: Lodging is available at Langford
Resort Hotel, E. New England Ave., and
Park Plaza, 307 Park Ave. S.,Winter Park,
Fla. 32789. There is no camping.
Of interest in the area are Disney World
and Sea World.
Ticket information: A ticket to all 5
events (4 concerts and 1 lecture) is $20.
Admission to each individual event is
$6. The tickets are sold only the week
before the Festival. Reservations for $20
tickets are taken by the Bach Festival
Secretary at the address above.
How to get there: The concerts are at
Knowles Memorial Chapel on the campus
of Rollins College, Winter Park.

New College Music Festival
5700 N. Tamiami Trail, Sarasota, Fla.
33580
Chamber music
Three weeks beginning in early June
The first New College Music Festival
was held for 1 week in July 1965. By
1967 it had grown to its present length
of 3 weeks. Major concerts are performed on weekends; during the week
student participants take classes in
instruments and breathing techniques
and study under faculty artists in chamber ensembles.
The 6 major concerts take place in Van
Wexel Performing Arts Hall (seating
capacity 1,776). About 10 student concerts are performed on the New College
campus.
Director: Dr. Arthur T. Borden, Jr.
Accommodations/other items of interest
in area: There are many motels on N.
Tamiami Trail including the Allamonda,
Bay Breeze, Holt, Imperial, and Royal
motels. Camping is available within easy
driving distance at Myakka River and
Oscar Scherer state parks.
Nearby are beautiful sand beaches on the
Gulf of Mexico.
Ticket information: For major concerts,
tickets are $25 for series of 6 concerts,
$5 each concert. Student concerts are
free.
How to get there: Festival site is on
west side of U.S. 41 through Sarasota,
across from Sarasota-Bradenton airport

HAWAII

InterArts Hawaii
c/o UH Foundation, Hawaii Hall 6,
2500 Campus Road, Honolulu, Hawaii
96822
Classical, contemporary, dance, ethnic,
theater
June through August
This summer-long festival, aptly named
InterArts Hawaii, presents dance, drama,
contemporary, classical and national
music, literature events, films, art exhibits, and many lectures and workshops
by guest artists. The emphasis is contemporary, with the attendance of
such notables as John Cage, Speculum
Musicae, and Ensemble Nipponia, who
play contemporary Japanese music on
traditional Japanese instruments. Symphony Canada and others add a classical
dimension.
Concerts are held indoors at Kennedy
Theater, which seats 634, and at several
smaller auditoriums and theaters. Outdoor concerts are held at Andrews
Amphitheatre, which can accommodate
over 1,000, and the music department
courtyard is used for Gamelan concerts.
An umbrella is recommended in case
of "liquid sunshine."
Director: Marian Kerr
Sponsors: Univ. of Hawaii, Summer
Session; Univ. of Hawaii Foundation;
Hawaii Commission on Culture and the
Arts; and others.
Accommodations/other items of interest
in area: For information on lodging
and camping write to Hawaii Visitors
Bureau, 2270 Kalakaua Avenue, Honolulu, Hawaii 96822.
The Festival is 10 minutes from downtown Honolulu, 1 mile from Waikiki.
Manoa Valley and Paradise Park are
nearby.
Ticket information:Admission is about
$5. Some events are free. For tickets
write to Kennedy Theater Box Office,
1770 East-West Road, Honolulu, Hawaii
96822.
How to get there: From Waikiki take
McCully Street toward the mountains.
Turn right on Wilder Ave. after crossing
the freeway. Wilder borders one edge
of the Manoa campus (but name changes
to Dole Street).

ILLINOIS

Ravinia Festival
Ravinia Park, Highland Park, Ill. 60035
Classical and dance
Late June through mid-September
In 1979 the Ravinia Festival celebrated
its 44th anniversary. This event extends
over a 12-week period in the summer
each year, devoting the first 8 weeks to
music and the last 4 to dance. Although
the musical emphasis here is on classical
and opera, the festival also offers "special
concerts" of pop, jazz, and folk. Past
performers have included the Chicago
Symphony Orchestra, Leontyne Price,
Giuseppe Giacomini, Jean-Pierre Rampal, Misha Dichter, and the Joffrey
Ballet.
Programs are held outdoors; there is a
covered pavilion with a seating capacity
of 3,500 and an enclosed theater with
950 seats. In addition, there is unlimited
lawn space.
Director: Edward Gordon
Sponsor: Ravinia Festival Association
Accommodations: For information about
accommodations in the area, write to
Highland Park Chamber of Commerce,
Highland Park, Ill. 60035
Ticket information: Tickets range in
price from $1 to $16 depending on the
type of program, and they may be
ordered by mail after May 1 by writing
to Box 896, Highland Park, Ill. 60035
How to get there: Ravinia Park is
located 22 miles N. of Chicago, on
Edens Expressway

VIOLINIST ITZHAK PERLMAN REHEARSES WITH STUDENTS AT THE ASPEN MUSIC FESTIVAL (PHOTO PREVIOUS PAGE)

INDIANA

The Pendleton Festival "Summerfest"
421 E. State St., Pendleton, Ind. 46064
Classical, opera, ballet, theater
June through July
The Pendleton Festival Symphony had
its debut in 1976 with its founder George
Daugherty, then age 20, conducting
Metropolitan Opera soprano Roberta
Peters in operatic scenes. Maestro Daugherty continues to conduct first-rate artists
in such works as *La Boheme, Die Fledermaus* and *The Merry Widow* for the summer festival. Orchestral works, ballet and
theater are also part of the festival, as
well as free park concerts and chamber
music performances.
Concerts are held in the Paramount
Theater, which seats 1,600, Pendleton
First United Methodist Church, seating
500, and at Pendleton Falls Park, in the
open air.
Director: George Daugherty, Jr.
Accommodations/other items of interest
in area: Accommodations are available
at Holiday Inn and Sheraton Inn in
Anderson, Indiana, at the junction of
I-69 and Ind. 109. There are camping
facilities at Pearl Lake, Pendleton, Ind.
46064. Picnicking is allowed in Falls
Park, Pendleton.
The small town of Pendleton (population 2,500) is 35 miles from Indianapolis. Pendleton Falls Park is the setting
for Jessamyn West's historical novel,
The Massacre at Fall Creek.
Ticket information: Admission ranges
from $2 to $35. Write to the Festival
or buy tickets at the door.
How to get there: Pendleton is at the
junction of I-69 and Ind. State Road 38

KANSAS

Messiah Festival
Bethany College, Lindsborg, Kans.
67456
Classical and religious
From Palm Sunday through Easter
With its inauguration in 1882, this is the
oldest festival of its kind in the United
States. It revolves around two performances of Handel's *Messiah* on the two
Sunday afternoons, and on Good Friday
evening, the rendition of Bach's oratorio,
the *St. Matthew Passion,* which has been
performed here annually since 1929. The
Festival also includes a week of concerts
and recitals. The Midwest Art Exhibition
runs simultaneously.
Performances take place in Presser Auditorium (1,900 capacity) on the campus
of Bethany College.
Director: Dr. Elmer Copley
Sponsor: Bethany College
Accommodations/other items of interest
in area: Accommodations may be obtained
at the Viking Motel in Lindsborg or at
one of the major chains in Salina, 20
miles north. Camping is available with
hookups for a nominal fee. Trailers welcome.
The Eisenhower Museum in Abilene and
the Indian Burial Ground are additional
points of interest in the area.
Ticket information: Reserved seat tickets for the Handel and Bach oratorios
range from $3 to $9. For tickets, write
to Messiah Ticket Office, Bethany College, Lindsborg, Kans. 67456
How to get there: Lindsborg is 20 miles
S. of I-70, on I-35W

LOUISIANA

L.S.U. Festival of Contemporary Music
School of Music
Louisiana State University
Baton Rouge, La. 70803
20th-century music
February
Founded in 1944 by L.S.U. Professor
Helen Gunderson, the Festival includes
lectures as well as concerts.
Director: Dr. Dinos Constantinides
Ticket information: Admission is free

MAINE

Bowdoin College Summer Music Festival
Bowdoin College, Brunswick, Me. 04011
Classical
Mid-June through July
The Bowdoin College Summer Music
Festival is a weekly series of chamber
music concerts given on the campus by
the Aeolian Chamber Players, assisted
by noted guest artists. Since 1964, the
Aeolians have been the resident ensemble at the Summer Music Festival, where
they teach, hold master classes, and perform in the context of Bowdoin Summer
Music School. The Aeolians have been
presenting works for strings, winds,
and piano since 1961 and are well-known
for their recordings and performances
of contemporary works. Approximately
100 pieces have been written for the
group, including works by many of the
world's greatest living composers. Concerts are held in Kresge Auditorium on
the Bowdoin College campus (capacity
350) and in the First Parish Congrega-
tional Church in Brunswick (capacity 600)
Director: Robert Beckwith
Sponsor: Bowdoin College
Accommodations/other items of interest
in area: Motels in the area include the
Stowe House, the Holiday Inn, Maine-
line Motel, New Meadows Motel and
Inn, Star-Light Motel, and Siesta Motel.
There are camping facilities in the Brunswick area.
The coastal region of Maine, with boating, beaches, and so forth, is nearby.
Ticket information: Admission is $5 per
concert, $20 for series tickets.

MASSACHU- SETTS

Aston Magna Festival
30 Berkshire Heights Road, Great Barrington, Mass. 01230
Classical (17th and 18th centuries)
Mid-June through early July (3 Saturdays)
The Aston Magna Foundation for Music, founded in 1972, brings together artists, scholars, instrument makers and serious students to pursue a broad study of the glorious music of the 17th and 18th centuries—considering not only the instruments, techniques, and pitch and tunings proper to the music, but also the broader social and cultural context in which the music was created and originally functioned. The artistic results of these studies are embodied in the Aston Magna Festival, held each summer in Great Barrington.
The Festival consists of 3 Saturday evening concerts in St. James' Church. There is seating for 400.
Director: Albert Fuller
Accommodations: A list of accommodations in the Great Barrington and surrounding area can be obtained by writing to the Festival.
Ticket information: Admission for each concert is $8.50. For tickets, write to Aston Magna Foundation, 345 East 81st St., New York, N.Y. 10028. tel. (212)471-1122. After June 15th—(413) 528-3595.
How to get there: Great Barrington is reached via Route 7 and Route 23.

Boston Pops
Symphony Hall, 301 Mass Ave., Boston, Mass. 02115
Popular classical
May through mid-July
Since 1885 the Boston Pops has been an American institution drawing large audiences to popular classical, semi-classical, and band concerts.
Free concerts are held on the Esplanade, which allows lawn seating for 10,000. Indoor concerts take place at Symphony Hall, which seats 2,600.
Musical Director: John Williams
Ticket information: Esplanade concerts are free. Tickets for Symphony Hall concerts range from $4.50 to $10.50. Send a self-addressed envelope to the Symphony Hall Box Office at the address above for a schedule.

Sevenars Music Festival
Academy in South Worthington, Mass. (413)238-5854
Classical, vocal, chamber
Mid-July to late August, each Sunday at 5:30; in August, Fridays at 7:30 (in addition to Sundays)
Founded in 1968, coinciding with the town of Worthington's Bicentennial, this annual classical-music festival began with the Schrade family's concerts, held at the local church. As audience response increased, a historic Academy was renovated, and the concert series was expanded to include many well-known artists and prize-winning newcomers. In addition to the Schrade family of pianists, pianist David James, cellist David Wells, and Michael Rudiakov have been among performers in recent years. Arts and crafts exhibits of well-known New England artists take place before and after the Sunday afternoon concerts; refreshments are served to patrons.
Concerts are held in the Academy, which seats 300 and whose windows open onto a rural landscape.
Directors: Robert and Rolande Young Schrade
Sponsors: Sevenars Concerts, Inc.,with assistance of Commonwealth of Massachusetts Council on the Arts and Humanities
Accommodations: There are many hotels and motels in the Northampton, Pittsfield, Springfield, Amherst, and Worthington area. Camping is permitted at the Berkshire Park Campgrounds (413) 238-5918, and there are facilities for trailers.
Ticket information: Admission is by donation, with a suggested minimum per person ($2 in 1978). For ticket information, call (413)238-5854.
How to get there: The Academy is located just off Route 112, between Huntington and Worthington.

South Mountain Concerts
P.O. Box 23, Pittsfield, Mass. 01201
Classical
June through October
Located on a wooded slope in the midst

of the Berkshire Hills, South Mountain's Concert Hall has been the scene of distinguished music since its founding in 1918 by Mrs. Elizabeth Sprague Coolidge. An intimate atmosphere and fine acoustics provide a special setting for the performance of chamber music, recitals, and opera. Internationally known artists who have appeared include Leonard Bernstein, Alexander Schneider, Leontyne Price, Rudolf Serkin, the Juilliard Quartet, the Guarneri Quartet, Gary Graffman, the Beaux Arts Trio, and the Cleveland and Tokyo Quartets.

The Concert Hall has a capacity of 600 and is listed on the National Register of Historic Buildings.

Director: Mrs. Willem Willeke

Sponsor: South Mountain Association, Inc.

Accommodations/other items of interest in area: Accommodations can be obtained at the Berkshire Hilton Inn in Pittsfield or the Red Lion Inn in Stockbridge. Points of interest in the area include the Williamstown and Berkshire Theater Festivals, and the Pleasant Valley Bird Sanctuary.

Ticket information: General admission tickets are $6. For tickets, write to South Mountain Association, Box 23, Pittsfield, Mass. 01201.

How to get there: South Mountain is located 1 mile S. of Pittsfield on US routes 7 and 20.

Worcester Music Festival
Worcester County Music Association, Memorial Auditorium, Worcester, Mass. 01608
Classical
Late October to early November (2 weekends)

The Worcester Music Festival has been presenting music since 1858, when it began as a singing society. Each person who attended that first meeting paid twenty-five cents and was given vocal instruction and taught to sing in chorus. Over many years it grew into a major festival presenting orchestral music in addition to substantial choral music with distinguished soloists. Since 1944 full symphony orchestras have been associated with the Festival. The concert series is held annually over 2 weekends, with such major symphonies as the Boston Symphony, the Philadelphia Orchestra, and the Detroit Symphony, along with major vocal and instrumental artists. Other festival programs include a young artists competition, the Worcester chorus concerts, and outdoor pops concerts. Concerts are held in Mechanics Hall, which seats 1,579, and Memorial Auditorium, with seats for 2,846.

Director: Worcester County Music Association

Accommodations: The Holiday Inn, 70 Southbridge St., Worcester 01698; Sheraton-Lincoln Inn, 500 Lincoln St., Worcester 01605

Ticket information: Prices range from $6 to $12.50

MICHIGAN

Ann Arbor May Festival
University Musical Society, Burton
Tower, Ann Arbor, Mich. 48109
Classical
End of April or early May
The Ann Arbor May Festival has wel-
comed spring to the American Midwest
since 1894. It has recently featured 4
concerts by the Philadelphia Orchestra
and guest soloists. Over the past 86
years the most famous names in the
world of classical music have performed
at this festival. It is known throughout
the musical world as one of the oldest
and finest classical music festivals.
Concerts are held in Hill Auditorium,
which seats 4,177.
Director: Mr. Gail W. Rector
Accommodations/other items of interest
in area: There are many hotels and
motels in Ann Arbor which can provide
accommodations.
All the attractions of Ann Arbor and the
University of Michigan, a major city and
a major university, are available to patrons of the Festival.
Ticket information: Series tickets, depending on the seat, range from $14 to
$42. Single tickets are from $4 to $12.
Tickets can be obtained in person or by
mail.

Bay View Music Festival
Bay View, Mich. 49770
Classical, dance, theater
Late June to late August
The Festival was founded in 1875 to
provide summer resort patrons with
cultural, religious, educational, and
recreational programs.
Performances are by resident faculty and
take place in either the 1,700-seat John
M. Hall Auditorium or the 250-seat
Voorhies Hall.
Director: Ernest G. Sullivan
Sponsor: Bay View Association
Accommodations: Hotels and motels in
the area include the Terrace Inn and
Staffords Bay View Inn in Bay View, and
the Holiday Inn and Days Inn in nearby
Petoskey. There are parks near the
Festival available for camping and pic-
nicking.
Ticket information: Tickets are $3

How to get there: Take Mich. 131 at
Petoskey N. to Bay View

Detroit Concert Band Summer Festival Series
20962 Mack Ave., Grosse Pointe Woods,
Mich. 48236
Classical, light popular, marches
Early June to early August
Since 1946 this summer series under the
direction of Dr. Leonard B. Smith has
provided band music in the tradition of
John Philip Sousa. During its existence
it has performed over 2,600 concerts—
not only marches but classical and light
popular music with instrumental and
vocal soloists.
Performances are generally outdoors at
different locations in the Detroit area:
Hart Plaza, Band Shell, Belle Isle Park,
and Michigan State Fairgrounds. They
occur 5 nights per week with a different
program on each night.
Director: Leonard B. Smith
Sponsor: City of Detroit
Accommodations/other items of interest
in area: In Detroit, the Plaza Hotel, Pont-
chartrain Hotel, the Radisson Cadillac
Hotel, and many others can provide
accommodations. No camping available.
Detroit's new Renaissance Center Green-
field Village in nearby Dearborn, Mich. is
an additional point of interest in the
area.
Ticket information: Admission is free

Kalamazoo Bach Festival
Kalamazoo College, 1200 Academy St.,
Kalamazoo, Mich. 49007
Classical and baroque
Early December and late February to
early March
One of the major Bach festivals in the
U.S., the annual Kalamazoo Bach Festival has been a high point of Kalamazoo
cultural life for over 30 years. Taking
place over 2 consecutive weekends, it
includes 2 Young Artists Concerts, a
major choral work, and chamber concerts. There are also free noon-hour
concerts by young artists, which patrons
can enjoy while eating a bag lunch.
An Intermission Dinner between the 2-
part presentation of a major choral
work is a tradition of the Festival. Performances are by the chorus and orchestra of the Bach Festival Society, with

guest soloists. The performers of the Young Artists Concerts are the winners of a nationwide competition for young performers of baroque music. Concerts are held in Stetson Chapel, which seats 700. Those coming to Kalamazoo for the Festival should be prepared for cold weather.
Director: Dr. Russell A. Hammar
Accommodations: Accommodations are available at Kalamazoo Hilton in downtown Kalamazoo or at Valley Inn, N. Park St., Kalamazoo, Mich. There are no facilities for camping or picnicking.
Ticket information: Series Concert tickets are $12, or, for students (I.D required), $5. Single admission tickets range from $4 to $8 for each concert. Tickets can be obtained by mail from the Festival; however, Student Series tickets can only be purchased in person at The Bach Office, Room 210, Light Fine Arts Bldg., Kalamazoo College.
How to get there: I-94 to Business I-94 leads to Kalamazoo College

Matrix: Midland
Midland Center for the Arts, 1801 W. St. Andrews, Midland, Mich. 48640
Classical, dance
June
Matrix: Midland presents symphony concerts, lyric theater, dance, and arts exhibits. Past performers have included Aaron Copland, Morton Gould, Canadian Brass, and Michigan Opera Theater, among others. Science exhibits and lectures are also offered in the belief that it is good to see how the other half lives. Events are held in an auditorium seating 1,538, in an outdoor area which can accommodate 3,000, and in a smaller lecture theater and recital rooms.
Director: Judith O'Dell
Sponsor: Midland Center for the Arts
Accommodations/other items of interest in area: Lodging is available at Holiday Inn, 1500 W. Wackerly; Ramada Inn Central, 1815 Saginaw; and Ramada Inn, 2914 W. Midland Road. Camping facilities are available at Ramada Inn Campground at $10 per couple. Trailers are welcome but tents are not. There is picnicking in Emerson Park.
Of interest in the area are Dow Gardens and Chippewa Nature Center.
Ticket information: Admission to some events is free. Ticket prices range up to $10. For more information and tickets write to Matrix: Midland Tickets, P.O. Box 2206, Midland, Mich. 48640
How to get there: From Ann Arbor take Highway 23 to Highway 65, then W. on Highway 10 past Midland turnoff to Eastman Road. Matrix: Midland is at Eastman Road and St. Andrews (Midland Center for the Arts).

MONTANA

Adult Chamber Music Festival
Dept. of Music, Montana State University,
Bozeman, Mont. 59715
Classical chamber music
Late June to early July
This participation festival is for chamber
music players of at least high school pro-
ficiency. Visiting groups—a string quartet
or wind group—coach, demonstrate, and
perform a concert during the week-long
event. Usually participants play assigned
works (seven or so) and freelance for fun.
In addition, involvement in larger symphony groups, concertos, concerto
grossos, and playing of original compositions is available. Non-playing and playing family members are welcome. The
festival schedules one family mountain
picnic.
Director: Mary C. Sanks
Sponsor: Dept. of Music, Montana
State University
Accommodations: All participants
usually stay in the dormitory provided
on campus. Other accommodations available include the Holiday and Ramada
inns in Bozeman. Camping and trailer
facilities are available in the area.
Nearby attractions range from a fine
library, museum, pools, and theater, to
fishing, hiking, and visiting Yellowstone
National Park, 90 miles away.
Ticket information: Registration to play
all week costs $65. No registration fee
for non-performing family members.
Dormitory housing costs a nominal fee
per day. To register, write to Dept. of
Music, Montana State University, Bozeman, Mont. 59715

NEW HAMPSHIRE

**Chamber Music at Portsmouth
(formerly The Strawberry Banke
Chamber Music Festival)**
P.O. Box 1529, Portsmouth, N.H. 03801
Chamber music
July through August
Concerts by the Portsmouth Chamber
Ensemble, the Festival's resident trio,
are a mainstay. Many fine chamber
groups and performers join them for
this summer series of performances in
downtown Portsmouth.
Director: Frank S. Dodge
Sponsors: The New Hampshire Commission on the Arts, the National Endowment for the Arts, and others.
Accommodations/other items of interest
in area: Accommodations are readily
available at Holiday Motor Inn, Meadow-
brook Motor Inn, and Howard Johnson's,
all at Portsmouth traffic circle, Route
95.
Summer visitors to Portsmouth may
enjoy Prescott Park Arts Festival, Theater by the Sea, Strawberry Banke Historic Preservation Museum, art galleries,
craft shops, and fine restaurants.
Ticket information: Tickets may be had
at the door or by writing to the Festival.

New Hampshire Music Festival
P.O. Box 147, Center Harbor, N.H.
03226
Classical symphony, chorus, chamber
music
Early July to mid-August
The Festival features New Hampshire's
oldest professional orchestra, founded
in 1952. Its members include 30 players
from all over the U.S. and a chorus of
150 local singers. James Bonn, piano
soloist, was guest artist of note during
the 1979 season.
Concerts take place on Tuesdays, Wednesdays, Thursdays, and Sundays in 4
different halls (average capacity 500)
in Plymouth, Gilford, and Meredith.
Director: Thomas Nee, Music Director
and Conductor
Accommodations: The Meadows Motel
and Staffordshire Inn in Center Harbor,
and the Plymouth Inn in Plymouth, can

provide accommodations.
Ticket information: Tickets are $5 each
or 6 for $25 by mail, or call (603)253-
4331

NEW JERSEY

Waterloo Summer Music Festival
Waterloo Village, Waterloo Road, Stanhope, N.J. 07874
Classical and other
Weekends, June through September
The Waterloo Music Festival, held on
the grounds of a restored, Colonial
period hamlet, features classical orchestral and chamber music. The 90-piece
Festival Orchestra, led by Maestro
Gerard Schwartz, includes members
of the New York Philharmic and
students from Centenary College
summer music school. Past guest performers have included Pablo Casals, Isaac
Stern, Van Cliburn, and Beverly Sills.
Waterloo also hosts special 3-day festivals, among them a jazz festival and a
bluegrass festival. Pop, folk, and country
presentations are additional attractions.
Concerts are held in a covered, green-and-
white-striped tent, which seats about
3,000. In good weather, however, patrons
may chose to sit outdoors on the lawn.
Foul-weather clothing is recommended,
just in case.
Director: Mr. Percival Leach
Sponsor: Waterloo Foundation for the
Arts
Accommodations/other items of interest
in area: Accommodations are available
at Panther Valley Motor Lodge, Alla-
muchy, N.J. 07820; the Holiday Inn,
Ledgewood, N.J. 07852; and Fehers
Motor Inn, Newton, N.J. 07860. Open
field camping, with water available, is
allowed for the bluegrass festival only.
Picnicking is allowed at all times, anywhere on the grounds.
Waterloo Village Historic Restoration
has many points of interest, including
antique and craft shows. Wild West City,
in Netcong, N.J., is nearby.
Ticket information: Indoor seating
ranges from $6.50 to $8.50, with lower-
priced tickets sometimes available, and
lawn seating is $3.50, weather permit-
ting. For tickets, write to the Festival,
or call (201)347-4700.
How to get there: To get to Waterloo
take Interstate Route 80 (E. or W.),
exit 25 to US Route 206 N., and
go left at the second traffic light onto
Waterloo Road.

NEW MEXICO

The Santa Fe Opera
P.O. Box 2408, Santa Fe, N.M. 87501
Classical
June to August
Begun in 1957 by John O. Crosby, in its 23 seasons the Santa Fe Opera has presented 22 world or American premieres, in addition to staging operas from the standard repertory. The Santa Fe Opera is also well known for its apprentice programs for young singers and stage technicians.
The outdoor theater, partially covered, seats 1,765, with standing room for 150.
Director: John O. Crosby
Accommodations: Write to Chamber of Commerce, P.O. Box 1928, Santa Fe N.M. 87501. tel. (505)983-7317. Early reservations are recommended since hotels are usually filled to capacity during the opera season.
Of interest in the area are historic Santa Fe itself, the pueblos in the area, Indian crafts, and the Santa Fe Chamber Music Festival
Ticket information: Tickets in 1979 cost from $8 to $25, with $3 standing room tickets
How to get there: The theater is located 6 miles N. of Santa Fe on US 84-285 at the San Juan Ranch

NEW YORK

Caramoor Festival
Box "R", Katonah, N.Y. 10536
Classical (orchestra, chamber music, opera)
Mid-June through mid-August
Caramoor will celebrate its 35th season in 1980. Opened to the public as a museum in 1970, Caramoor was the Mediterranean-style country house of Walter Rosen and his wife Lucie Bigelow Rosen. The house was built between 1930 and 1939 as a setting for Mr. Rosen's vast collection of European and Chinese works of art. Every season includes special events for children. Programs in 1979 included "Discover the Renaissance"; "Discover Baroque"; "Discover Classical Winds"; and Haydn's The Apothecary, an opera for children.
Many of the world's leading artists have performed at Caramoor.
The Venetian Theater seats 1,500, the Spanish Courtyard 500. Both are out-of-doors and appropriate clothing for a summer afternoon or evening is suggested. Rain does not cancel a performance. Tickets purchased in advance of a performance provide protected seats in case of rain.
Director: Michael Sweeley, Director
Accommodations: The Festival recommends the Holiday Inn in Mt. Kisco, N.Y. 10549.
Ticket information: Tickets range from $7.50 to $15. The Children's Events tickets are $1.50 for a child and $3.50 for an adult accompanied by a child. The latter sell out quickly and advance orders are recommended. For tickets write or call (914)232-4206.
How to get there: For the Venetian Theater only, special Caramoor buses leave the rear of the State Theater, Lincoln Center (New York City), 62nd St. off Columbus Ave., at 6:30 P.M. promptly. Round trip costs $7.50. If you plan to drive, write the Festival for information.

Chautauqua Institution
Chautauqua, N.Y. 14722
Classical
Mid-June through late August
This festival offers 24 symphony concerts by the Chautauqua Symphony

Orchestra and 6 operas, as well as dance and some jazz. Additional musical events include presentations of light classical and popular music. Chautauqua also presents an extensive series of lectures by notables in the political, scientific, and art and literary worlds.

Events are held in a covered amphitheater which seats 5,000 and in Norton Hall which seats 1,400. Sweaters and jackets are recommended for cool evenings.

Director: Dr. Robert R. Hesse

Accommodations: Contact Chautauqua Institution at the above address for information on lodging. There is no camping or picnicking.

Ticket information: Admission varies according to event and length of stay

How to get there: Chautauqua Institution is between Buffalo, N.Y. and Erie, Pa., off I-90

Heritage of New York Festival

The Center for Music, Drama, and Art
Saranac Ave. at Fawn Ridge, Lake
Placid, N.Y. 12946
Classical, theater, dance
July 4 to Labor Day

Lake Placid—scene of the 1980 Olympic Winter Games—is the setting for an annual festival which provides classical concerts on Mondays and Wednesdays, plays on Fridays, Saturdays, and Sundays, films on Tuesdays, and lectures on Thursdays for most of the summer. In addition there are daily classes, workshops, and exhibitions. Performers in the past have included the Paul Taylor Dance Company, Virgil Fox, Cantilena Chamber Players, Roberta Peters, Lake Placid Sinfonietta, and the McLaughlin/Beswick Dance Theatre.

Concerts are given either in a 353-seat auditorium or outdoors in a bandshell at a local park.

Director: Ken Lawless

Accommodations/other items of interest in area: For a list of hotels and motels in the area, write to Lake Placid Chamber of Commerce, Lake Placid, N.Y. 12946. Olympic site, John Brown's grave, and Seven Nations Museum are some other attractions in the area.

Ticket information: General admission is $5; $3 for students and seniors. Subscription discounts and group rates available. Write for tickets or call (518)523-2512.

Lake George Opera Festival

Box 425, Glens Falls, N.Y. 12801
Classical
July to August

The purpose of the Lake George Opera Festival is to bring opera in English, performed by gifted young artists, to the thousands of vacationers and year-round residents of the scenic Adirondack area. Its first season was in 1962. Artists who have appeared at the Lake George Opera Festival include Diana Soviero, Henry Price, Michael Devlin, Frances Bible, Gimi Beni, Charles Roe, Catherine Malfitano, and Beverly Sills. Performances are in an air-conditioned auditorium which seats 876.

Director: David Lloyd

Accommodations: For information on hotels, camping and picnicking facilities, and other items of interest in the area, write: The Adirondack Regional Chambers of Commerce, 206 Glen Street, Glens Falls, N.Y. 12801; or Lake George Chamber of Commerce, Canada Street, Lake George, N.Y. 12845.

Ticket information: Tickets are $6 to $12. Special senior citizen, student, and group discounts are available. Mail orders and telephone orders are accepted (518) 793-3858.

Maverick Concerts

Box 102, Woodstock, N.Y. 12498
Classical (chamber music)
July and August, through mid-September

The Maverick Sunday Concerts, the oldest continuous chamber concert series in the U.S., presents outstanding artists of international reputation. In its woodland setting, the Maverick Concert Hall provides indoor and outdoor seating for approximately 375. Chamber music concerts are presented each Sunday afternoon throughout the season and on Tuesday evenings in August. Those who have performed in previous years include the Tokyo String Quartet, Lorin Hollander, Paula Robison, Orpheus Trio, the Dorian Wind Quintet, Richard Goode, Ani and Ida Kavafian, and Jaime Laredo.

Directors: John Ebbs, Chairman; Leo Bernache, Music Director

Accommodations/other items of interest in area: In Woodstock, the Pinecrest Lodge and Fernwood Acres can provide lodging.

The town of Woodstock is filled with

shops, galleries, restaurants, and theaters.
Ticket information: Admission ranges
from $2.50 (outside) to $4.50
How to get there: Take the New York
State Thruway to exit 19. Maverick is
2 miles southeast of the center of
Woodstock.

Music in May

New York Philharmonic, Avery Fisher
Hall, 65th & Broadway, New York,
N.Y. 10023
Classical
May
The New York Philharmonic Orchestra
presents 18 special May concerts with
such well-known conductors as Zubin
Mehta, Pinchas Zukerman, Alexander
Schneider and Andre Kostelanetz. These
popular musical evenings provide a per-
fect introduction to light classical and
Baroque music.
The concerts are at Avery Fisher Hall.
Sponsor: The New York Philharmonic
Accommodations: Lodging is plentiful
in New York City.
Ticket information: Admission ranges
from $4 to $12.50, depending on seat-
ing and the particular concert.

Saratoga Performing Arts Center

Saratoga Springs, N.Y. 12866
Classical and other
Mid-June through August
On the 1,500-acre Saratoga Springs
State Park, near a lake, is an amphi-
theater, "its shape and color those of
nature," which seats 5,103 and has room
for 10,000 more on gently sloping lawns.
This is the Saratoga Performing Arts
Center, the summer home of Maestro
Eugene Ormandy and the Philadelphia
Orchestra, which performs during
August, and George Balanchine and the
New York City Ballet, which performs
during July. The Center also presents
rock groups, folk singers, country-
western artists and top entertainers in
show business. It hosts the Newport
Jazz Festival and a special country
music weekend.
Director: Mr. Herbert A. Chesbrough
Accommodations/other items of interest
in area: The Gideon Putnam
Hotel is located near the Center. For
more information contact Chamber of
Commerce, 297 Broadway, Saratoga
Springs, N.Y. 12866, tel. (518)584-3255.

Camping is not allowed, but there are
picnicking facilities.
As regards other-than-musical events,
the Acting Company performs in a 500-
seat theater which is part of the Performing Arts Center, and nearby are
the nation's oldest active thoroughbred
race track, museums, points of historical
interest, mineral baths, facilities for
many sports, and entertainment for
children
Ticket information: Ticket prices range
from $4 to $11. For more information
and a season brochure write to the
Arts Center, or call (518)584-9330;
box office (518)587-3330.
How to get there: The Center is 30
minutes from Albany, Troy and
Schenectady and 3½ hours from New
York City, Boston and Montreal at
exit 13-N of I-87.

Spring Festival

Crane School of Music, State University
College, Potsdam, N.Y. 13676
Classical
April
Since 1930 the Crane School Chorus and
Symphony Orchestra have presented 2
performances, with a renowned guest
conductor during the 2-day Annual
Spring Festival. Past guest conductors
have included Stanley Chapple, Aaron
Copland and Sarah Caldwell. Classical
and/or contemporary works, which can
show the mettle of the 250-voice chorus
and full symphony orchestra, are chosen.
An informal 50-minute talk with the
guest conductor is open to the public.
The concerts are held at Helen M. Hos-
mer Concert Hall of the Crane School of
Music which seats 1,400.
Director: Robert W. Thayer
Sponsor: Student Government Associa-
tion-State University College
Accommodations/other items of interest
in area: There are numerous motels and
hotels in Potsdam in a radius of 10
miles. There is no camping.
Potsdam is in the Adirondack region.
Of interest in the area are the Adirondack Mountains, St. Lawrence Seaway,
and rural countryside. Canada is 45
minutes away.
Ticket information: Admission is $4

NORTH CAROLINA

Brevard Music Festival
P.O. Box 592, Brevard, N.C.
Classical, musical comedy, opera
Late June to mid-August
More than 40 performances of symphony, chamber, and choral music, in addition to recitals, musical comedy, and opera are provided by this festival, which is linked with the Brevard Music Center, a training center for young musicians.

The principal performing group is the Brevard Music Center Orchestra, made up of the instrumental artists-faculty and advanced students. In addition, guest artists of note also appear. Some of these in recent years were Van Cliburn, Lille Kraus, Mary Costa, Enrico Di Giuseppe, Benny Goodman, and Doc Severinsen.

Performances take place either at the 1,700-seat Whittington-Pfohl Auditorium or the 450-seat Straus Auditorium.

Director: Dr. Henry Janiec
Sponsor: Brevard Music Center
Accommodations: The Imperial Motor Inn and Brevard Motel, both in Brevard, can provide accommodations. Camping is available nearby in the Blue Ridge Mountains and the Pisgah National Forest.

Ticket information: Season tickets are $75, while prices for individual performances vary from $3.50 to $6.00. For tickets, write to Brevard Music Center, P.O. Box 592, Brevard, N.C.

Eastern Music Festival
712 Summit Ave., Greensboro, N.C. 27405
Classical
Mid-June through early August
Eastern Music Festival, a 6-week summer classical music festival and institute of music studies at Guilford College, has been described as a "classical music turn-on." Annually, E.M.F. establishes a resident musical community of 80 teacher/performers drawn from leading orchestras and 200 talented young student musicians. These professional and student performers, as well as guest artists of international stature, present over 35 orchestral and chamber music concerts. Master classes by artists-in-residence are open to season ticket holders. There are also pops concerts at local parks, and mini concerts on the lawn, for the enjoyment of picnicking patrons.

Director: Sheldon Morgenstern
Accommodations/other items of interest in area: Major motels provide nearby accommodations.

Festival patrons may also attend the Shakespeare Festival in High-Point or the American Dance Festival in Durham or visit the Southeastern Center for Contemporary Art and Old Salem in Winston-Salem.

Ticket information: Season tickets are about $33, individual tickets about $7.

How to get there: Take I-85 to its junction with I-40; go W. on I-40 to the Guilford College exit. Turn right and follow College Road to the gates of Guilford College. By air, fly to Greensboro/High Point airport; limousine service is available to Guilford College. Greensboro can also be reached by train and bus.

OHIO

Baldwin-Wallace Bach Festival
Kulas Musical Arts Building, Berea, Ohio
44017
Classical
Weekend in mid-May
The Baldwin-Wallace Bach Festival
begun in 1932 is the second oldest of
its kind in the country. Usually works by
Bach are performed on Friday and
Saturday evenings, but other composers,
such as Vivaldi, who greatly influenced
Bach, are sometimes also chosen.
Performances take place at a covered
auditorium which seats 650.
Director: Dwight Oltman
Sponsor: Baldwin-Wallace College
Accommodations: No camping
available
Ticket information: Guarantors who
contribute $40 receive 2 tickets to the
Festival events. Five minutes before
each event, the public is invited to
occupy any remaining seats.

Cincinnati Opera Summer Festival
Cincinnati Music Hall, 1241 Elm St.,
Cincinnati, Ohio 45210
Grand Opera
Mid-June through mid-July
The Cincinnati Opera, founded in 1920,
performed in an outdoor pavilion at the
Cincinnati Zoo until moving to the
Music Hall in 1972. For years it was the
only grand opera in the United States
with summer performances. Virtually
every well-known opera star from
Beverly Sills to Richard Tucker, Jan
Peerce, and Lily Pons, has appeared
with the Opera.
Director: James de Blasis
Accommodations/other items of interest
in area: Accommodations are plentiful
in the Cincinnati area. For information,
write to the Convention and Visitors
Bureau, Cincinnati, Ohio 45202.
Other items of interest in the area include the Cincinnati Reds, Kings Island,
the Cincinnati Art Museum, the Cincinnati Playhouse in the Park, and the
Showboat Majestic (on the Ohio River).
Ticket information: For series tickets,
write to the Subscription Manager,
Cincinnati Opera, 1241 Elm St.,
Cincinnati, Ohio 45210. Single tickets

are available from the opera office (at
1241 Elm Street) until June 1, and
afterwards from the ticket office, 7th
and Race Streets, Cincinnati, Ohio
45202.

Lakeside Music Festival
236 Walnut Ave., Lakeside, Ohio 43440
Classical
Late July to late August
Over 100 years old, this festival has its
own symphony orchestra-in-residence
performing as many as 9 concerts during
the season. In addition, artists such as
Ferrante and Teicher, Fred Waring,
Indianapolis Ballet, and George Shear-
ing perform in concert.
Concerts take place in a covered hall
which seats 3,200 people.
Director: Robert L. Cronquist
Sponsor: Lakeside Association
Accommodations/other items of interest
in area: Fountain Inn, Hotel Lakeside
and Richards House in Lakeside can provide accommodation. Camping possible
at Lakeside's trailer camp.
Nearby points of interest include the
Lake Erie Islands and the Sandusky Bay
area.
Ticket information: Tickets, available
only at the gate, are $3 per day
How to get there: Take the Ohio Turn-
pike to Route 13, go N. to 250, W. to
Lakeside

May Festival
Music Hall, 1241 Elm Street, Cincinnati,
Ohio 45210
Classical, choral
May
Because of its large population of British
and German people, who brought with
them their love of choral music, Cincinnati has always been a musical city. The
May Festival, which celebrated its 100th
anniversary in 1973, is the oldest continuing festival of its quality in the
Western hemisphere. It has featured
world-renowned musicians as soloists
and guest conductors. The Festival now
consists of 4 concerts of major choral
works; there is also a Saengerfest,
audience sing-along of favorite choral
masterpieces, and a carolfest, audience
sing-along of Christmas carols.
Concerts take place in the Music Hall,
a newly renovated 100-year-old building in downtown Cincinnati whose audi-

torium seats 3,631.
Directors: James Conlon, Music Director
Steven Monder, General Manager
Sponsor: Cincinnati Musical Festival
Association
Accommodations/other items of interest
in area: The following Cincinnati hotels
provide convenient accommodations for
festival patrons: Netherland Hilton, W.
5th St.; Cincinnati Terrace Hilton, W. 6th
St.; Cincinnati Stouffer's, W. 6th St.
Other items of interest in the area are
the Cincinnati Opera Association, the
Cincinnati Ballet Company, the Cincinnati Playhouse in the Park, and many
fine museums.
Ticket information: Tickets range from
$4 to $13 and may be obtained by writing to May Festival Tickets, 29 W. 4th
St., Cincinnati, Ohio 45202; or by
phone: (513)381-2661

OREGON

Peter Britt Music and Arts Festival
Jacksonville, Ore.
Classical
Early August for 2 weeks
Peter Britt was one of Oregon's first
horticulturists and photographers. The
lush gardens that he created in Jacksonville, which are now a historical landmark, form the setting for this annual
two-week festival. The varied programs
include orchestral works, recitals, ballet,
and choral presentations.
Indoor recitals are held at the U.S. Hotel
ballroom in downtown Jacksonville,
which seats 200. For outdoor concerts
at the gardens there is some seating on
benches, but it is recommended that
patrons bring a blanket or folding chair.
Concertgoers are encouraged to come
early to the gardens and bring a picnic
supper.
Director: John Trudeau, Music Director
Sponsors: Oregon Arts Commission,
National Endowment for the Arts
Accommodations/other items of interest
in area: For accommodations, write to
Jacksonville Chamber of Commerce, 185
North Oregon St., Jacksonville, Ore.
97530.
Jacksonville is near Ashland, home of
the renowned Oregon Shakespeare
Festival.
Ticket information: Prices are $5 for
adults, $3 for students and senior citi-
zens. For tickets, write to Britt Music
Festival, P.O.. Box 1124, Medford, Ore.
97501.

Music in May
Pacific University School of Music
Forest Grove, Ore. 97116
Mostly classical
Three days in May
Music in May was begun in 1948 to encourage string, band, and chorus music
in the public schools of the Northwest.
Each year, 500 selected high-school
musicians—from Oregon, Washington,
Idaho, Alaska, and Hawaii—gather at
Pacific Univ. to perform mostly classical
music in band, choir, and orchestral
ensembles. There are 3 days of events
for the student musicians, culminating
in an evening performance, held indoors,
in the Pacific Univ. Gymnasium.

Director: Roger Hanna
Sponsor: School of Music, Pacific Univ.
Accommodations: For information on
accommodations, write to the Festival
Ticket information: Admission is $2
How to get there: Forest Grove is 22
miles W. of Portland on Highway 8

University of Oregon Summer Festival of Music
University of Oregon School of Music,
Eugene, Ore. 97403
Classical
Early to mid-July
The Festival has grown from one performance in 1970 to 16 or more in recent years. Now almost two weeks long, its musical focus is Bach but a wide cross-section of repertoire by other composers such as Verdi, Beethoven, and Mendelssohn is always included and performed by orchestra, chorus, chamber ensembles, and solo singers and instrumentalists.
Professional musicians from throughout the U.S., Canada, and Europe take part. Performers in recent years have included Helmuth Rilling, conductor; Arleen Auger (Germany), Alyce Rogers (Portland), soloists; The Musical Offering (Los Angeles) and Syrinx Woodwind Quintet (Germany), chamber groups. In addition during the Festival there are workshops in choral conducting, noon musicology lectures, and informal recitals. Concerts are held in Beall Hall on the University of Oregon campus. The hall seats 555.
Directors: H. Royce Saltzman, Administrative Director; Helmuth Rilling, Artistic Director
Sponsor: University of Oregon School of Music
Accommodations: The Greentree Motel and New Oregon Motel on Franklin Blvd. in Eugene can provide lodging. The U.S. Forest Service can give information on the many campgrounds in the area.
Ticket information: Tickets range from $1.50 to $8.50 for concerts

PENNSYL-VANIA

Bach Choir of Bethlehem Annual Festival
Packer Memorial Chapel, Lehigh University, Bethlehem, Pa.
Classical
Second and third weekends of May
The Bach Choir of Bethlehem was founded in 1898 in order to perform the baroque master's intricate *Mass in B Minor.* Then, as now, it was comprised of steel plant workers, housewives, farmers, business people, teachers and students from the Lehigh Valley. The choir has achieved international recognition; in 1976 it presented the *Mass in B Minor* at an international Bach festival in Germany. The choir has also performed in major U.S. cities. Devoted completely to the choral works of J.S. Bach, the choir features about 175 singers and an accompanying 45-piece orchestra.
Festival performances take place in the Packer Memorial Chapel, which seats more than 1,000.
Director: Dr. Alfred Mann
Accommodations: Hotel Bethlehem, Holiday Inn East, and Howard Johnson's can provide accommodations in the area. No camping available.
Ticket information: Tickets range from $12 to $28 for 4 concerts. For tickets, write to The Bach Choir of Bethlehem, 423 Heckewelder Place, Bethlehem, Pa. 18018.

International Boy Singers Festival
125 S. 4th St.
Connellsville, Pa. 15425
Classical and light choral music
Late December
This 5-day boys' choir festival has been held annually since 1969 in various cities of the United States, and in Holland, France, Canada, and Mexico. In past festivals 27 boys' choirs from several countries have participated.
Director: George Bragg
Sponsor: Americas Boychoir Federation
Ticket information: Admission is free. For tickets, write to Americas Boychoir Federation, 125 S. 4th St., Connellsville, Pa. 15425.

Music at Gretna

Box 356, Mt. Gretna, Pa. 17064
Classical (chamber) and jazz
June through August
This summer festival consists of 12 concerts on Sunday and Thursday evenings.
It features performances of the best
works from the chamber music repertoire of the past 300 years. The Audubon
Quartet is the nucleus of the Festival's
varied performing groups; winners of gold
medals in 2 international competitions,
they were named "Young Artists to
Watch" by *Musical America*. Additional
non-subscription jazz concerts are also a
part of the Festival.
Concerts are held in The Chautauqua
Playhouse and Campmeeting Tabernacle,
2 identical 80-year-old auditoriums, each
seating 700 persons, with unique vaulted
ceilings. They provide perfect shelter and
excellent acoustics in a rustic, outdoor
atmosphere.
Director: Carl Ellenberger
Sponsor: The Pennsylvania Chautauqua
Accommodations/other items of interest
in area: For a list of selected motels near
Mt. Gretna write to the Festival at the
address above. Nearby camping facilities
are provided by Distelfink Campground
at Pa. Turnpike exit 20.
Mt. Gretna is a quiet wooded place in the
foothills of the Appalachians. Swimming,
boating, hiking, tennis, summer stock
theater, and Victorian architecture may
be of interest to visitors.
Ticket information: Admission is $3 to
$5; season tickets (12 concerts) are $25.
Write to the Festival for tickets or (if
any are left) get them at the door.
How to get there: Mt. Gretna and the
Festival are between Lebanon and Lancaster on Route 117, 20 miles E. of
Harrisburg. Take Pa. Turnpike exit 20.

Robin Hood Dell Summer Festival

Robin Hood Dell West, 52nd & Parkside
Aves., West Fairmount Park, Philadelphia,
Pa.
Classical
Mid-June to early August
One of the few festivals of its type featur-
ing a major orchestra—the Philadelphia
Orchestra—which has free general admis-
sion. In recent years the American Ballet
Theater and the Metropolitan Opera
Company have also performed. Guest
conductors and soloists have included
some of the best known names in clas-
sical music: Eugene Ormandy, Leonard
Bernstein, Zubin Mehta, Pinchas Zuker-
man, Shirely Verrett, and Van Cliburn.
A covered hall at Robin Hood Dell in
West Fairmount Park provides seating
for 5,000. Events on the lawn have room
for 10,000.
Director: Helen Martin
Sponsors: Robin Hood Dell Concerts,
Inc., supported by the City of Philadel-
phia and Friends of the Dell
Accommodations: Marriott Hotel and
Holiday Inn on City Line Avenue
Ticket information: Free tickets dis-
tributed through coupons in daily news-
papers
How to get there: Located at 52nd and
Parkside Aves., in West Philadelphia

RHODE ISLAND

Newport Music Festival
50 Washington Square, Newport, R.I.
02840
Classical, chamber music
July
The musical events of this unusual 10- to
12-day Romantic revival take place in
elegant Newport Mansions and at several
outdoor sites. In addition to chamber
ensembles, the Festival presents American
recital debuts for young artists of international acclaim. Despite the grandeur
of the setting an informal festive atmosphere prevails. Cruise-wear is appropriate
at morning or afternoon concerts. For
evening events many guests are in formal
attire, though it is not required.
Director: Mark P. Malkovich III
Accommodations/other items of interest
in area: For information on accommodations contact Newport County Chamber
of Commerce, 10 America's Cup Ave.,
Newport, R.I. 02840; tel. (401)847-1600.
Newport boasts many historical and
resort attractions and has excellent
beaches.
Ticket information: Ticket prices range
from $7.50 for morning concerts to
$12.50 for evening performances. Write,
or phone (401)849-4343. Early reservations are advisable.
How to get there: By car from New York
City, travel via the New England Turnpike to signs for the Newport Bridge
(3½ hours); from Boston, go via Route
24 (1¼ hours). There is air taxi service
available to Newport from Providence.

TENNESSEE

Sewanee Summer Music Festival
Sewanee Summer Music Center,
Sewanee, Tenn. 37375
Classical
Late June to late July
Weekend concerts feature chamber
music ensembles each Saturday and
symphony orchestras (there are 3 at the
Center) on Sundays. At the end of July
are 4 days of performances.
Students and faculty present all concerts
with occasional appearances by guest
conductors and artists such as Henri
Temianka, conductor, California Cham-
ber Orchestra; Arthur Winograd, con-
ductor, Hartford Symphony; Kishiko
Suzumi, violinist; and Julian Martin,
pianist.
Performances take place in Guerry Hall,
which seats 1,000.
Director: Martha McCrory
Sponsor: The University of the South
Accommodations: Lodging is available
at the Sewanee Inn in Sewanee and at
the Holiday Inn in Monteagle. There are
also camping and trailer facilities in
Monteagle.
Ticket information: Tickets are $2.
How to get there: Sewanee is between
Chattanooga and Nashville, 5 miles
from the Monteagle exit on I-24

TEXAS

International Festival at Round Top
P.O. Box 89, Round Top, Tex. 78954
tel. (713) 249-3129. Festival site:
Festival Hill, Round Top, Tex.
Classical, solo piano, chamber music,
orchestral performances
Weekend evenings, early June to early
July
Founded in 1971, this classical-music
festival is one of the youngest in the
U.S. and the first of its kind in Texas.
In addition to Mr. James Dick, the
founder, performers in recent years
have included Sylvia Rabinof, Michael
Sellers, Young-Uck Kim, Yo-Yo Ma,
and Yehuda Hanani.
The site is called Festival Hill, a large,
grass-covered meadow which can accom-
modate 3,000 people.
There is a resident Festival-Institute,
which was founded by concert pianist
James Dick, and it serves as an educational center which has expanded in
scope from solo instruments, orchestral
and chamber music studies to year-
round performances, master classes, and
seminars. For information about prices,
times, and availability of classes at the
Festival Institute, write to Festival Hill,
Round Top, Tex. 78954.
Director: James Dick, Artistic Director
Accommodations: Round Top has no
guest accommodations, but there are
many motels in nearby Giddings, La
Grange, and Brenham
Ticket information: Admission for all
concerts is $3.50 for adults, $2 for
children under 12. Tickets go on sale 1½
hours before concerts at the box office
at Round Top. Admission to each
seminar is $2 per person.
How to get there: Festival Hill is on
Highway 237, one-half mile from the
Town Hall Square in Round Top, Tex.
Round Top is about 1 hour from both
Houston and Austin and 2 hours from
San Antonio.

UTAH

**Brigham Young University Summer
Piano Festival and Gina Bachauer International Piano Competition**
C-550 HFAC, Brigham Young University,
Provo, Ut. 84602
Classical (piano)
Last week in June
Each day of this week-long festival offers
concerts (group piano, recitals and cham-
ber music), a Master Class, lectures, semi-
finals and, at the end of the week, the
finals of the Gina Bachauer Competition
at which the Utah Symphony Orchestra
accompanies the contestants. Past per-
formers and leaders of Master Classes
have included Daniel Pollack, Mischa
Dichter, Nelita True, Joanne Baker,
Grant Johannesen and many other artists.
Concerts are held at Madsen Recital Hall
which seats 500 and DeJong Concert
Hall seating 1,500.
Director: Dr. Paul Pollei
Sponsor: Brigham Young University
Accommodations/other items of interest
in area: Lodging is available at BYU
General Services, LIDH, Provo Ut. 84602
and Royal Inn, 55 E. 1230 N. Provo, Ut.
84601; other hotels and motels are avail-
able in Provo and the surrounding area.
Provo is a city of 50,000 immediately
next to the spectacular Wasatch moun-
tains. Of interest in the area are Robert
Redford's Sundance Resort, Heber
Creeper scenic steam railroad on Mt.
Timpanogos (12,000 ft.) and Salt Lake
City (40 miles).
Ticket information: Admission is
about $4

VERMONT

Marlboro Music Festival

Marlboro, Vt. 05344
Classical
Early July through mid-August
Violinist Adolf Busch founded Marlboro
Music School and Festival in 1951 with
his brother Herman, son-in-law Rudolf
Serkin, and Marcel, Louis, and Blanche
Moyse. Their rehearsals and concerts
that first summer were held in the converted barns and farm buildings that
formed the campus of the newly established Marlboro College. The founders
felt that Marlboro Music should be more
than just a school or festival. It should
be a kind of musical retreat where musicians come together to work in an atmosphere free from the distractions of
everyday life. Fifteen weekend concerts
are held in an indoor hall with an adjacent canopied area.
There is indoor seating for 668, canopied
seating for 200.
Director: Rudolf Serkin
Accommodations/other items of interest
in area: For a list of accommodations,
write to Chamber of Commerce, 180
Main St., Brattleboro, Vt. 05301; or
Vermont Information Service, Montpe-
lier, Vt. 05602. Camping and picnicking
are not permitted on grounds.
In the vicinity are Molly Stark State Park,
Clark Art Institute, lakes, hiking, charming New England villages.
Ticket information: Prices range from
$2.50 (outside) to $9. Reserved seats
outside are in a canopied area. For tickets, write to 135 S. 18th St., Philadelphia, Pa. 19103 (before June 12); Marlboro, Vt. 05344 (after June); or phone
(802)254-8163.
How to get there: Marlboro is 10 miles
west of Brattleboro, Vt., off Route 9.
Bus service from New York City to
Brattleboro and planes (Air New England) to Keene, New Hampshire. Keene
is a 1-hour drive from Marlboro. Numerous airlines fly to Hartford, Conn., which
is approximately 2 hours away.

Southern Vermont Music Festival

Manchester, Vt.
Classical
Late June through July
For over 5 years the Southern Vermont

Music Festival has been in operation in
conjunction with the school of music
which has 50 students from leading
music schools in the U.S. and foreign
countries. On the weekends, faculty and
students present chamber music concerts.
"House Music" concerts, by less advanced players, are also presented.
Concerts are given at Arkell Pavilion,
which is covered and seats 500.
Directors: Eugene List, Carroll Glenn,
Francis Tursi
Sponsor: Southern Vermont Art Center
Accommodations/other items of interest
in area: Lodging is available at: 1811
House, Barnstead Motel, Coburn House
Hotel, and Four Winds Motel. There is
camping at Emerald Lake Park at moder-
ate cost. Picnicking is allowed.
Manchester-In-The-Mountains is a resort
village nestled in a valley at the base of
Mt. Equinox in the Taconic. The cool
summer climate is ideal for hiking, swimming, golf and tennis. Marlboro, Tanglewood and Saratoga Festivals are all less
than 2 hours away.
Ticket information: Admission is $3 to
$6.50. Contact the Festival at (802)362-
1405 for tickets.
How to get there: From Albany, take
Vermont Route 7. From New York City,
take the Taconic Parkway or N.Y. Thruway (the Festival is about 4½ hours
from New York City).

Vermont Mozart Festival

P.O. Box 512, Burlington, Vt. 05402
Classical chamber music
Mid-July through mid-August
Concerts by nationally and internationally known soloists and ensembles, together
with music workshops and master classes,
are presented by the Vermont Mozart
Festival. During the 3-week festival
there are about 20 concerts. The emphasis is on Mozart, but works of other
"durable" composers are also performed.
Most of the events are held on Shelburne
Farms in Burlington. Concerts in the coach
yard can accommodate 700, and concerts
on the south porch of the main house
have lawn seating for 1,000. Guests
should bring blankets or folding chairs.
Some concerts will also be given in other
parts of Vermont.
Director: Melvin Kaplan, Music Director
Sponsor: Vermont Festival Association
Accommodations/other items of interest

in area: Information on lodging may be obtained from the Greater Burlington Hotel and Motel Owners Association, Burlington, Vermont.

Of interest in the area are Shelburne Museum and Champlain Shakespeare Festival. Festival guests might also enjoy hiking and camping in the Green Mountains or sailing and swimming on Lake Champlain.

Ticket information: Admission is about $6

VIRGINIA

Shenandoah Valley Music Festival
Box 12, Woodstock, Va. 22664
Classical
Weekends, from late July through early August

The Shenandoah Valley Music Festival was begun in 1963 in cooperation with the American Symphony Orchestra League Conductors' workshops. The concerts are held in Orkney Springs.

A covered pavillion seats 800, with lawn seating for 1,000.

Director: Larry Tynes
Sponsor: Shenandoah Valley Music Festival Committee, Inc.

Ticket information: Tickets cost from $2.50 to $6; group rates are available. Tickets are available at the gate or by mail. Write, or call (703)459-3396.

How to get there: From the north on I-81, take exit 69 at Mt. Jackson, Va., turn S. on US-11 through Mt. Jackson to Va. 263. Turn W. to Orkney Springs. From the south on I-81, take exit 68. Turn N. on US-11 to Va. 263 W.

WASHINGTON WISCONSIN

The Pacific Northwest Wagner Festival
Seattle Opera, P.O. Box 9248,
Seattle, Wash. 98109
Opera
Mid-July through early August
This festival presents two complete cycles
of Richard Wagner's four operas, *Der
Ring des Nibelungen,* presented in both
German and English. The Festival became
the first organization in the world to pre-
sent both German and English Ring
Cycles. This production schedule has
been continued since 1975 attracting
yearly visitors from around the world.
The performances are in the Seattle
Opera House which seats over 3,000.
Director: Glynn Ross
Sponsor: Seattle Opera Association
Accommodations: For information on
lodging write: Seattle King County
Convention and Visitors Bureau, 1815
Seventh Ave., Seattle, Wash. 98101.
There is no camping. There are very
nice picnicking areas near the fountain
on the Center grounds
Ticket information: Complete Cycle
tickets range from $54 to $160
How to get there: The Festival is on the
Seattle Center Grounds

Peninsula Music Festival
Fish Creek, Wis. 54212
Classical
Middle to late August
Founded by Thor Johnson in 1975 and
now directed by Michael Charry, the
Peninsula Music Festival features a series
of classical music concerts in August of
each year. Performers in previous festivals have included John Browning, Grant
Johannesen, Nathaniel Rosen, Zara Nel-
sova, Donald Gramm, Shirley Verrett,
George Boulet, and William Masselos.
Concerts are held in the Gibraltar Audi-
torium in Fish Creek, Wis. which seats
725.
Director: Michael Charry
Sponsor: Peninsula Arts Association
Accommodations: There are many motels
and resorts in the area, as well as village,
state, and private campgrounds where
trailer facilities are available. For information, write to Door County Chamber
of Commerce, Sturgeon Bay, Wis. 54235.
In addition to the music festival, Fish
Creek plays host to a summer theater.
Ticket information: Admission is $5.50
per concert. For tickets, write to Peninsula Music Festival, Ephraim, Wis. 54211.
How to get there: Air, bus, or auto to
Sturgeon Bay, Wis.

WYOMING

Western Arts Music Festival
Box 3037 University Station,
University of Wyoming, Laramie,
Wyo. 82071
Classical chamber music
Mid-June to mid-July
Since the early '70s this annual festival
has been providing a program of chamber
music on the campus of the University of
Wyoming. Performers in recent years
have included the Western Arts Trio,
Pro Arte Quartet, Wyoming Woodwind
Quintet, Sylvia Jenkins, and Raymond
Ocock. An additional event during the
season is the Symposium on New
American Music. An indoor concert hall
provides seating for 600 people.
Directors: David Tomatz and Werner
Rose
Accommodations: Hotels and motels,
camping and picnicking are available in
the area
Ticket information: No admission charge.
Enrollment fee for Symposium if taken
for credit at the university.

JAZZ

CALIFORNIA

Glen Helen Invitational Jazz Festival
Glen Helen Regional Park, 2555 Devore
Road, San Bernardino, Calif. 92407
Jazz
Saturday in mid-May
Primarily a contest festival for college
big bands and jazz combos, the Glen
Helen Invitational also features guest
bands such as the Jim Linahon Big Band
and the University of Redlands Studio
Band.
Performances take place outdoors in Glen
Helen Park in an area which seats approxi-
mately 1,000 people.
Director: Dave DeLille
Sponsor: San Bernardino County
Regional Parks Department
Accommodations: In San Bernardino
there are the Travelodge, the Hilton Inn,
and the Holiday Inn. Camping is $3 per
unit per night at the Festival site; facilities such as restrooms, showers, barbecue
grills and a disposal station are on the
grounds. Trailers up to 35 ft. are
welcome.
Ticket information: There is an entrance
fee of $1 per vehicle; performances are
otherwise free
How to get there: Glen Helen Regional
Park is 10 miles northwest of San Bernardino, via I-15 at the Devore Road off-
ramp

Monterey Jazz Festival
P.O. Box JAZZ, Monterey, Calif. 93940
Jazz
Third weekend in September
The Monterey Jazz Festival presents
well-known jazz greats as well as "jazz
stars of tomorrow." The 5 concerts
which make up the 3-day festival are
held in a partially covered outdoor
arena which seats 7,000. Excellent
sound equipment enables everyone to
hear equally well. Between shows there
is entertainment outside the arena.
Warm clothing is advised for evening
concerts.
Director: James L. Lyons
Accommodations: Hotel and motel accommodations are available. Write to
Monterey Peninsula Chamber of Commerce, Box 1770, Monterey, Calif.
93940, or phone (408)649-3200.
Ticket information: Season tickets range
from $34.50 to $44; single performance
tickets range from $6 to $10. All concerts
are usually sold out, so tickets must be
purchased early. Write to the Festival at
the above address.
How to get there: Concerts are held on
the Monterey County Fairgrounds 1
mile from downtown Monterey. The
Fairgrounds are situated 5 minutes from
the bus and airline depots.

Vintage Sound
Paul Masson Mountain Winery, Pierce
Road, Saratoga, Calif.
Jazz
July through September
Weekend jazz concerts at Paul Masson
Mountain Winery present jazz greats
such as Dizzy Gillespie, Carmen McRae,
Cal Tjader, and many more. There is
complimentary wine during intermis-
sions. The Winery, with its Romanesque
facade, is a picturesque setting for these
outdoor concerts. Audiences are limited
to 1,000.
Director: Mr. Jan Wells
Sponsor: Paul Masson Vineyards
Accommodations: There is no camping
or picnicking at the Vineyards. For in-
formation on lodging in the area contact
the Festival at the address below.
Ticket information: Admission is about
$7. For tickets write to Vintage Sounds,
P.O. Box 97, Saratoga, Calif. 95070.
How to get there: Write to the Festival
for directions.

MINNESOTA

Augsburg Jazz Festival
731 21st Ave. S., Minneapolis, Minn.
55454
Jazz
March
There are jazz concerts on both evenings
of this 2-day festival, and clinics for
young musicians during the day. Past
performers at the Festival have included
Gary Foster and Bobby Shew, Randy
Purcell and Eddie Daniels, Jon Faddis
and Gary Niewood, and Lin Biviano and
Bruce Johnstone.
Events are held in Si Melby Hall with a
seating capacity of 1,200.
Director: Monica Maye, Fine Arts Coor-
dinator
Sponsor: Augsburg College
Accommodations: Accommodations are
available in downtown Minneapolis at
the Radisson, Masquette Inn, and the
Holiday Inn. There is no camping.
Ticket information: Admission is $3
Tickets may be obtained from the Festi-
val at the address above, or at the gate.

MISSOURI

National Ragtime Festival
Goldenrod Showboat, 400 Wharf St.,
St. Louis, Mo. 63102
Ragtime and jazz
Mid-June for 1 week
Much of the music in this week-long
festival is presented on the decks of a
showboat in the Mississippi River. Past
performers at this ragtime and tradi-
tional jazz festival have included Turk
Murphy, the Salty Dogs, the St. Louis
Ragtimers, the 1926 Jazz Band, the
Royal Society Jazz Orchestra, and the
New Orleans Jazz Band. There is contin-
uous music nightly throughout the
Festival. Food and drinks are available.
Director: G. William Oakley
Sponsors: Goldenrod Showboat
Accommodations/other items of interest
in area: For a list of accommodations,
write to the Festival director.
Other items of interest in the area in-
clude the St. Louis Gateway Arch and
Six Flags over Mid-America.
Ticket information: Admission is $9
and $10. For ticket information, write
or call Goldenrod Box Office, 400
Wharf St., St. Louis, Mo. 63102;
tel (314)621-3311.
How to get there: The showboat is on
the St. Louis levee of the Mississippi
River

NEW YORK

Newport Jazz Festival—New York
New York City, Saratoga Springs, N.Y., and Waterloo Village in Stanhope, N.J.
Jazz
Mid-June to beginning of July
The Newport Jazz Festival began in 1954 in Newport, R.I., and moved to New York City in 1972. The Festival has become famous for the quality, variety and breadth of jazz it presents—prompting even President Jimmy Carter to pay it tribute. Every major jazz artist has participated, among them Ella Fitzgerald, Count Basie, George Benson, Herbie Hancock, Thelonius Monk, Miles Davis, Stan Getz, Lionel Hampton, Stan Kenton, Chick Corea, and Dizzy Gillespie.
In New York City, concerts take place at Carnegie Hall, Avery Fisher Hall, N.Y.U. Loeb Center, and various outdoor locations. In Saratoga Springs performances are at the Saratoga Springs Performing Arts Center; in Waterloo Village they take place outdoors.
Director: George Wein
Sponsor: Jos. Schlitz Brewing Co.
Accommodations: In New York City, the New York Sheraton is the official Newport Jazz Festival headquarters and has special rates for festival patrons. A hotel list may be obtained from New York Convention and Visitors Bureau, Inc., Dept. J., 90 E. 42nd St., New York, N.Y. 10017.
Ticket information: Tickets range from $7.50 to $15. For tickets, write to Newport Jazz Festival—New York, P.O. Box 1169, Ansonia Station, New York, N.Y. 10023.

OHIO

The KOOL Jazz Traveling Festivals
3380 Erie Ave., Cincinnati, Ohio 45208
Jazz, soul, rhythm and blues
From late May to early August
All summer the KOOL Jazz Festivals, begun in 1974, tour the nation's major cities, among them Oakland, Milwaukee, San Diego, Houston, Kansas City, Atlanta, Cincinnati, New Orleans, New York, and Hampton, Va. Most of the events take place in large outdoor stadiums for 1 or 2 nights on the weekend. (The Houston Astrodome, Louisiana Superdome, and Hampton Coliseum are covered.) Most of the well-known names in jazz and soul music have taken part: George Benson, The Commodores, Aretha Franklin, Natalie Cole, Gladys Knight & the Pips, Johnnie Taylor, and B.B. King, to name only a few. Among the Festival's features are giant color television screens which bring front-row views to the entire audience.
Most festival nights start at 8:00 P.M. and end at 12:30 A.M.
Sponsor: KOOL (Brown and Williamson Tobacco Company)
Accommodations: Contact convention and visitors bureaus in each city of interest for information about accommodations
Hotel and travel assistance is available in Atlanta, Milwaukee, San Diego, Houston, and New Orleans through Right Way Productions, 4319 Degnan Blvd., Los Angeles, Calif. 90008.
Ticket information: Prices for tickets range from $7.50 to $12. For summer season schedule and ticket information write to The KOOL Jazz Festivals at the above address. Tel. (513)321-6688.

THE NEW ORLEANS JAZZ AND HERITAGE FESTIVAL (PHOTO PREVIOUS PAGE)

TEXAS

Texas Jazz Festival
Corpus Christi Coliseum, Corpus Christi,
Tex.
Jazz
Early July
The Texas Jazz Festival was the first
free jazz festival in the world which
featured top name entertainment. Greats
such as Stan Kenton, Al Hirt, Arnette
Cobb, and Louis Gasca participated in
past festivals. The Festival continues
to present the best in jazz—at the
Corpus Christi Coliseum, which seats
15,000, on a sightseeing jazz cruise, and
at churches and clubs in Corpus Christi.
There is jazz at the airport when the
stars arrive, and open rehearsals. The
Festival also sponsors music clinics where
students can learn from the Festival's
guest artists.
Director: Al "Beto" Garcia
Sponsors: Miller Brewing Co., and Musicians Union #644 Local Membership.
Ticket information: Admission ranges
from $5 to $6. Tickets can be obtained
from Corpus Christi Tourist Bureau,
613 S. Shoreline, Corpus Christi, Tex.
78403

FOLK

ALABAMA

Bluegrass Fiddle Jamboree—Arts and Crafts Fair

Route 3, Box 218, Danville, Ala.
Folk and bluegrass
May
Singers, musicians, and dancers compete for prizes and the honor of being the best during this 2-day festival. The competitions include old-time country, folk and gospel singing, mandolin, harmonica, guitar, bluegrass bands, bluegrass banjo, senior fiddle (51 years and up), junior fiddle (under 50 years), buck dancing, and clogging. Some fine bluegrass bands will also play for entertainment.
The Festival is held near Decatur, Ala., at the Southeastern Horse Center, which is covered and provides seating for about 10,000. There's plenty of parking and good food available.
Director: Bob Myers
Sponsor: Morgan and Lawrence Legal Secretaries Assn.
Accommodations: Motel accommodations are available at Decatur Inn and Holiday Inn on Highway 31 North. Camping is allowed with hook-ups and water for $6 per day. There are facilities for trailers. Picnicking is discouraged; food concessions are conveniently located.
Ticket information: Admission ranges from $2 to $3 at the gate only
How to get there: The Festival is 10 miles E. of Decatur and 3 miles E. of I-65 on Highway 67

Bucks Pocket Old Time Fiddlers' Convention

Route 1, Section, Ala. 35771
Bluegrass
First Saturday in November
Since it started as a small event to raise money for community projects, this bluegrass and country festival has grown to be one of the larger amateur events of its kind in the southeast U.S.
Performances take place at the Macedonia Junior High Auditorium, which has seating for 1,000.
Director: Rabon Allen
Sponsor: Macedonia Junior High School
Accommodations: The Holiday Inn and Liberty Inn in Scottsboro can provide accommodation. Camping is available at Bucks Pocket State Park.

Ticket information: Ticket price to be established; tickets available only at the door
How to get there: Section is 12 miles from Scottsboro

Dixie Bluegrass

Lockwood Park, Chatan, Ala.
Bluegrass
May and September
Twice a year, in spring and fall, 4-day bluegrass festivals are held in Lockwood Park. Past performers have included Bill Monroe, Lester Flatt, Osborne Bros., Jim and Jesse, Ralph Stanley, James Monroe, and Carl Story.
Concerts are held outdoors; in case of rain a shed is available with a capacity of 1,000.
Director: Margie Sullivan
Accommodations: Camping facilities are available. Trailer hookups are also available. Picnicking is allowed.
Ticket information: Four-day tickets are $20 and 3-day tickets are $16. They can be purchased at the gate.
How to get there: Lockwood Park is 5 miles off Highway 17 in Washington County

The Dixie Bluegrass Boys North Alabama Bluegrass Festival

Highway 72 West, Barton, Ala.
Bluegrass
A weekend in mid-August
Initiated in 1974, the Festival takes place during a 3-day weekend in an uncovered outdoor area which seats 5,000.
Director: The Dixie Bluegrass Boys
Sponsor: Lin Michael
Accommodations/other items of interest in area: The Holiday Inn and Howard Johnson's in Florence can provide lodging nearby. Camping is available in the area.
The Tennessee River, with the T.V.A. Wilson Dam and its swimming, camping, and boating, flows nearby.
Ticket information: Tickets are $3 Friday, $4 Saturday, and $3 Sunday. Available only at the gate.

Dixie Land Bluegrass Festival

P.O. Box 186, Gantt, Ala. 36038
Bluegrass and folk
October
This 3-day festival presents bluegrass and folk music, clogging, and buck dancing. It boasts entertainment for the whole

family. The Festival is outdoors, and patrons are advised to bring chairs. Food is available at the Festival, and there is also picnicking.

The Festival is held at Riverview Campground and Music Park.

Director: B.R. Wagner

Sponsor: B.R.W. Enterprises.

Accommodations: Lodging is available at motels in the area. There is camping with complete facilities at a cost of $10 for 3 days; trailers are also welcome. Open fires, fishing, tenting and Indian-style camping are all possible at Riverview Campground.

Ticket information: Admission is $10 for the 3-day weekend. For tickets or more information contact the Festival.

How to get there: There will be signs to Riverview Camp on Route 82 between Red Level and Gantt, Ala.

Southern States Bluegrass Festival
P.O. Box 698, Cullman, Ala. 35055
Bluegrass
Late July

This southern-style bluegrass festival has featured such groups as the Free State Boys, Dixie Mountain Boys, the Southern Strangers, the Country Ramblers, Dixie Express, the Campbell Trio, Shades of Bluegrass, Lonesome Pine Fiddlers, and the Lawrence Millbillies.

Events are outdoors and guests should bring lawn chairs.

Director: James Terry

Sponsor: Parks & Recreation

Accommodations: Motel accommodations are available in the area. Camping in the rough is available at a cost of $4 for 2 people. Trailers are permitted.

Ticket information: Two-day tickets are $7 in advance, $8 at the gate. Day tickets range from $3 to $5. They can be obtained by mail from Parks & Recreation, P.O. Box 698, Cullman, Ala. 35055.

**Tennessee Valley Old-Time Fiddlers'
Convention**
Athens State College, Athens, Ala.
Old-time fiddling and related early rural music
First full weekend in October

In the early 1960s a Nashville newspaper columnist lamented the apparent death of old-time fiddling, but a survey by a few devotees of old-time music in the Tennessee Valley area revealed the opposite. It was found that a lot of old-time musicians, unknown to the general public, regularly met in their homes to play, thereby maintaining their skill in the old art.

After an enthusiastic response to 2 local fiddling contests held in Limestone County (Athens), Alabama, as a test, the Tennessee Valley Old-Time Fiddlers' Assn. was formed in the summer of 1967 and an annual convention established. The first full weekend in October has been established as the permanent date for the annual convention, with Athens State College as host. The authentic old-time music to be heard at this event is predominantly southeastern in style; however, other styles, such as Canadian, Texan, northeastern and northwestern may be enjoyed also. Events include contests in old-time fiddling and concerts in related early rural music.

Events are held outdoors on the college campus—in the gym in case of rain.

Director: Bill Harrison, 305 Stella Dr., Madison, Ala. 35758

Sponsor: Tennessee Valley Old-Time Fiddlers' Assn.

Accommodations: Accommodations include the Athens Motel (205)232-0131; the Travelway Motel (205)232-3933; and the Welcome Inn (205)232-6944. Picnicking and primitive camping are permitted in the area. There are no special facilities for trailers.

Ticket information: Admission is $2 and $3.

How to get there: Athens in midway between Nashville and Birmingham, at the junction of US-72 and I-65.

ARIZONA

Arizona Old-Time Fiddlers' Contest
Payson Chamber of Commerce, P.O. Drawer A, Payson, Ariz. 85541.
tel. (602)474-2994
Traditional, fiddle music
Late September
Payson's Old-Time Fiddlers' Contest attracts contestants from all over the southwest, who perform danceable folk tunes played in old-time fiddling fashion. In addition to the fiddlers, there is a guest band and square dancing. The 2-day contest is held at the Payson rodeo grounds, with seats for 4,000.
Director: Larry H. Stanton
Sponsor: Payson Chamber of Commerce
Accommodations: There is ample motel space in the area, as well as free camping and facilities for trailers
Ticket information: Tickets are available at the gate

Old-Time Country Music Festival
Payson Chamber of Commerce, P.O. Drawer A, Payson, Ariz. 85541.
tel. (602)474-2994.
Old-Time Country Music
Late June
The 2-day old-time country music festival is held at Payson's rodeo grounds.
Director: Paul Berryman
Sponsor: Payson Chamber of Commerce
Accommodations: Motels, free camping, and trailer facilities are available
Ticket information: Tickets are available at the gate

Old-Time Gospel Music Festival
Payson Chamber of Commerce, P.O. Drawer A, Payson, Ariz. 85541.
tel. (602)474-2994
Late May
The high pine country north of Phoenix provides the setting for this 2-day gospel music festival, which features various gospel groups from the southwest. The Festival is held at the rodeo grounds, seating approximately 4,000. Foul-weather clothing is recommended.
Director: Pat Watson
Sponsor: Payson Chamber of Commerce
Accommodations: Motels, free camping, and trailer facilities are available
Ticket information: Tickets are available at the gate

ARKANSAS

Albert E. Brumley Sundown to Sunup Singing
Springdale, Ark.
Gospel singing
Early August
For 3 nights in the Parsons Rodeo Arena (13,000 capacity) in Springdale, gospel music fans gather to hear groups such as the Kingsmen, the Blackwood Bros., the Singing Hemphills, and the Dixie Echoes. In case of rain the program is held in 2 large auditoriums. A talent contest for best amateur or semi-pro gospel with $175 in cash prizes is also held.
Director: Bob Brumley
Sponsor: Springdale Chamber of Commerce
Accommodations: Special parking area free for self-contained campers. Many motels in Springdale can provide accommodations, such as the Flamingo Motel, the Holiday Inn, and Holiday Motel, all on Highway 71 S.
Nearby Beaver Lake, one of the largest man-made lakes in the nation, offers fishing, swimming, and boating.
Ticket information: Advance tickets for 3 nights are $10, or $4.50 each night. For tickets, write to Springdale Chamber of Commerce, Springdale, Ark. 72764.
How to get there: Springdale is in northwest Arkansas on US highways 71 and 62

Northwest Arkansas Bluegrass Music Festival
Route 2, Box 12, Harrison, Ark. 72601
Folk and bluegrass
August
Well-known local bands and others, like the Tennessee Gentlemen, perform bluegrass music at this 3-day festival. There are also contests for flat-top guitar, banjo, and fiddle. Sunday morning gospel singing is a festival tradition.
The show is at the Harrison Roundup Club Arena, with an outdoor stage and plenty of shade.
Director: Ardith Yancey
Accommodations: There is camping on the fairgrounds where the Festival is held. The fairgrounds are close to motels and restaurants.
Ticket information: Admission ranges from $2 to $5. A 3-day ticket is $9.

Tickets can be purchased at the gate.
How to get there: The Festival is on the
Northwest Arkansas Fairgrounds, which
is ½ mile S. of Harrison, Ark.

Ozark Folk Center
Mountain View, Ark. 72560
tel. (501)269-3851
Folk, gospel, traditional
May through October
The Ozark Folk Center is an Arkansas
State Park dedicated to the preservation
and sharing of the Ozark Mountain way
of life. Throughout the season the center
offers evening music programs featuring
traditional instruments such as acoustical
guitar, 5-string banjo, fiddle, mandolin,
autoharp, mountain dulcimer, and
picking bow. Singers perform ballads,
gospel songs, and other traditional music
learned in the homes of friends and
family through oral transmission. Dancers present the square and round dances
of the Ozarks as well as the jig. The
performers are the people from Mountain View and neighboring communities
who have brought their traditional music
to the center for visitors. The annual
Arkansas Folk Festival, now in its 17th
year, is a 2-weekend event held at the
center in late April. There are several
weekend festivals and contests throughout the center's season. The music
auditorium seats 1,060.
Director: Jack Quaill
Sponsor: Arkansas State Parks
Accommodations: In addition to the
Ozark Folk Center Lodge (on the Folk
Center grounds) there are many motels
and campgrounds in the Mountain View
area. For information, write to the
center.
Ticket information: Admission to folk
musicals is $2, at the gate only.
How to get there: For travel information, contact the Arkansas Department
of Parks and Tourism, State Capitol,
Little Rock, Ark. 72201. tel. (501)371-
1511.

Turkey Track Bluegrass Music
Highway 250, Waldron, Ark.
Bluegrass
Mid-June
Popular bluegrass bands perform in the
beautiful Ouachita mountains at this
weekend festival at Turkey Track Farm.
Past performers have included Mac Wiseman, Joe Stuart, Kenny Cantrell and the
Tennessee Gentlemen, to name only a
few. There is also an arts and crafts display.
Events are on a back porch stage, with
unlimited outdoor space for the audience. Folks should be prepared for cool
evening weather.
Director: Bill Churchill
Accommodations/other items of interest
in area: Lodging is available at Aloha
and at Southern Hills, Waldron. Camping
is free with electric hook-ups at $2 per
day; there is no charge for trailers. There
is a picnicking area close to the Festival's
concession. Fishing, swimming and scenic
drives are available around Waldron.
Ticket information: Admission is about
$4 to $5 at the gate. A 3-day pass is
about $11.
How to get there: Turkey Track Farm is
2 miles S. of Waldron on 71-B, then 7½
miles E. on Highway 250

CALIFORNIA

Art Festival and Oldtime Fiddle Jamboree
Museum Park, P.O. Box 595, Shasta, Calif. 96087
Folk and fiddle
May
The Oldtime Fiddle Jamboree, sponsored by the California State Oldtime Fiddling Association, District 6, is held during the Art Festival and Children's Art Fair. Guitarists, banjoists, bassists and harp players are invited to perform from 11 A.M. to 5 P.M. on the 2 festival days. All music is acoustical.
The Festival is outdoors.
Director: Jeri Fallis
Sponsor: Shasta Service Guild
Accommodations/other items of interest in area: Lodging is available in Redding. Free camping is available at Whiskeytown Lake, 3 miles W. of Shasta.
Of interest in the area are Shasta Museum, Shasta Lake, and Whiskeytown Lake.
Ticket information: Admission is free
How to get there: Museum Park is in Shasta State Historic Park on Highway 299-W, 3 miles W. of Redding

Calico Hullabaloo; Calico Spring Festival; Calico Days Celebration
Calico Ghost Town, Ghost Town Road, P.O. Box 638, Yermo, Calif.
Country and western, bluegrass, barbershop, ragtime
Late March, late May, and 3-day weekend in mid-October
The Calico Hullabaloo features a country and western dance and other attractions such as the Tobacco Chewing and Spitting Championship (the current distance record is 28' 10"), Horseshoe Pitching Championship, Old Miner's Stew Cookoff, and Greased Pole Climb. The Calico Spring Festival features a country dance, bluegrass under the stars, fiddle, banjo, guitar, group competitions, and barbershop and ragtime music. The Calico Days Celebration recreates the Old West for 3 days with a western dance, a moonshine jamboree (bluegrass music), a gunfight stunt championship, an old prospector's burro run, a country gospel show, and old-fashioned contests of all

kinds. Some of the musicians who have played in recent years include Joe and Rose Lee Maphis, Bodie, Mountain Express, and the Gloryland String Band. Activities take place in the Calico Silver Bowl, an uncovered outdoor facility which seats 1,000.
Director: Don V. Tucker
Sponsor: San Bernardino County Regional Parks Dept.
Accommodations: Camping at the site is available at $4 per night per unit. Facilities include restrooms, showers, barbecue grills, and a disposal station. Trailers up to 35 ft. long are welcome. The Holiday Inn, Vagabond Motor Hotel, Howard Johnson's, and Travelodge, all on Main Street in Barstow, can provide accommodations.
Ticket information: Entrance fee is $1 per vehicle per day

49er Banjo, Fiddle and Guitar Festival
California State University, Long Beach, Calif.
Folk and bluegrass (traditional and contemporary)
Late April
This 1-day student-sponsored campus festival features advanced competition in banjo, fiddle, guitar, bluegrass bands, and miscellaneous instruments. Guest performers are also a part of the show.
The Festival, held outdoors, can accommodate 7,000, and is usually sold out.
Director: Rowland Kerr
Sponsor: Associated Students, CSULB
Accommodations: Lodging is available in the area. There is no camping on campus, but picnicking is allowed, and food will be sold by campus organizations.
Ticket information: Admission is $4. Tickets can be obtained from Associated Students, CSULB, 1212 Bellflower Blvd., Long Beach, Calif. 90804.

Golden West Bluegrass Festival
Silver Lakes Park, Norco, Calif.
Bluegrass
The last weekends in January, April, and October
The Golden West Bluegrass Festival is considered to be the oldest bluegrass music festival in California. Don Reno, Jim and Jesse, Bill Monroe, Ralph Stanley, Lester Flatt, and the Country Gentlemen are among those who have performed in this lovely outdoor setting.
Director: Dick Tyner

Accommodations: Nearby accommodations include the Corona Inn in Corona and the Pine Tree Motel in Chino. Camping is available at $2 a night; there are no hook-ups, but trailers are allowed. Picnic facilities, a swimming pool, hot showers, and horseback riding are all available. Ticket information: Tickets are $5 on Fridays, $6 on Saturdays and Sundays. They are available from Dick Tyner, P.O. Box 341, Bonsall, Calif. 92003. How to get there: Silver Lakes Park is 65 miles E. of Los Angeles

Grass Valley Bluegrass Festival
Nevada County Fairgrounds, Grass Valley, Calif.
Bluegrass, old time, gospel
Summer—3rd weekend in June
Fall—3rd weekend in September
The success of this summer festival at the foot of the Sierra Mountains prompted the initiation in 1979 of a fall festival as well. Regional and local bands take part in 3 days of bluegrass, gospel and old-time country music. In addition there are workshops in bluegrass-related instruments.
Performances take place outdoors in an area with a covered stage. The audience may bring folding chairs.
Sponsor: California Bluegrass Association
Accommodations/other items of interest in area: There are motels and hotels in Grass Valley and nearby Nevada City. Camping at the site is available with limited hook-ups. Trailers are welcome. Cost is included in admission tickets.
Ticket information: Three-day tickets cost $14; Friday and Sunday, $5 each day; Saturday, $7.50. For tickets, write to California Bluegrass Association, P.O. Box 11287, San Francisco, Calif. 94101
How to get there: The fairgrounds are E. of Grass Valley (on State Route 49) on McCourtney Road
How to get there: Calico Ghost Town is on Ghost Town Road off I-15, 10 miles N. of Barstow, Calif.

Huck Finn Jubilee
Mojave Narrows Regional Park, P.O. Box 361, Victorville, Calif.
Bluegrass, country and western
Father's Day weekend in June
This 2-day event is designed to provide some of the fun Tom Sawyer and Huck Finn had nearly 100 years ago. There are

fiddlers' contests, river-raft building contests, fish derbies, rowboat races, hot-air ballon rides, and a fence-painting championship.
The jubilee's setting is a regional park and activities take place outdoors.
Director: Don V. Tucker
Sponsor: San Bernardino County Regional Parks Dept.
Accommodations: Hilton Inn, Green Tree Inn, and Motel 6 in Victorville can provide accommodations. Camping at the site is available at $3 per night per unit. Facilities include restrooms, showers, barbecue grills, and a disposal station. Trailers up to 35 ft. long are welcome.
Ticket information: Entrance fee is $1 per vehicle
How to get there: Mojave Narrows Regional Park is off I-15, 7 miles on Bear Valley Cutoff across railroad tracks to Ridgecrest, and then left on Ridgecrest 3 miles

International Chili Society Bluegrass Jamboree
Tropico Mine, Rosamund, Calif.
Bluegrass
A weekend in late October
This bluegrass festival and contest originated as a supplementary attraction around the Annual World Championship Chili Cookoff (cooking contest), which is still an important feature of the weekend. Performances, by local talent, are held outdoors.
Director: Dick Tyner
Accommodations: The Antelope Valley Inn is in nearby Lancaster, Calif. Camping, picnicking, and trailers are permitted without cost.
Ticket information: Admission is $5 each day. For tickets, write to Dick Tyner, P.O. Box 341, Bonsall, Calif. 92003.
How to get there: Fifty miles N. of Los Angeles on Route 14

International Folk Dance Festival
Dorothy Chandler Pavilion, Los Angeles Music Center, Los Angeles, Calif.
Folk
Dates vary considerably; in 1980 it was held on January 26
As many as 1,000 folk dancers from 18 nations now participate in this 1-day festival which began in 1937. Everything from American Indian ceremonial dances to Spanish flamenco to Korean traditional dances are performed at the

Dorothy Chandler Pavilion in the afternoon and evening.
Director: Irwin Parnes
Sponsor: International Concerts Exchange
Accommodations: There are many hotels and motels in Los Angeles
Ticket information: Tickets range in price from $3.75 to $8.75

Lake Gregory Summer Fest
Lake Gregory Regional Park, P.O. Box 656, Crestline, Calif. 92325
Bluegrass and swing
Early July
This 1-day event features bluegrass and swing music for its evening dance. In addition there are kayak and paddleboard races, relays, a 2-man volleyball championship, and a fireworks show.
West Coast groups like Bodie Mountain Express, Phiddle Harmonics, and Sum Fun Band perform in an outdoor setting which can seat approximately 800 people.
Director: Dave DeLille
Sponsor: San Bernardino County Regional Parks
Accommodations: No camping available
Ticket information: Entrance fee is $.75 per person
How to get there: Lake Gregory Regional Park is on Lake Gregory Drive in Crestline

Old-Time Fiddlers' Convention
Univ. of California, Santa Barbara, Calif.
Folk (traditional)
Mid-October
Each year this 1-day festival honors one of the outstanding old-time musicians. The celebration occurs outdoors in the park-like area of the campus diamond, which can comfortably accommodate 4,000, with the Santa Ynez Mountains forming a scenic backdrop.
The Festival sponsors performances by bluegrass and old-time bands, and a number of contests for both beginning and advanced folk musicians and singers.
Director: Peter Feldman
Sponsor: UCSB Arts and Lectures
Accommodations/other items of interest in area: Lodging is available at Motel 6, the Holiday Inn, and Turnpike Lodge in Goleta. No camping is allowed on campus, but there are facilities nearby at El Capitan Beach. Picnicking is

allowed and food will be sold at the Festival.
Santa Barbara is known for its excellent beaches. Also of interest in the area are Santa Barbara Mission and the village of Solvang.
Ticket information: Admission is $3. Tickets can be obtained at UCSB Arts and Lectures Ticket Office in person, by mail, or at the gate.
How to get there: Take Highway 101 to UCSB. The Festival is on the campus diamond lawn.

Salt Flats Hoedown
Salinas Community Center, N. Main St., Salinas, Calif.
Country and bluegrass
July
This "hoedown" is primarily a western regional fiddle contest, along with entertainment provided by bluegrass bands and other special entertainment. It was begun in 1975. A rodeo follows the hoedown program.
The event takes place in an auditorium seating 1,600 people at the Salinas Community Center.
Director: Grace Stewart
Sponsor: California Rodeo Association
Accommodations: There are many hotels and motels in the area. Reservations are recommended. (Two hotels offer opportunities for free jamming—Quality Inn and Town House.) No tent camping is permitted but campers and trailers are welcome at the site.
Ticket information: For information write to Grace Stewart, Coordinator of Annual Salt Flats Hoedown, 1044 San Simeon Drive, Salinas, Calif. 93901

San Diego Bluegrass Jamboree
On the Indian Reservation, Alpine, Calif.
Bluegrass
One day early in April and one day in late June
The jamboree is held in a large oak grove on the reservation of the Viejas Indians, who are said to have resided there for over 1,000 years. The Festival was founded in 1975 and has featured such performers as the Country Gentlemen, the Osborne Brothers, and Dan Crary.
Director: Dick Tyner
Accommodations: There are several hotels and motels in Alpine, 5 miles from the Festival site. Camping costs $2 a night, and trailers are permitted. Facilities in-

clude a pool, a general store, and a Jacuzzi.

Ticket information: Tickets are available at $5 per day from Dick Tyner, P.O. Box 341, Bonsall, Calif. 92003

How to get there: Thirty-five miles E. of San Diego on I-8

Topanga Banjo Fiddle Contest
University of California at Los Angeles, Westwood, California
Folk, bluegrass, traditional, country
Early July (one day)
This annual all-day event features fiddle, banjo, and singing contests in both bluegrass and traditional styles. Contestants compete for cash prizes, merchandise, and trophies. In addition to the contests there are guest performers, and patrons are encouraged to bring their own instruments for jam sessions. There is dance instruction in clog, country, and square dancing.
The Topanga Banjo Fiddle Contest began 19 years ago in Topanga Canyon. In recent years the event has alternated between the campuses of the University of California at Santa Barbara and at Los Angeles. The Festival is held outdoors.
Director: Dorian Keyser
Sponsor: Santa Monica Friends Meeting House
Accommodations: There are many hotels and motels in the Santa Monica/West Los Angeles area
Ticket information: Admission is $3. Tickets are available only at the gate. For information, write to Dorian Keyser, 5922 Corbin Ave., Tarzana, Calif. 91356. tel. (213)345-3795.

Vista Bluegrass Jamboree
Vista, Calif.
Bluegrass
One day in mid-July
Local bands perform in an outdoor setting
Director: Dick Tyner
Accommodations: There are many hotels, motels, and camping sites in the area
Ticket information: Tickets are $3.50 for the day, and are available from Dick Tyner, P.O. Box 341, Bonsall, Calif. 92003
How to get there: The Jamboree is 40 miles N. of San Diego between I-5 and I-15 in Vista, Calif.

Zen Crook Music Festival
Prado Regional Park, 16700 Euclid Ave., Chino, Calif. 91710
Country and western, bluegrass
Last weekend in August
This festival provides 3 days of country and bluegrass music by well-known performers (Merle Travis, Dan Crary, Joe and Rose Lee Maphis, and Riverside Citrus Belters Barbershop Chorus have appeared) as well as the West Coast Flat-Picking Guitar Championship, on Sunday.
Located in the gentle rolling hills of Prado Regional Park, the Festival takes place outdoors. Seating is provided by the audience.
Director: Dick Tyner
Sponsors: San Bernardino County Regional Parks Dept. and Dick Tyner Productions
Accommodations: Camping at the site is available at $4 per night per unit. Facilities include restrooms, showers, barbecue grills, and a disposal station. Trailers up to 35 ft. long are welcome. Accommodations are available from Pine Tree Motel in Chino and Ontario Travelodge in nearby Ontario.
Ticket information: Ticket prices are not yet determined. For information, write to San Bernardino County Regional Parks Dept., 825 E. Third St., San Bernardino, Calif. 92415, or the Festival address above.

CANADA

Atlantic Folk Festival
Moxsom Farm, Hardwood Lands, Mants County, Nova Scotia, Canada
Folk
Late July to early August
This 3-day folk festival presents the best of down-east Canadian folk music, as well as folk artists from other parts of Canada and the U.S. Valdy, Buffy St. Marie, Wilf Carter, Jonathan Edwards, Ryan's Fancy, and John Allan Cameron have all performed, as well as many others.
The Festival is held on a working farm. Besides the main stage, there is a traditional stage and a stage for jam sessions. Regional musicians have been invited to play at the camping areas. There is also a large children's area.
Director: Brooks Diamond
Accommodations: There will be areas on Moxom Farm set aside for camping for about 15,000. Facilities include running water and cold showers. The cost is included in the Festival ticket price. Food concessions will provide over 20 different foods. Lodging is also available at Keddy's Motel and Glengarry Motel in Truro, Nova Scotia.
Ticket information: Tickets are about $20 Canadian for the weekend or $10 Canadian per day if ordered in advance; or $24 and $12 at the gate. Tickets can be ordered from Rm. 212, S.U.B. Dalhousie Univ., Halifax, Nova Scotia, B3H 3H4, Canada.
How to get there: Take Highway 102 from Halifax, drive 40 miles and take exit 9 to Rout 14, then drive 3 miles along Route 14 to Moxsom Farm

Back 40 Bluegrass Festival and Competition
127 Keats Drive, Woodstock, Ontario N4S 8C1, Canada
Bluegrass
Mid-June
This 3-day festival presents bluegrass by a variety of bands, an open bluegrass jam, and gospel singing on Sunday. A competition for bluegrass and old-time bands is a central event. There is also a hog-calling contest.
The Festival takes place outdoors, on the shores of a lake. Bring lawn chairs.

Director: Wayne Uncer
Accommodations: There is free camping in the rough on the Festival site. Lodging is available at many hotels and motels in the area.
Ticket information: Weekend tickets are $10. Day tickets range from $2 to $6.
How to get there: The festival is at Pittock Conservation Area which is 1 mile N. of Woodstock, Ontario, on Highway 59

Bluegrass Canada
Carlisle P.O., Carlisle, Ontario LOR 1HO, Canada
Bluegrass
First full weekend in June
Bluegrass Canada, now in its 7th year, is the largest Canadian bluegrass festival. The annual 3-day event is held in Courtcliffe Park and includes concerts, a bluegrass band contest, gospel singing, square dancing, and a crafts fair. Past festivals have included such performers as Doc Watson, Bill Monroe, and Lester Flatt. Festival seating is out-of-doors, uncovered, and foul weather clothing is recommended.
Directors: Court and Rad Weaver
Accommodations: Camping is permitted on the park grounds. Water and electric hook-ups are available by reservation. There are food concessions at the Festival. Hotels in Hamilton, Ontario, include the Royal Connaught Hotel and the Terminal Towers.
Ticket information: Admission to the 3-day festival, including camping, is 25 Canadian dollars. Admission for Sunday only is 15 Canadian dollars. Tickets are available at the gate.
How to get there: Courtcliffe Park is E. of the town center on Carlisle Rd.

Bluegrass Festival
Box 332, R.R. 1, Kingston, Ontario K7L 4V1, Canada
Bluegrass
Early July
This 3-day festival is held outdoors on the banks of the Cataraqui River. The Festival has featured well-known groups from Tennessee, Virginia and Pennsylvania, as well as many Canadian performers.
Patrons are advised to bring lawn chairs.
Director: Dean L. Northey
Accommodations: Lodging is available

in the immediate area. Camping is available on the Festival grounds at a cost of $2.50 per day. Trailers are allowed, and there is picnicking.

Ticket information: Day tickets range from $5 to $7, and a weekend pass is $15

How to get there: The Festival is on Highway 15, 2¾ miles S. of Interchange 104 on Highway 401

Canadian National Open Banjo Competition
R.R. #4, Durham, Ontario, Canada
Banjo contest
Mid-July
This 2-day banjo competition includes contests in the following areas: open class, 5-string, tenor, and plectrum. There is also a contest for women and for those under 16.

The competition is held indoors at the District Community Center in Durham. Seating capacity is 4,500.
Director: Mrs. K. Van Geem
Sponsor: Durham and District Community Centre Board
Accommodations: Camping is allowed in the area at a cost of $3 per night
Ticket information: Admission is $3

Canadian Open Old-Time Championship Fiddlers' Contest
Shelburne, Ontario, Canada
Old-time fiddlers' contest, folk
Early August
This annual old-time fiddlers' contest is now in its 29th year. Approximately 200 contestants compete during the 2-day event. Participants in past contests have included Sleepy Marlin, Al Cherney, Graham Townsend, and Rudy Meeks. Additional events include a Giant Fiddle parade and an antiques and crafts show. The contest is held indoors in the Shelburne Recreation Complex, with a seating capacity of 4,000.
Director: Kenneth Gamble
Sponsor: Shelburne Rotary Club
Accommodations: In Shelburne there are the Hyland and the Timberline motels. Camping is permitted and there are facilities for trailers. There are some accommodations in private homes during the contest.
Ticket information: Friday admission is $2, available at the door. Saturday tickets are $5 and $6, by mail order only. For Saturday tickets, write to Box 27, Shelburne, Ontario, Canada, enclosing price of admission.
How to get there: Shelburne is 60 miles N. of Toronto and approximately 50 miles N. of Malton International Airport

Festival of Friends
Gage Park, Office 21, Augusta St., Hamilton, Ontario, Canada
Folk
Mid-August
Performances are going on simultaneously on 4 stages during the 3 days of this folk festival. Past performers have included Bruce Cockburn, Silvia Tyson, Valdy, Noel Harrison, John Allan Cameron, the Good Brothers, Robert Paquette, CANO, and many, many others. Other events include dance and children's art workshops, theater, and the largest outdoor display of pre-judged art in Canada.

Everything is outdoors. There's room for everyone who comes; recent festivals have had an attendance over 3 days of about 200,000.
Director: William B. Powell
Accommodations/other items of interest in area: Lodging is available at the Royal Connaught at 112 King East and at the Holiday Inn at 150 King-East. There is no camping, but there is picnicking. There is a children's museum on the grounds of Gage Park. In Hamilton, festival-goers may want to see the Botanical Gardens, Football Hall of Fame, and the Art Gallery.
Ticket information: Admission is free

Gates Town Jamboree
R.R. 2, Bauss Corners, Nova Scotia, Canada
Bluegrass, country and western, old-time fiddle
Mid-August
This 3-day jamboree in "The Singing Hills of Stanburne" was begun in 1975 to bring country and western music, bluegrass, and fiddling in Nova Scotia back to where it used to be. The popularity of this festival testifies that the goal has been met; audiences of about 50,000 have gathered to hear over 200 performers. The Jamboree also sponsors various games.

The Festival is outdoors, and guests should provide their own seating arrangements.
Directors: Mr. Harold Gates and Miss

Minnie Gates

Accommodations: Lodging is available in Bridgewater at the Mariner Motel on Aberdeen Rd.; Bridgewater Motor Inn at 35 High St.; and Wandlyn Motor Inn at 50 North St. There are facilities for camping, and for trailers, at a cost of 15 Canadian dollars for the weekend, or 18 Canadian dollars with hook-ups. Picnicking is allowed.

Ticket information: Admission is 1 Canadian dollar per person per day at the gate

How to get there: Gates Jamboree is on Gates Farm in Stanburne, 90 miles from Halifax, 20 miles from Bridgewater, 5 miles from New Germany, 2½ miles from Bauss Corners. Signs will be up at the end of the 3 roads leading to Stanburne.

Hillsburgh Country Bluegrass Jamboree
Box 124, Hillsburgh, Ontario, NOB 1ZO, Canada
Bluegrass
Early July
Begun in 1975, this 1-day jamboree provides 12 hours of continuous music outdoors in a park in Hillsburgh Village with room for 10,000 people. At dinnertime, an open stage welcomes anyone willing to try their hand at banjo or guitar. Some of the groups who have played include the Good Brothers, the Dixie Flyers, Jim Hale and the Chicken Spankers, and Larry Sparks and the Lonesome Ramblers. Arts and crafts sales and demonstrations and children's events are additional attractions.

An alternate rain-out facility is available.

Sponsor: Hillsburgh Festival Committee

Accommodations: Camping and lodging are available nearby

Ticket information: Tickets are 6 Canadian dollars in advance, 7.50 Canadian dollars at the gate

How to get there: Hillsburgh is on Highway 25, northwest of Georgetown, Ont.

Mariposa Folk Festival
525 Adelaide St. E., Toronto, Ontario M5A 3W4, Canada
Folk
June
Mariposa represents a broad spectrum of folk music in all its forms. It brings together fine representatives of Ontario's regional traditions and weaves them with both traditional and contemporary performers from across North America, the British Isles, and, indeed, the world. For the 3 days of the Festival several stages are in operation from morning until dusk with continuous concert and informal workshop sessions. Folk dance, carefully chosen crafts displays and demonstrations, a Native People's segment, and children's activities are also a part of the Festival.

The Festival is outdoors; seating is on the ground, and attendance is limited.

Director: Estelle Klein, Artistic Director; Rob Sinclair, Manager

Accommodations/other items of interest in area: For information on lodging write to the Convention and Tourist Bureau, the Toronto Eaton Centre, 220 Yonge St., Box 510, no. 110, Toronto, Canada, or call (416)979-3133.

Of interest in the area is the Ontario Science Centre and Metro International Caravan.

Ticket information:Weekend admission is $27 Canadian; single-day admission is $11.

How to get there: The Festival is at Toronto Islands Park. Take the public ferry from the docks at the foot of York Street, which is downtown.

Maritime Old-Time Fiddling Contest
Mailing address: 30 Guysborough Avenue, Dartmouth, Nova Scotia, Canada
Folk
Early July
This annual old-time fiddling contest is in its 30th year, and it takes place over a 3-day period in July. The program consists of a contest in four different classes: open, Scottish, 16-and-under, and 60-and-over. Contestants compete for cash prizes and trophies. In addition to the contest, on Sunday there is an afternoon-long outdoor event featuring noncompetitive, old-time musical entertainment; it is held at Beazley Sports Field, which can accommodate 4,000 spectators.

The contest is held in the Prince Andrew High School Auditorium which seats 1,200. (For information about contest rules, write to the Festival.)

Director: James Delaney

Sponsor: Saint Thomas More Council of Catholic Men

Accommodations: Camping costs $6 per day; trailer facilities with water and electrical hookups are available

Ticket information: Tickets cost $4 for

adults and $2.50 for children under 12; they can be obtained at the door on the night of the event or ordered in advance

Miramichi Folksong Festival
356 Water St., Newcastle, New Brunswick, Canada EIV 1X3
Folk
Early July
In 1947 historian Louise Manny began a collection of New Brunswick folk songs. Singers and storytellers from all over the Miramichi brought her a mixture of songs of long ago (some were brought over by their forefathers from the old country) and songs of present events—shipwrecks, disasters, songs of the lumber woods. As they contributed to the collection they gradually became aware of the folk culture of the Miramichi, and the group of songs they assembled reflects that culture. The annual 3-day festival, part of Newcastle's Canada Week festivities, is in its 21st year. It features well-known folksingers from the area, as well as a step-dancing violin contest.
The Festival is held in the Newcastle Town Hall.
Director: Mrs. Leo Mitchell
Ticket information: Admission is $2

Northern Lights Festival Boreal
P.O. 1236, Stn. B, Sudbury, Ontario, P3E 457, Canada
Folk, blues, bluegrass, regional
Mid-July
Concerts are held on a number of small stages on the shore of Lake Ramsay and in an outdoor auditorium, all in a beautiful park. The program includes folk, blues, bluegrass, Quekecquios groups, and native music. Some of the past performers have been Jackie Washington, Valdy, Robert Paquette, Barde, Sukay, Hang the Piper, Alanis Obonsawin, Tom Jackson, and John and Riki.
The Festival also provides crafts exhibits and a children's area.
Sponsor: Elected board
Accommodations/other items of interest in area: The park in which the Festival is held is near the center of town, where hotel accommodations are available. There are nearby camping sites, some of which can accommodate trailers. There is picnicking.
Sudbury is in the heart of a great hunting,

camping and fishing area.
Ticket information: Admission is 6 Canadian dollars per evening, or 15 Canadian dollars for all 3 evenings. Daytime activities are free.

Nova Scotia Bluegrass and Old-Time Festival
Festival site: Green Valley Campgrounds, Nine Mile River, Nova Scotia, Canada
Mailing address: Lantz, Nova Scotia BON 1RO, Canada
Bluegrass and old-time
July
Only acoustical music is allowed at this 2-day festival of bluegrass and old-time music. A large number of folk performers provide entertainment for an audience of about 4,000.
The Festival is outdoors at Green Valley Campgrounds.
Directors: Mel Sarty, Fred Isenor, Fulton Isenor, Charles Fullerton
Sponsor: Nova Scotia Bluegrass Committee
Accommodations: Lodging is available at the Windcrest Motel in Rawdon, Nova Scotia, and at the Airport Motel at Halifax International Airport. There is primitive camping at Green Valley Campgrounds for 5 Canadian dollars per unit for the weekend. For hookups, contact Green Valley Campgrounds well in advance.
Ticket information: Weekend tickets are 7 Canadian dollars in advance or 8 Canadian dollars at the gate. Day tickets are 4 Canadian dollars. Tickets can be obtained by mail from Fred Isenor, Lantz, Nova Scotia, Canada.
How to get there: To get to Green Valley Campgrounds and the Festival, turn off Highway 102 (the main highway through Nova Scotia) at exit 8, to Highway 214

Owen Sound Summerfolk Festival
P.O. Box 521, Owen Sound, Ontario N4K 5R1, Canada
Folk
Third weekend in August
Three days at the Owen Sound Summerfolk Festival is a good way for folk enthusiasts, and just plain folks, to cap the summer. There are 35 concerts by accomplished folk musicians, singers and songwriters, 42 workshops in wood-

carving, spinning, weaving, milking, and harmonica, to name just a few. There is also square dancing, and a lot of mingling on the outdoor grounds which can comfortably accommodate 4,000 people enjoying themselves. The Festival has a children's area which provides continual activities designed to please the kids, such as storytelling, puppet shows, clowns, concerts, and a variety of workshops.

Events take place rain or shine. Foul-weather clothing is recommended.
Director: Tim Harrison
Sponsor: Georgian Bay Folk Society
Accommodations/other items of interest in area: For information on hotel and motel accommodations, write to the Festival. There are some camping facilities, for $3 Canadian, per night, near the Festival; other campgrounds are available 1 to 2 miles away.
Of interest in the surrounding area are the Blue Mountain Slide Ride, Sauble and Wasaga Beaches, and Scenic Caves.
Ticket information:Weekend tickets are $12 Canadian, ($14 at the gate). Saturday or Sunday tickets are $7 and a ticket for the Friday night concert is $4.
How to get there: Owen Sound Summerfolk Festival is approximately 120 miles N. of Toronto on Highway 10

Southern Ontario Bluegrass Festival
Medad Forest Park, R.R. 1, Millgrove, Ontario, Canada
Bluegrass
Late June to early July
This is a recently established 4-day festival. It features concerts by groups such as Cody, White River Bluegrass Band, the Dixie Flyers, the Humber River Valley Boys, White Birch Bluegrass, the Golden Bluegrass Boys, Rudy Meeks and Station Road, and Bob Paisley and the Southern Mountain Boys. There is also a bluegrass band concert.
The Festival is outdoors; there is a pavilion in case of rain. Patrons are advised to bring umbrellas and lawn chairs.
Director: Jack W. Buttenham
Sponsors: Canadian Bluegrass Review and Something Bluegrass
Accommodations/other items of interest in area: Hotel and motel accommodations are available in the area. Rough camping is free; facilities include limited water hook-ups and clean washrooms.

There is swimming, and a play area for children.
Of interest in the area are the Rockton Lion Safari and Ontario Place.
Ticket information: Weekend tickets are 12 Canadian dollars in advance, or 10 Canadian dollars at the gate. Day tickets range from 3 to 6 Canadian dollars. For advance tickets, write Canadian Bluegrass Promotions, Box 143, Waterdown, Ontario, Canada L0R 2H0.

Southwestern Ontario Fiddle Contest
Royal Canadian Legion Branch 216, Box 733, Ontario, Canada
Folk
Fourth weekend in June each year
This annual 2-day event features fiddle contests of the Canadian old-time type. Contestants compete for cash prizes and trophies. In addition to the contests, there are guest performers at a jamboree, and there is a dance on Saturday night after the finals.
The Southwestern Ontario Fiddle Contest was founded in 1969, and it is held outdoors in the Petrolia Arena, in Petrolia, Ontario.
Directors: Gerald Bailey and Mrs. H. Mosienko
Sponsor: Royal Canadian Legion Branch 216, Petrolia
Accommodations: There is a campground next to the arena, and it has trailer facilities; no tents are allowed
Ticket information: Friday night admission: Adults, $2 Canadian; children under 14, $ .50. Saturday night admission: adults, $3; children, $ .50 (admission includes show and dance).
How to get there: The arena is located on Petrolia Street E. of Sarnia and W. of Highway 21

Vancouver Folk Music Festival
453 West 12th Ave., Vancouver, B.C. V5Y 1V4, Canada
Folk
Mid-July
The organizers of this 3-day folk festival have scoured the back alleys and juke joints of North America and abroad to bring to Vancouver the best folk music being played today. The format of the Festival is daytime workshops and small concerts, and large concerts each evening. The music to be heard includes bluegrass, Cajun, old-timey, blues, con-

temporary songs, Irish, African, Quebecois, British Isles, and Yiddish, as well as dance and storytelling. In addition, there will be good food, an arts and crafts area, and a children's area. The Festival is outdoors with space for about 8,000.
Directors: Mitch Podolak and Gary Cristall
Sponsor: Heritage Festival Society
Accommodations/other items of interest in area: Lodging is readily attainable in Vancouver. There is no camping, but there is picnicking in the park where the Festival will be held.
Besides the many attractions of the city of Vancouver, the area has wonderful scenery and fishing.
Ticket information: A 3-day ticket is about $20 Canadian. To obtain one, or for more information, write to the Festival.

Western Canada Amateur Olde-Tyme Fiddling Championship
P.O. Box 203, Swift Current, Saskatchewan S9H 3V6
Folk
End of September
1980 will be the 15th year of the Olde-Tyme Fiddling Championship. Legion Hall, seating 600, is the home of the event. During the 3-day event, fiddlers perform on open air stages throughout Swift Current. Other activities include old-time dance, a pancake breakfast and the Fiddlers' Banquet.
Director: A. F. (Tony) Juffinger
Accommodations: For information on accommodations, write to the above address. Camping and picnicking are allowed and facilities are available for trailers as well.

Winnipeg Folk Festival
171 Lilac Street, Winnipeg, Manitoba R3M 1S1, Canada
Folk (acoustic)
Early July
Founded in 1973, this annual 3-day event is held outdoors in a park near Winnipeg. Featuring a series of all-day and evening concerts, the Festival is dedicated to the continuation of folk music. Past performers have included Dave Van Ronk, David Amram, Tom Paxton, Odetta, Bill Price, Utah Phillips, and Lucille Edmond, among others. Concerts are held outdoors at 6 loca-

tions around the park. There are many food and drink stands, a picnic ground, and arts and crafts exhibits. It is suggested that patrons bring foul-weather gear.
Director: Mitch Podolak
Accommodations: There is a campground nearby with facilities for trailers. Accommodations there cost $3 Canadian per night.
Ticket information: Tickets may be bought at the gate for $25 for the weekend; they may be purchased in advance for $22
How to get there: The Festival site is located 8 miles N. of Winnipeg on Highway 59

CONNECTICUT

The Annual New England Fiddle Contest

P.O. Box 854, Hartford, Conn. 06101
Traditional
Memorial Day weekend
This began as a downtown festival in
1972 with an audience of about 2,500
as part of the Peace Train effort to en-
liven city living. Last year it drew about
25,000 people with 90 contestants. It
is an old-time, old-fashioned fiddle contest for contestants (and audience) of all
ages. There is heavy family attendance.
The festival is held in Bushnell Park
(uncovered), with room for 30,000 to
50,000 people.
Director: Paul LeMay
Sponsor: Peace Train Foundation, Inc.
Accommodations: There are many hotels
and motels in Hartford
Ticket information: Admission is free
How to get there: Follow signs on I-91
or I-84 for the capitol. Bushnell Park is
at the foot of the State Capitol Building.

Canaan Valley County Musical Festival

Canaan Valley Sporting Club, Canaan,
Conn. 06018
Folk, country, bluegrass
Second Sunday in June, third Sunday in
August, fourth Sunday in September
Bands play in the rotunda of the Canaan
Valley Sporting Club clubhouse, while
the audience, on chairs or blankets they've
brought for the occasion, cheers them on
from the lawn. In case of rain there is a
125-ft. porch area for cover.
Director: Col. John J. Koneazny
Sponsor: Canaan Valley Sporting Club
Accommodations/other items of interest
in area: Iron Masters Motel and the Inter-
Laken Inn, both in Lakeville, Conn., and
the Stagecoach Hill Inn in nearby Shef-
field, Mass., can provide accommodations. No camping at the site.
Within a ½-mile hike of the club is
Campbell Falls.
Ticket information: Admission is free
How to get there: From signs on Route
44 at East Canaan and Route 7 at the
Canaan barracks, follow small arrow
signs to Canaan Valley

Wesleyan Folksong Festival

Graduate Summer School, Wesleyan
Univ., Middletown, Conn. 06457
Folk
Mid-July
This folk song festival, held on the
campus of Wesleyan University,
has presented singers and musicians
such as Almeda Riddle, Peter Bellamy,
Joe Heaney, Margaret MacArthur, and
many more too numerous to list. The
Festival also presents contradance,
sacred harp, and shaped-note singing.
Many workshops are offered, both indoors and outdoors.
Main events take place in two 400-seat
air-conditioned halls.
Director: Dr. James L. Steffenson
Sponsors: The John and Clara Higgins
Foundation Graduate Summer School
and the Center for Creative Youth
Accommodations: Write to the Festival
for an information sheet on hotel and
motel accommodations. There is camping in the state parks, which are 15
miles away. Picnicking is allowed on
the Wesleyan campus.
Ticket information: Admission is $6,
series tickets are $15 and $10; some
events are free.
How to get there: Wesleyan University
in Middletown, Conn., is midway between Boston and New York City, and
midway between Hartford and New
Haven, Conn.

DELAWARE

Delaware Bluegrass Festival
Gloryland Park, Porter Road, Glasgow, Del.
Bluegrass
A 3-day weekend at the beginning of September
The Delaware Bluegrass Festival has been presenting nationally famous bluegrass bands since 1972 in a covered arena seating 4,000 people. Performers have included Bill Monroe, Ralph Stanley, Lester Flatt, Jim and Jesse, the Virginia Boys, and Jimmy Martin.
Director: Carl Goldstein
Sponsor: Brandywine Friends of Old-Time Music
Accommodations: Hotels in the area include Howard Johnson's in Newark and Gateway in New Castle. Camping is available for a nominal fee; there are no facilities. Picnicking is allowed.
Ticket information: Tickets are available at the gate; cost is $5 for Friday and $7 each day for Saturday and Sunday
How to get there: Take I-95 to the Delaware 896 (S.) exit

DISTRICT OF COLUMBIA

Festival of American Folklife
Washington Monument Grounds, 14th St. and Constitution Ave. NW, Washington, D.C.
Folk and traditional
October
Since the Smithsonian's Festival of American Folklife was established in 1967, it has presented more than 9,000 craftspersons, musicians and dancers to over 6 million festival visitors. The participants have come from 38 foreign countries, over 60 unions and labor organizations, 116 Native American tribal groups, and every region in the U.S. and its possessions. The aim has been to bring to the National Mall the rich variety of folk traditions which comprise the roots of American culture.
Director: Ralph Rinzler
Sponsor: The Smithsonian Institution
Accommodations: A variety of lodging is available in Washington, D.C. There is no camping, but picnicking is allowed on the National Mall.
Ticket information: Admission is free

FLORIDA

Cerebral Palsy Bluegrass Festival
United Cerebral Palsy, 506 E. Colonial
Drive, Orlando, Fla. 32807
Bluegrass and country
May
This 3-day festival is held on Mother's
Day weekend. It features top bluegrass
bands, clogging, guitar and banjo picking,
and good country singing. Events are
held in tents at Yogi Bear's Jellystone
Camp Resort. Food is available, and
there is also picnicking. There are prizes
for the oldest, youngest, and most
prolific mothers.
Director: Ms. Nadine Ziglar
Accommodations/other items of
interest in area: Lodging is available at
the Holiday Inn, TraveLodge and Day's
Inn. Trailers are welcome. There are
nearby places to swim.
Of interest in the area are Disneyworld,
Sea World and related attractions.
Ticket information: Evening and day
tickets range from $5 to $8. Three-day
tickets are $14.
How to get there: To get to Jellystone
Camp Resort take Exit 75 on the
Florida Turnpike, go W. on I-4 to
Florida 528A, then follow the signs

Florida Folk Festival
Box 265, White Springs, Fla.
Folk
Mid-May
This 4-day family festival is held in the
250-acre Stephen Foster Center overlooking the Suwannee River. The main
concerts are in an amphitheater with
hillside seating for about 5,000. The
Festival features folk musicians and
singers, musicians playing unusual instruments such as the Biblical psaltry, clog
and ethnic dancers, and bluegrass. Music,
dance, song, and storytelling workshops
are also a part of the Festival. There
are crafts demonstrations and Southern-
style home-cooked food.
Rain gear is recommended; the show
goes on, rain or shine.
Director: Thelma A. Boltin
Sponsors: Stephan Foster Center and
Florida Federation of Music Clubs
Accommodations: For information on
lodging contact the Chamber of
Commerce in White Spring. There is
limited camping at the Stephan Foster
Center. The cost is $12 for two people
for the weekend. If self-contained, trailers are welcome. There is picnicking.
Ticket information: Admission is $3
per day at the gate only
How to get there: For directions, con-
tact the Stephan Foster Center (at the
Festival address)

GEORGIA

Bluegrass and Old Time Fiddlers' Reunion
Highway 117 South, Rhine, Ga.
Folk and bluegrass
Third weekend in June and September
This bluegrass and old-time music get-together happens twice during the summer over 3-day weekends. Events take place outdoors before a covered stage (tent provided for inclement weather) within walking distance of Spring Lake on the 2,000 acre JMB Ranch.
Performers such as Chubby Anthony and Tall Timber Bluegrass, Cedar Creek, Front Porch String Band, and the Cross Family have been participants.
Director: Bob Couey
Sponsor: Spring Lake Enterprises, Inc.
Accommodations: Stuckey's Carriage Inn in Eastman and Abbeville Motel in Abbeville can provide accommodations. Free primitive camping is available. Electrical hook-ups and water are $3 a day. There is free swimming and fishing at nearby Spring Lake.
Ticket information: Tickets cost $15 for 3 days (day tickets are available), obtainable at gate only
How to get there: The Festival is located 8 miles S. of Rhine on Highway 117

Dahlonega Bluegrass Festival
P.O. Box 98, Dahlonega, Ga. 30533
Bluegrass
June and September
Mountain Music Park presents two 3- to 4-day bluegrass festivals, one in June and one in September. They feature such groups and performers as Mac Wiseman, Chubby Anthony and Tall Timber, Don Reno and the Tennessee Cutups, and many more. A band contest is a highlight of the Festival. Events are held outdoors, with seating for 2,500. The facilities are covered.
Director: Norman Adams
Accommodations/other items of interest in area: For information on motel accommodations and camping, write to the Festival. There are camper hook-ups, for $3 per night, and free camping in the rough for festival patrons.
There is gold panning ½ mile N. of Mountain Music Park.
Ticket information: Admission ranges from $5 to $8. Four-day tickets are

$20; 3-day tickets are $18.
How to get there: Mountain Music Park is 1 mile S. from Dahlonega, Ga., on Highway 60

Georgia's Best Bluegrass Festival
North Georgia State Fairgrounds, Marietta, Ga.
Bluegrass
First weekend in May and first weekend in October
This festival began in October 1969, and since then there have been two weekend festivals per year, one in May and one in October. Approximately 50 bands perform during each weekend, with no electrical instruments allowed.
The Festival is held in the exhibit building of the North Georgia State Fairgrounds. There is seating for 1,000.
Director: Dillard Rogers and Jimmy Jones
Accommodations/other items of interest in area: There are more than a dozen motels in the Marietta area. Campers and mobile homes are allowed in the fairgrounds area at no cost. There are a limited number of hook-ups.
Marietta is in the Atlanta area, within a few minutes of Six Flags Over Georgia.
Ticket information: Admission is $4 per day. Tickets are available at the gate.
How to get there: The Fairgrounds are located on Calloway Road in Marietta, which is northwest of Atlanta

New Year's Bluegrass Festival
Jekyll Island, Ga.
Bluegrass and old time
Late December to early January
Celebrate the year's end with bluegrass. This New Year's Weekend festival presents many popular bluegrass groups, such as the Country Gentlemen, the Lewis Family, Jim and Jesse, the Osborne Brothers and many more.
The festivities are indoors at the Convention Center, which can accommodate over 3,000.
Director: Vinson Dover
Accommodations/other items of interest in area: For information on lodging write to Jekyll Island—State Park Authority, Jekyll Island, Ga. 31520. There is free camping for festival patrons in the Convention Center's parking lot, but there are no facilities. Camping with complete facilities is available at Cherokee Campground

for $5.50 per day. There are wonderful areas for picnicking.

Jekyll Island has ocean beaches, beautiful scenery, excellent fishing, historical sites, good restaurants, and sports facilities. Winter temperatures average about 50 degrees.

Ticket information: Day tickets range from $5 to $7. To order them in advance contact Jekyll Bluegrass, Box 731, Dahlonega, Ga. 30533.

How to get there: Jekyll Island is 9 miles by causeway from Brunswick, Ga. It is readily accessible to boats.

Spring Music and Crafts Festival; Georgia Mountain Fair; Fall Country Music and Bluegrass Festival

P.O. Box 444, Hiawassee, Ga., 30546
Country, bluegrass, fiddling, gospel
May, August, and October

The *Spring Music and Crafts Festival* is held over 2 consecutive 3-day weekends in May. Country music and gospel music are emphasized the 1st weekend; fiddling and bluegrass the 2nd. There are competitions for fiddle, banjo, guitar, mandolin, and bluegrass bands, and displays of crafts as well. Events are held outdoors on the shores of Lake Chatuge.

The *Georgia Mountain Fair* spans 12 days in August and offers country, bluegrass, and gospel music. Many well-known groups participate. In addition to concerts and shows, there are mountain crafts displays and demonstrations, clogging, and a pioneer village to visit, among other attractions. The fair is held alongside Lake Chatuge.

The *Fall Country Music and Bluegrass Festival,* held 2 weekends in October, features country musicians, bluegrass bands, and old-time fiddlers. There are also displays of arts and crafts and clogging. Events during this fall festival are held in an enclosed pavilion with seating for 3,600.

Sponsor: Georgia Mountain Fair
Accommodations/other items of interest in area: Camping is $2, or $4 with a hook-up. There is picnicking.
The area is by beautiful Lake Chatuge.
Ticket information: Tickets are $2 at the gate
How to get there: Intersection of US 76 and Ga. 75, 100 miles N. of Atlanta

Yellow Daisy Festival and Bluegrass Music Contest

Stone Mountain Park, P.O. Box 778, Stone Mountain, Ga. 30086
Bluegrass
Early September

Named after the rare Confederate yellow daisy which grows only within a 30-mile radius of Stone Mountain, this festival sponsored by Stone Mountain Park provides a 3-day weekend of everything from bluegrass music contests to hog calling. The Georgia State Fiddle Championship is part of the Festival, as are art and flower shows, craft exhibits, barbecues, forestry field events (crosscut sawing, ax throwing, greased pole climbing, etc.), band concerts, and buck dancing and clogging.

Competitions are held in a 5,000-seat covered coliseum. Up to 90,000 spectators appear for weekend activities.

Director: Kathi Hayes
Sponsor: Stone Mountain Park
Accommodations/other items of interest in area: Camping and motel facilities are available in the Park. A 1-time parking permit of $2.50 is required to enter the Park. Recreational vehicle sites are $5.50/night, with sewer hook-ups $.50 more, all with electricity and water. Tent sites are $4.50/night and are without electricity.

Park attractions include a beach, Swiss skylift, 732-bell carillon, riverboat, and the world's largest sculpture, carved out of Stone Mountain.
Ticket information: No charge for festival other than $2.50 parking permit
How to get there: Take I-285 E. to the Stone Mountain Freeway and follow signs 7 miles to the Park

IDAHO

National Oldtime Fiddlers' Contest

8 E. Idaho, Weiser, Id. 83672
Folk and oldtime fiddling
Third full week in June
It was fiddle music that accompanied
the wagon trains across the plains 100
and more years ago. As towns replaced
the old mining and settlers' camps, the
music stayed for hoedowns and square
dances. The first fiddling contest was
held in Weiser in 1914, although the
present National Oldtime Fiddlers'
Contest was inaugurated in conjunction with Idaho's Centennial year in
1963. The contest, and the festival accompanying it, is designed to perpetuate
the oldtime fiddlers' art. Audience and
participants are all asked to wear dress
of pioneer America, if possible, and
prizes are awarded for best costumes.
On Saturday there is an oldtime parade
with floats. A visit to the National Fiddlers' Hall of Fame, with its archives of
fiddle tunes and mementos, is a must.
Anyone is eligible to compete, and fiddlers come from all over the U.S. and
Canada to play in the Weiser High
School Gymnasium, which seats 2,500
people.
Director: Bill Scott
Sponsor: Weiser Chamber of Commerce
Accommodations/other items of
interest in area: Contact the Chamber of
Commerce for information about motels
and rooms in private homes. There are
several camping areas.
America's deepest gorge, Hell's Canyon,
is a nearby sight to see.
Ticket information: For tickets write to
Chamber of Commerce, 8 E. Idaho,
Weiser, Id. 83672. Tickets range in price
from $1 on Monday to $6 on Saturday.
There are lower rates for children and
general admission (not reserved) Monday
through Thursday.
How to get there: The contest site is
about 1½ miles northwest of Weiser

Northern Rockies Folk Festival

Sun Valley Center, Box 656, Sun Valley,
Idaho 83353
Folk
Early to mid-August
This festival emphasizes the authenticity
of its concerts. It has presented per-
formers of the ilk of Rosalie Sorrels,
Utah Phillips, and the Desert String
Band.
The Festival is located in the midst of
a large wilderness area.
Director: Richard Hart
Sponsors: National Endowment for the
Arts, and corporate support
Accommodations: For information on
lodging and camping write to Sun Valley
County G.D., Sun Valley, Id. 83353.
Ticket information: Admission is free

ILLINOIS

Bluegrass Music Festival
Rockome Gardens, Route 2, Arcola, Ill.
61910
Folk and bluegrass
July
This 2-day festival is held outdoors at
Rockome Gardens, a fine site for a folk
festival if ever there was one. The Festival
features local musicians and bands such
as Chet Kengery and the Knights of Blue-
grass, Kenny Dace and the Downstate
Ramblers, and the Ambraw River Boys.
There is limited seating on benches;
patrons are advised to bring blankets or
chairs.
Director: Leesa Willis
Sponsor: Rockome Gardens
Accommodations/other items of interest
in area: Hotel and motel accommodations
are available. For information write to
Rockome Gardens at the above address.
There is no camping. Picnicking, however,
is allowed.
Rockome Gardens is in the heart of
Illinois Amish Country. Rockome Gardens
aims to provide a relaxed look back into
the past and offers a touch of everything from rocks and flowers to antiques
and apple butter. The rock and flower
gardens comprise about 7 acres of the 20-
acre grounds.
Ticket information: The music is at no
extra cost beyond gate admission to the
park. For more information write to
Rockome Gardens.
How to get there: Rockome Gardens is 5
miles W. of Arcola just off I-57 and US
45

**Crazy Horse Campground Bluegrass
Festival**
R.R. 1, Ashland, Ill. 62612
Bluegrass
Late May and early June
This 3-day bluegrass festival features top
Midwest bands such as the Harmon Trio,
Sally Mountain Show, Ozark Mountain
Trio, Over the Hill Gang, Cedar Hill
Grass, Bluegrass Related and more. There
are also lively fiddle and banjo picking
contests. The show is outdoors; guests
may bring lawn chairs.
Directors: Dale and Joan Tripp
Accommodations/other items of interest
in area: Holiday Inn and Star Lite Inn on

Highway 39 offer motel accommodations.
Camping at $10 per weekend is available;
facilities include water, electricity, toilets,
hot showers, and garbage disposal. Trailers
and tents are welcome. Picnicking is fine;
there is also a snack bar and grocery
store on the grounds. Crazy Horse Campground offers many outdoor sports and
family activities.
The campground is located centrally in
historic Lincoln County.
Ticket information: Weekend admission
is $10

Harmony Pines Bluegrass
Gibson, Ill.
Bluegrass
May and July
Local groups such as Cedar Hill Grass,
Bluegrass Five, Sally Mountain Show,
Ozark Mountain Trio, Bluegrass Related,
and Special Consensus Bluegrass Band
perform at these 3-day spring and sum-
mer festivals. Events are held outdoors;
there is plenty of space for everyone who
comes.
Guests should bring lawn chairs and
come prepared for foul weather.
Director: Oliver Smith
Sponsor: Knoxville Jaycees
Accommodations: Lodging is available in
Galesburg, Illinois, at Sheraton Motor Inn
and the Holiday Inn. Camping in the
rough is free with a festival weekend
ticket. Camper trailers are welcome.
Ticket information: Weekend tickets are
$8 and day tickets range from $2 to $5.
They are available at the gate, or by
mail from Oliver Smith, R.R. 2, Box 151,
Gibson, Ill.
How to get there: The Festival is 5 miles
S. of I-74 (on Route 97), then ½ mile W.

Lake Wildwood Haven Bluegrass Festival
Lake Wildwood Haven Campground,
Bushnell, Ill.
Bluegrass
Late September
During a 3-day weekend this festival
provides bluegrass music for up to 2,000
people in an outdoor setting. In case of
bad weather a large recreation hall will
house the show and about 800 people.
Performers such as Don Brown & Ozark
Mountain Trio, Sally Mountain Show,
Bluegrass Related, and Warren's Crossing
have appeared in recent years.
Director: Delbert Spray
Accommodations: The Holiday Inn in

Macomb, Illinois, 15 miles from the site, and the Bushnell Motel, 4 miles away, can provide accommodations. Camping, at $6 per weekend, with modern restrooms, showers, water, and electricity, is available at the site along with trailer facilities. Boating, fishing, and swimming are also offered at the campground.
Ticket information: For information, write to Delbert Spray, R.R. 1, Kahoka, Mo., 63445. Tel. (314)853-4344.
How to get there: The campground is 4 miles E. of Bushnell

Southern Illinois Folk Festival
DuQuoin State Fairgrounds, DuQuoin, Ill.
Folk
Late September
This regional festival was founded in 1972. It features country and bluegrass music, and offers demonstrations of old-time crafts and pioneer farm skills. For children who attend the Festival, there are games and activities enjoyed by children 100 or more years ago.
The Festival can accommodate 8,000.
Director: Mrs. M. R. Prusacki
Sponsor: Southern Illinois Folk Festival, Inc.
Accommodations: Lodging in DuQuoin is available at the Hub Motel and Motel DuQuoin. Accommodations are also available in the nearby towns of Benton and Carbondale. Camping is available at a cost of $6, or $6.50 with hook-up. Trailers are also welcome. There is picnicking.
How to get there: DuQuoin State Fairgrounds are on US 51, S. of DuQuoin

INDIANA

Blue Grass
Route 1, Box 126, Glenwood, Ind. 46133
Bluegrass
Mid-July
This annual 2-day event features banjo and dance contests in addition to bluegrass music. Music is presented outdoors, on a 300-acre site. Past performers have included Ralph Stanley, the Wilson Brothers, Ed Hamilton, and many others.
Director: Carol Hammons, tel. (317)679-5210
Accommodations: There are camping facilities in the area
Ticket information: Admission is $10 for the entire festival
How to get there: The Festival site is 6 miles southeast of Glenwood, Ind.

Indiana Fiddlers' Gathering and Other Old-Time Musicians
Tippecanoe Battlefield, P.O. Box 225, Battle Ground, Ind. 47920
Traditional
July
One of the best traditional music festivals in the Midwest, this celebration of traditional music takes place over 2 weekends. It features workshops, Sunday morning gospel sings, and jam sessions, as well as concerts. Performers are traditional folk artists from the Midwest, and folk groups from other parts of the country.
The Festival is held outdoors, but moves inside in case of heavy rain.
Director: D. Clarke Evans
Sponsor: Battle Ground Historical Society
Accommodations/other items of interest in area: Motel accommodations are readily available. There are camping facilities in Tippecanoe County. Write to the Festival requesting camping and hotel and motel guides.
Of interest in the area are Fort Quiatenon Historical Park Museum, Purdue University, Tippecanoe County Historical Museum, and Columbia Park of Lafayette.
Ticket information: Tickets are sold at the gate or may be bought in advance by writing to the Festival

How to get there: The Festival is 7 miles N. of Lafayette—follow highway signs to Tippecanoe Battlefield

Jayland Bluegrass Festival
Jay County Fairgrounds, Portland, Ind.
Bluegrass
June
Featured at this 3-day festival are such groups as the Moore Brothers, the Fox Brothers, Yesterday's Grass, Bittersweet String Band, the Johnsons, Collins Cisco and Kentucky Grass, and others. The music, all acoustical, can be heard from the grandstand and in a shady grove area with seats, but there is usually spontaneous music happening all around the fairgrounds. The Festival includes banjo and fiddlers' contests.
There is also an antique show and sale, arts, crafts, and a flea market. Food is available on the grounds. Patrons are advised to bring lawn chairs.
Directors: Don. R. McNees, Woody Turner
Accommodations/other items of interest in area: Jay Motel, Terrace Lodge Motel and Limberlost Motel can provide accommodations. Camping, including trailers, is permitted at $6 per unit per weekend. Picnicking is permitted.
How to get there: The Festival is 3 blocks E. of the junction of highways 27 and 67 in Portland

Stoneyrun Bluegrass
8507 East 137th Street, Leroy, Ind. 46355
Bluegrass
August
During the 2 days of this festival, 2 bluegrass programs are presented, with groups such as James Monroe and the Midnight Ramblers, Piper Road Spring Band, Northwind, and Crown Point. Banjo and fiddle contests are also held. Events take place outdoors at Stoneyrun County Park.
Directors: Marcia Glesener and Phyllis McNeill
Sponsor: Lake County Parks and Recreation Dept.
Accommodations/other items of interest in area: Lodging is available at the Holiday Inn and Red Roof Inn, both in Merrillville. There is no camping in the park but there is picnicking.
Of interest in the area is a working gristmill at Hobart.

Ticket information: Admission is $3 per day or $5 for 2 days, at the gate
How to get there: Take I-65 to Route 231, then take 231 E. until you see Stoneyrun's signs

Stonycreek Farm Bluegrass Festival
222 Stony Lane, Noblesville, Ind.
Folk
September
The setting of this 3-day late-summer festival is a meadow—a natural amphitheater in the woods. As well as concerts of folk music, there is a fiddle contest and a band contest. Festival performers have included First Annual Farewell Reunion, Bittersweet String Band, Wildwood Flowers and others.
In case of rain, there is a shelter which can accommodate 2,000.
Director: Mrs. Jan Schmierer
Accommodations/other items of interest in area: Lodging is available in Anderson, 20 minutes from the Festival, and in Indianapolis, 35 minutes away. Primitive camping, at no cost, is allowed on the Festival grounds. Picnicking is permitted. Festival guest may enjoy the nearby ponds and creeks for fishing, farm animals, and horse-drawn hayrides.
Ticket information: Admission is $4.
How to get there: The Festival is 2 miles E. of Noblesville on Highway 38

IOWA

The Bluegrass Music Festival of Iowa

Iowa State University, Iowa State Center,
Ames, Iowa
Bluegrass
Weekend in early October
This festival, first held in 1978, features
nationally known bluegrass musicians as
well as local bands. Recent well-known
performers include Ralph Stanley and the
Clinch Mountain Boys, Fox River Grass,
Bill Monroe and the Blue Grass Boys,
Hotmud Family, Possum Trot, and the
Onion Creek Cloggers.
Banjo, guitar, fiddle, mandolin, dobro,
singing, and clogging workshops are led
by bluegrass musicians. In addition, arts
and crafts from all over the Midwest are
shown and sold.
Afternoon concerts are outdoors or, in
bad weather, indoors in Benton Auditori-
um (450 seats). Evening concerts are
held in C.Y. Stephens Auditorium (5,000
seats).
Directors: Martin G. Miller and Robert
Dagitz
Sponsors: Iowa State University and
the Iowa State Center
Accommodations: In the Ames area,
Gateway Center, Holiday Inn, and the
Silver Saddle Motel provide accommoda-
tions. Camping is available nearby.
Ticket information: Tickets are $10 for
the weekend, $6 for evening concerts.
Write to Iowa State Center Box Office,
Ames, Iowa 50010.
How to get there: Take the exit at
Elwood Drive from Highway 30
How to get there: The Festival is held at
Westfair, located 6 miles E. of Council
Bluffs on Highway 6, next to the I-80 and
I-29 Exchange.

Chariton Valley Bluegrass Jamboree

County Fairgrounds, Chariton, Iowa
Bluegrass
Late June and early July
Bluegrass is the word at this 3-day festival.
Groups such as Corders Bluegrass Show,
Morningstar Express, Bobby Allen, Last
Pony Mine Bluegrass Show, and Short
Line Grass provide good entertainment.
The Festival also includes a flea market,
crafts fair, and square dance.
Events are outdoors, but in case of rain
everyone will move to an indoor arena.

Director: John Sipes
Sponsor: Chariton Jaycees
Accommodations: There is free camping
in the rough
Ticket information: For information on
tickets, lodging, and directions write to
the Festival Director, John Sipes, at 813
Armory, Chariton, Iowa 50049

Council Bluffs Iowa Old-Time Country Music Contest and Pioneer Exposition

106 Navajo, Council Bluffs, Iowa 51501
Folk, country, bluegrass
Early September
This festival was organized to preserve
the type of entertainment enjoyed by
settler families. Annually, during the
Labor Day weekend, over 300 entrants
compete in 20 categories, some of which
are bluegrass band, fiddle, gandy dancing,
folk singing, country singing, guitar,
banjo, mandolin picking, poetry reading
and storytelling, and more. There are
also dancing exhibitions, a gospel sing,
arts and crafts demonstrations and exhibitions, and many more events.
The Festival occurs in an amphitheater
with a capacity of 20,000 and in 5 indoor spaces, each with a capacity of
2,500.
Director: Bob Everhart
Sponsor: Westfair and Council Bluffs
Chambers of Commerce
Accommodations/other items of interest
in area: Lodging is available at Chalet
Best Western Motel, 16th and Ave. G,
Council Bluffs. Camping facilities are
available for $1 per day; no hook-ups.
Trailers are welcome. There is picnicking.
The Festival takes place in beautiful
bluff country. Of interest in the area are
the Lewis and Clark Monument, Bayliss
Park and fountain, and the Dodge
House Historical Landmark. Longs Land-
ing is a fishing, boating and camping area
on the Missouri River, and Lake Manawa
State Park offers recreation and camping.
Ticket information: Tickets are $4 per day
or $10 for the weekend. They are avail-
able at the gate.

KANSAS

National Flat Picking Championship
Box 245, 117 E. 9th, Winfield, Kans. 67156
Folk, old time, and bluegrass
A weekend in mid-September
The Festival provides a 3-day weekend of concerts, contests, workshops, and arts and crafts exhibitions at the Winfield Fairgrounds and its all-weather facilities. In recent years musicians like Norman Blake, Bryan Bowers, the Lewis Family, the McLain Family Band, Doc Watson, and Lester Flatt have appeared on one or another of the Festival's 3 stages. The contests have $10,000 in awards for the winners of national competitions in flat-picking guitar and hammered dulcimer and local ones in mandolin, fiddle, and banjo.
Director: Bob Redford
Sponsor: Walnut Valley Association
Accommodations: Camping and picnicking are available on the site at no charge with a weekend ticket. Trailers are welcome.
Ticket information: Tickets cost $8 per day, $20 for the 3-day weekend (not available in advance)
How to get there: Winfield is at the junction of highways 77 and 160

Walnut Valley June Jamboree
Box 245, 117 E. 9th, Winfield, Kans. 67156
Folk, old time, and bluegrass
First weekend in June
After its success over the years with its National Flat-Picking Championship every September, the Walnut Valley Association inauegerated this summer event in 1979. This festival, like its counterpart in September, is comprised of 3 days of concerts, contests, workshops, and arts and crafts displays. The contests—National Finger-Picking Guitar Championship, National Mountain Dulcimer Championship, and the Walnut Valley Old Time Banjo Championship—have $4,000 in awards for the top players.
Events take place at the Winfield Fairgrounds which provides all-weather facilities.
Director: Bob Redford
Sponsor: Walnut Valley Association
Accommodations: Camping and picnicking are available on the site at no charge with a weekend ticket. Trailers are welcome.
Ticket information: Tickets cost $8 per day, $20 for the 3-day weekend (not available in advance)
How to get there: Winfield is at the junction of highways 77 and 160.

KENTUCKY

Bluegrass Music Festival of the United States
2125 Citizens Plaza, Louisville, Ky. 40202
Bluegrass
Late May and early June
This festival was instituted in 1973 by Louisville Central Area, Inc., a non-profit promotion and development organization for downtown Louisville. Concerts are held over a 3-day weekend on Riverfront Plaza, a 6-acre public plaza in Louisville, in an outdoor setting with a capacity of 5,000; seating to be provided by the audience. Some of the best known bluegrass musicians have participated—Bill Monroe, Ralph Stanley, Jim and Jesse, John Hartford, Norman Blake, Vassar Clements.
There are also workshops in bluegrass instruments, hammer dulcimer, and dance.
Director: John I. Trawick
Sponsors: Louisville Central Area, Inc. and Louisville-area businesses
Accommodations/other items of interest in area: Galt House, on Fourth and River, and Rodeway Inn, 101 E. Jefferson, can provide accommodations in Louisville. Other attractions in the area include the Belle of Louisville, an authentic paddlewheel steamboat, and the downtown Main Street historic district.
Ticket information: Admission is free
How to get there: Located at Fifth and Main streets in downtown Louisville

Celebration of Traditional Music
College Box 2336, Berea, Ky. 40404
Appalachian traditional music
Late October
The purpose of this 4-day celebration, begun in 1973, is to give recognition to Appalachian folk artists and to bring younger people into contact with them. The Festival presents strictly old-time traditional music, instrumental workshops, ballads and songs, string music, hymn singing, a symposium, and square dancing.
Events are held in an indoor auditorium which can accommodate 1,500. A street dance is held outdoors.
Director: Loyal Jones
Sponsors: Berea College and National Endowment for the Arts

Accommodations/other items of interest in area: Lodging in Berea is available at the Boone Tavern Hotel, Holiday Motel, Prince Royal Motel, Edloo's Motel, Moore's Motel, Wilderness Trail Motel, and Hart's Motel. For campers and trailers there is the Walnut Meadow Travel Park, ½ mile W. of I-75 at Ky.-21. Of interest in the area are Berea College, Renfro Valley Barn Dance, Shakertown, and numerous craft shops.
Ticket information: Admission is $2 for evening programs, at the door. All other events are free.
How to get there: The Festival is on the Berea College campus, which is just off I-75

The Festival of Bluegrass
Masterson Station Park, Lexington, Ky. (Mailing address: Box 272, Georgetown, Ky. 40324)
Bluegrass
Early June (3 days)
This bluegrass festival has been held annually near Lexington, Ky., since 1974. In past years Lester Flatt, Jim and Jesse, and the Country Gentlemen have played to large crowds at this 3-day event, held outdoors in an uncovered facility with no seating limits.
Director: Jean C. Cornett
Accommodations: Camping is allowed, and trailer hookups are available; there is no charge for camping, but there are no sewers and only limited electricity. There are motels in Lexington, among them a Holiday Inn and a Ramada Inn.
Ticket information: Tickets may be bought at the gate or purchased in advance by writing to the Festival. One-day tickets cost $8; tickets for the entire weekend cost $15 if purchased at the gate and $12.50 if purchased in advance.
How to get there: Masterson Station Park is situated 3½ miles W. of Lexington on US-421

Kingdom Come Swappin' Meetin.
Cumberland, Ky. 40823
Folk
October
Begun in 1965, this 2-day festival draws people from many states. It stresses authentic folk music. Past performers have included Jean Ritchie, the Fraley Family, the Appalachian Folk, the McClane Family, John Jacob Niles,

EDNA RITCHIE AND JEAN RITCHIE (HOLDING AUTOHARP) PERFORM WITH THEIR SISTERS.

the Roadside Players, Yvonne Belmont Gregory, and Arthur Johnson. The Festival also sponsors demonstrations, crafts, exhibits, and contests. Some events are held in SECC little theater, which can accommodate 250. About 3,000 people attend this festival each year.

Director: Harold L. Patterson

Sponsor: Southeast Community College (SECC)

Accommodations/other items of interest in area: Lodging in Cumberland is available at Cumberland Motel and Gillian Motel. There is camping at Kingdom Come State Park at no charge. Facilities include bathrooms, picnic shelters, and a children's playground.

This is a good hiking area. Black Mountain, the highest point in the state, and Raven's Rock, a stone formation with a large cave opening at the top, are nearby.

Ticket information: Many events are free; for those which are not, admission varies. Tickets, when required, can be obtained at the gate.

How to get there: The Festival is located in extreme southeastern Kentucky on US routes 119 and 160

Mac Wiseman Bluegrass Festival

Renfro Valley, Ky. 40473

Bluegrass

Mid-July

This annual 3-day festival at Renfro Valley is now in its 9th year. Performers at previous festivals have included Doc Watson, Lester Flatt, the Osborne Brothers, Jimmy Martin, the Lewis Family, Ralph Stanley, the Country Gentlemen, Lula Belle & Scotty, Charles Monroe, and J. D. Crowe.

Concerts are held outdoors, in a wooded grove. There are concessions and other conveniences at the site.

Director: Mac Wiseman

Accommodations: There is ample motel space in nearby Richmond, London, Berea, Mt. Vernon, and Renfro Valley. Camping is free with the purchase of concert tickets. Trailer hook-ups are available.

Ticket information: Tickets are available through TICKETRON or the Renfro Valley office, Renfro Valley, Ky. 40473. Tel. (606)256-2664.

How to get there: Renfro Valley is located on I-75 near Mt. Vernon and Berea,

Ky., 50 miles S. of Lexington

Mountain Folk Festival

Box 287, Berea College, Berea, Ky. 40404

Folk dance and song

Early April

The 1st Mountain Folk Festival was held in 1935 and it has now grown to 4 days of workshops in traditional dance and song, attended primarily by members of dance centers in Appalachia, capped by a public performance on the last evening. The public performance takes place in Seabury Gymnasium (2,000 capacity).

Director: John M. Ramsay

Sponsor: Berea College

Accommodations: There are many motels in Berea, including Hart's, the Holiday Motel, Mountain View, and Prince Royal, all on I-75 at Ky-21. For campers and trailers there is the Walnut Meadow Travel Park, ½ mile W. of I-75 at Ky.-21

Ticket information: Public concert is free. Cost for full participation as dancer is $2.

Official Kentucky State Championship Old Time Fiddlers' Contest

1017 Brandenburg Road, Leitchfield, Ky. 42754

Old Time and bluegrass

Mid-July

The 3rd week in July has been proclaimed Old Time String Music Week in Kentucky, and it culminates in this 2-day official state fiddle contest. The contest is at Rough River Dam State Park, in a shady area, but moves indoors if there is rain. Contestants have come from 17 states, Canada, Ireland and Sweden, and there have been audiences of 4,000 to 5,000. Besides fiddle, there are also competitions for harmonica, banjo, guitar, bands, mandolin, and jig dancing. The contest was started in 1973 by the Grayson County Teen Action Program to benefit the March of Dimes. In 1975 it was made the official state championship.

Guests should remember to bring their lawn chairs.

Directors: Sodie Hall and Leo Mudd

Sponsor: Grayson County Teen Action Program

Accommodations: Lodging is available at Rough River State Lodge, Sarvers Motel, and St. Clar Motel, all located in Falls of Rough, Ky. 40119. Camping,

either primitive or with electricity and water, is available at $2 per day. Trailers are welcome. There is picnicking. The park has good recreational facilities, including swimming, boating, golf, and an archery range, as well as concessions and restaurants.
Ticket information: Day tickets are $2 and $3 at the gate

MARYLAND

Autumn Glory Festival
Courthouse, Oakland, Md. 21550
Folk and country
Four-day weekend in mid-October
Going strong since 1967—now attracting upwards of 40,000 people each year—this 4-day event features banjo and fiddle contests as well as concerts by well-known performers such as, in recent years, Stella Parton, the Seldom Scene, Cal Smith, Grandpa Jones, and Kenny Price.
The 5-String Banjo Competition, the Maryland State Fiddle Championship, and the concerts take place at the Southern High School Gym in Oakland.
Director: Cindy Hanks
Sponsor: Deep Creek Lake-Garrett County Promotion Council
Accommodations: There are many private campgrounds in addition to campgrounds at several state parks. Foul-weather gear is recommended.
Ticket information: Tickets for the main concerts are $6 for adults and $4 for children. Banjo and fiddle contest tickets are $4 for adults, and $3.50 for children.

Deer Creek Fiddlers' Convention
Norrisville Flats on Channell Road, near Norrisville, Md.
Bluegrass and old time
Early to mid-June, early to mid-July, and early to mid-August
Three times every summer, on the Sunday nearest the full moon in June, July, and August, Norrisville Flats is filled with the sounds of bluegrass and old-time bands and individual musicians competing for prizes. Music, dancing, and picnicking go on from noon until 10 PM. Those in the know say that you should bring a picnic supper, a blanket or lawn chair, and feet for dancing. Start out early; Norrisville Flats is hard to find, and after the first 1,000 people arrive, late-comers have to be turned away. "Noting the crowds and poor sound systems of some conventions, we decided to make a small good sound in a beautiful location," says our source. The festivities are all outdoors. Days tend to be hot and evenings chilly.
Director: Dave Greene

Accommodations: There is no camping, but food is available on the grounds
Ticket information: Tickets are $5 at the gate or $4 in advance. Children (of any age to 95) *with parents* are free. Tickets can be obtained from Dave Greene at 500 East 42nd St., Baltimore, Md. 21218.
How to get there: Norrisville Flats is about 3 miles E. of Norrisville and may be reached by traveling east from Norrisville for 1 mile on Route 136 (called Harkins Road); turn left onto Carea Road for 1 mile, then turn right onto Channell Road for one more mile. After the road drops into the valley and crosses a small bridge, turn right into the convention grounds. Norrisville is located on Maryland Route 25 about 25 miles N. of Baltimore and about 5 miles E. of I-83.

Susquehanna Campgrounds Bluegrass Festivals

Mt. Zoar Road, Conowingo, Md. 21918
Bluegrass and old time
Late May, early July, and mid-September
These three, 3-day festivals, Memorial Weekend Bluegrass Festival, Independence Weekend Bluegrass Festival, and Harvest Moon Bluegrass Festival, present many bluegrass and old-time performers, as well as contests, workshops, craft shows and clogging exhibitions.
The events are held in a shaded, outdoor, fenced-in amphitheater. Foul-weather clothing is recommended for all these festivals.
Director: Fred Graybeal
Sponsor: The Graybeal Family
Accommodations: Lodging is available at El Capitan in Perryville, Md. Camping facilities are free with a 2- or 3-day ticket. Hook-ups for trailers are available, and there are tables for picnicking.
Ticket information: Day tickets are $4 to $6 at the gate.
How to get there: From Route 1 at Conowingo, go 1 mile N. on Route 222 and left on Mt. Zoar Rd. for ¾ mile to Susquehanna Campgrounds

MASSACHU-SETTS

Hampshire Folk Festival

P.O. Box 1324, Hampshire Coll., Amherst, Mass. 01002
Folk (U.S. and international traditional)
Last weekend in April and first weekend in May
This is a small, special New England festival that was initiated by students at Hampshire Coll. Weather permitting, it is held outdoors on campus annually; performance halls are also available. The sponsors prefer to limit attendance to about 1,000 in order to provide an intimate setting. Utah Phillips, John Jackson, Alistair Anderson, Leadbelly, and Jean Redpath are among those who have performed at the event in past years.
Sponsor: Students of Hampshire Coll.
Accommodations: There are many hotels and motels in the Amherst area
Ticket information: Admission is $7 for the whole weekend. Tickets are available only at the Festival.
How to get there: I-91 to Amherst; follow signs to Hampshire Coll.

Pinewoods Camp Folk Music Week

Pinewoods Camp, Plymouth, Mass. 02360
tel. (617)224-3480
Folk (Anglo-American folk music)
Mid-August
The Country Dance and Song Society of America has been running dance and music weeks at Pinewoods Camp for over 40 years. Folk Music Week began about 20 years ago and continues to offer the finest folk music in a beautiful setting. For those interested in British and American folk music and in sharing that interest with others, there is a residential week of classes, workshops, and concerts with traditional folk musicians. Performers in previous summers have included Jean Ritchie, Lou Killen, and Frank Warner, among others. The camp capacity is 115.
Director: Joan Carr
Sponsor: Country Dance and Song Society, 55 Christopher St., N.Y., N.Y. 10014
Accommodations: All participants live

at camp (in cabins and cottages), and all meals are included

Ticket information: The fee for 1-week room, board, and tuition is $190 (full-week registration only). For registration information, write to the sponsor.

How to get there: Directions to the camp will be sent to all participants

S.M.U. Eisteddfod Festival of Traditional Music and Crafts

S.M.U. Eisteddfod, North Dartmouth, Mass. 02747

Folk

September

This is a festival of traditional folk music and crafts. Roy Harris, Joe Heaney, Caber Feidh, Bob White, the Folktellers, Connie Regan, and Barbara Freeman are among those who have appeared at the Festival in the past. Both indoor and outdoor facilities are available, depending on the weather.

Director: Howard Glasser

Sponsor: Southeastern Massachusetts Univ.

Accommodations: There is no camping in the area

Ticket information: All afternoon events are free; evening concerts are $5, children and senior citizens, $3. Write to the Festival, or purchase tickets at box office on the day of the event.

MICHIGAN

Charlotte Bluegrass Festival

Fairgrounds, S. Cochran Ave., Charlotte, Mich.

Bluegrass

Last full weekend in June

This annual festival—4 big days of bluegrass—is held outdoors under large shade trees or indoors in case of rain. Begun 7 years ago, it has grown into a major bluegrass festival and attracts people from many states as well as Canada. Performers in past years have included Bill Monroe, Lester Flatt, Jim and Jesse, the Osborne Brothers, Ralph Stanley, the Country Gentlemen, and the McLain Family Band.

Director: Gary V. Lyons

Accommodations: The Sundown and Crestview motels are on I-69, within 2 miles of the Festival. Camping on the Festival grounds is available at $5 per day per vehicle; trailer facilities are available.

Ticket information: Tickets are available in advance from Gary V. Lyons, 142 Laurel Bay Blvd., Laurel Bay, S.C. 29902, or at the gate. Admission for all 4 days is approximately $10 per person.

How to get there: Charlotte is about 20 miles S. of Lansing, the state capital, and East Lansing, home of Michigan State Univ.

Pioneer Bluegrass Festival

Delta College, University Center, Mich. 48710

Bluegrass

Mid-May

The 2nd week in May is bluegrass time at Delta College. Performers such as J. D. Crowe and the New South, the RFD Boys, Domestic Delivery, the Chicken String Band, and Willio and Phillio keep things lively.

Events take place at the college gym.

Director: Dick Priehs

Sponsor: Student Activities Board

Accommodations/other items of interest in area: Lodging is available at Best Western, Bay Road (M-84), or Bay Valley Inn, just off Bay Road. There is no camping, but picnicking is permitted. Of interest in the area are Midland Center for the Arts and Dow Gardens.

How to get there: Delta College is located

between Bay City, Saginaw, and Midland, Mich., just off I-75.

Southeastern Michigan Bluegrass Festival

Northfield Township Park, Whitmore Lake, Mich.
Bluegrass
Mid-July, 3-day weekend
Only recently born, in 1978, the Festival is located on 65 acres of camping area with wooded trails and a shaded stage area. Performers such as Curly Dan, Wilma Ann, John Hunley's Kentuckians, Blue Velvet, and the Laurel Mountain Boys have played. Events take place outdoors. Bring your own lawn chairs.
Director: Charlie Chase
Accommodations: Local motels and free camping in the rough are available
Ticket information: Advance tickets for 3 days cost $20. Write to Marvin Ramsey, 8705 Nollar Road, Whitmore Lake, Mich. 48189.
How to get there: East of Whitmore Lake at the corner of Seven Mile and Nollar roads

Sugar Bush Campgrounds Bluegrass Music

257 South Sand Lake Road, Hillsdale, Mich.
Bluegrass and gospel
August
Three days of the sweetest music in the Irish Hills of Michigan. This festival presents bluegrass concerts, workshops, gospel music, and a band contest.
The festivities are outdoors. Patrons are advised to bring umbrellas and lawn chairs.
Director: Sugar Bush Operations
Accommodations: Lodging is available at motels in the nearby towns of Jonesville and Hillsdale. Camping is about $2 per vehicle, with complete facilities. Trailers are welcome.
There are many good spots for picnicking. There is also a lake on the campgrounds.
Ticket information: Day tickets are $4 to $6 at the gate

Wheatland Festival

5220 N. Sherman Road, Lake, Mich. 48632
Folk
Weekend after Labor Day

The Wheatland Festival was initiated in 1974 as a benefit for a rural food co-op and has continued since as an occasion for the presentation and preservation of traditional American music and crafts. Performers such as the Red Clay Ramblers, the Hot Mud Family, Martin, Bogan and Armstrong, Carl Story, and the Williams Family have appeared in recent years for this 3-day gathering. There are competitions in flat-foot dancing and in the banjo, band, old-time, and bluegrass categories.
Performances are outdoors or in a tent with 1,500 capacity at Centennial farm outside Remus.
Director: Craig Turnbull
Sponsor: Wheatland Music Organization
Accommodations: The Holiday Inn in Mt. Pleasant, Mich., and the Blue Lake Inn, Mecosta, Mich., can provide accommodations. Camping in the rough is available at the site at no charge with festival ticket.
Ticket information: Three-day tickets cost $8 (advance). For tickets, write to Wheatland Music Organization, Box 1, Remus, Mich. 48632.
How to get there: Centennial farm is 4 miles northwest of Remus

MISSISSIPPI

Atwood Bluegrass Festival

Atwood Water Park, Monticello, Miss.
Bluegrass and country
May
This 2-day festival has featured Doc
Watson and Lester Flatt, Grandpa Jones
(Hee Haw), the Haggar Brothers, Dave
and Sugar, Kurt Kilpatrick and top
regional bluegrass groups. In addition to
musical entertainment, there are sports
and contests for the whole family.
Events take place in tents and outdoors;
patrons are advised to bring lawn chairs
or blankets.
Director: Donald Vince
Sponsor: Monticello-Lawrence Chamber
of Commerce
Accommodations: Accommodations are
available at Monticello Motel, Monticello,
Miss. 39654, the Jeffersonian, Prentiss,
Miss. 39474, and the Holiday Inn,
Brookhaven, Miss. 39601. Camping is
allowed; there is a primitive camping area
with fire rings. Comfort stations and
showers are available. There are also
facilities for trailers. Tables are available
for picnicking. Atwood Water Park has
tennis courts, arts and crafts booths,
children's events, playgrounds, canoeing,
and numerous competitions.
Ticket information: Admission is about
$5. For tickets or information write to
Atwood Bluegrass Festival, P.O. Box
5332, Jackson, Miss. 39216.
How to get there: Atwood Water Park
is on Highway 84 at the Pearl River
Bridge in Monticello

John W. Kyle Folklife Festival

c/o Anna Maher
Sardis Dam, Sardis, Miss. 38666
Folk
July
There is a square dance and recreational
activities, including a field day. Events
take place in an uncovered amphitheater.
Director: Anna Maher
Sponsor: John W. Kyle State Park
Accommodations/other items of interest
in area: There are motels, and the park
has vacation cabins. Camping is avail-
able for $5 per day (water and electricity
included); trailers are welcome.
Sardis Dam is one of the largest earth-
filled dams in the world. There is a
natural sand beach in the area.
Ticket information: There is no charge

Magnolia State Bluegrass Festival

Wiggins, Miss.
Bluegrass and gospel
First weekend in June
Performers at this festival have included
Bill Monroe and the Bluegrass Boys, the
Sullivan Family, Dub Crouch, Norman
Ford, and the Bluegrass Rounders.
Director: Margie Sullivan
Sponsor: Radio Station WIGG
Accommodations: There is camping.
Trailer hook-ups are $3 per day.
Ticket information: Admission is $5 on
Friday, $6 on Saturday, and $10 for the
2 days. Tickets are available at the gate.
For further information, write to Margie
Sullivan, St. Stephens, Ala. 36569
How to get there: The Festival is 1 mile
N. of Wiggins on Highway 49

MISSOURI

Don Brown's Bluegrass Festival

213 Chambers Rd., St. Lewis, Mo.
63137
Bluegrass
August
This is a 3-day bluegrass music festival.
Past performers have included Don
Brown and the Ozark Mountain Trio,
Bob Black, Al Murphy and the Spon-
taneous Mountain Boys, the Last
Kentuckians, the Whiskey Ridge Boys,
the Gospel Tones, Sinking Creek, and
Paul Brahe and the Bluegrass Limited.
Director: Don Brown
Accommodations: Motels are located
9 miles from the Festival. There is free
primitive camping.
Ticket information: Day tickets range
from $3 to $4. A weekend pass is $8.
They can be obtained in advance.
How to get there: The Festival is 9 miles
W. of Perryville on Highway T

Frontier Folklife Festival

Jefferson National Expansion Memorial,
11 N. Fourth St., St. Louis, Mo. 63102
Folk
Early September
For 3 days this Midwest regional festival,
held at Gateway Arch on the banks of
the Mississippi River, celebrates the
folkways prevalent during the period
of westward expansion. Musicians play
and sing the blues, ballads, gospel, old-
time, and Cajun and other ethnic music.
There are also crafts displays.
Performances are outdoors under tents,
with lawn seating for 500 in each tent.
Directors: Jane Bergey and Joe Pfeffer
Sponsors: Jefferson National Expan-
sion Historical Association, Missouri
Friends of the Folk Arts, National
Park Service, others
Accommodations/other items of interest
in area: Lodging is available at the Holi-
day Inn, Fourth and Pine; Hilton Inn,
Fourth and Washington; Stouffer's
Riverfront, Fourth and Walnut; and at
many other hotels on both sides of the
Mississippi. There is no camping in
the immediate area.
Points of interest nearby include the
Museum of Westward Expansion, Old
Courthouse, Old Cathedral, and Forest
Park.

Ticket information: All events are free
How to get there: The Gateway Arch is
on the Mississippi Riverfront in St.
Louis and is accessible from I-44, I-55,
and I-70

Hill & Hollow Folk Festival

Powell, Mo. 65730
Country and western, gospel, bluegrass
Last weekend in September
This gathering, occurring annually since
1968, attracts thousands of people from
more than 20 states. Old-time music and
singing, folklore, and arts and crafts provide the attraction over a 3-day weekend. Performers have included such musicians as Ernest Tubb and the Texas
Troubadours, Lester Flatt, Grandpa
Jones, the Kingsmen, and Lonzo and
Oscar. An art contest for best scenic
paintings in watercolor or oil is also
held.
Bring your own lawn chair for all events.
Director: Bill and Bob Brumley
Sponsor: Powell Community
Ticket information: Tickets available
only at gate. Admission charge of $2 for
each vehicle and $3 for trailers and recre-
ational vehicles on Saturday and Sunday.

Kahoka Festival of Bluegrass Music

Clark County Fairgrounds, Kahoka, Mo.
Bluegrass
Second weekend in August
This 4-day event has brought bluegrass
players from all over the Midwest each
year since 1972. Some of those who
have performed include Buck White and
the Down Home Folks, Mike O'Roark
and the Freeborn Men, Sally Mountain
Show, Bluegrass Related, and Possum
Trot. A fiddlers' convention and a band
contest on Saturday morning also take
place at the Festival.
Bands play in a covered amphitheater
which has room for 1,500 people.
Director: Delbert Spray
Accommodations: Lodging is available at
Kahoka Mötel adjacent to the festival
grounds, or at the Holiday Inn in Kahoka.
Camping, with modern facilities, is
available at no cost. Trailers are welcome.
There is picnicking and swimming.
Ticket information: Tickets are available
at the gate or by mail.
How to get there: The Festival is on
Highway 136

FATS KAPLAN AND ROY BOOKBINDER (PHOTO PREVIOUS PAGE)

Land of Mark Twain Bluegrass Festival
Lucky Lakes Campground, Palmyra, Mo.
Bluegrass
First weekend in June
This year, performances were by the
Sally Mountain Show, the Downstate
Ramblers, the Schell Brothers, and the
Strong Family String Band, among
others. A fiddle contest with money
prizes was one of the events.
Sponsor: The Tri-State Bluegrass
Association
Accommodations: There is camping
available, with electricity, a general
store, a large wooded area, and fishing
lakes
Ticket information: The ticket prices
are Friday, $3; Saturday, $5; and Sun-
day, $4. A weekend pass is $9. Children
under 12 are admitted free. For tickets
and information write to Sec., Tri-State
Bluegrass Association, R.R. #1, Kahoka,
Mo. 63445, or call (314)221-5722 or
853-4344.
Palmyra

Mountain Folks Music Festival
Silver Dollar City, Mo.
Folk
Early to mid-June
This festival is held in addition to the
attractions at Silver Dollar City park.
Approximately 40 folk groups perform
outdoors in various locations around
the park.
Directors: Ken Bell and Ron Jett
Sponsor: Silver Dollar City
Accommodations: There are numerous
motels in the area, as well as campsites
Ticket information: Admission is $8.95

Old-Time Fiddlers' and Pickers' Festival
Community Park, Graham, Mo.
Old-time music
Early August
Fiddlers and pickers from the entire
Midwest arrive for this weekend festival
and its contests with over $1,000 in
prize money. Judges are winners from
previous years or those knowledgeable in
the field. No entry fee for contestants.
Contests are held in Community Park
with some large tents available for shade.
Bring your own seats. In case of rain
the event will be held in the Graham
Community Building.
Director: Joe O. Mowry
Sponsor: Graham Community Better-
ment Assn.

Accommodations: Motels are available
in Maryville, Mound City, and Saint
Joseph. Camping is $2.50 per hook-up.
Trailers are welcome.
Ticket information: Tickets are $2 per
day, available only at the gate
How to get there: Graham is located
9 miles W. of US-71, in northwest
Missouri

Ozark Mountain Bluegrass Festival
Box 428, Eminence, Mo. 65466
Bluegrass
Early July
This 4-day bluegrass festival, held
annually for the last 10 years, is in the
heart of the Ozark Mountains. Events
include fiddle, banjo, and flat pick contests. Among the performers at previous festivals have been the Country
Gentlemen, Jim and Jesse, Buck White,
Don Reno, and Larry Sparks. The Festival site is outdoors and uncovered.
Director: Ken Seaman
Accommodations: Motels in Eminence
are Harveys, the Riverside, and the
Pinecrest. Camping is available at no
charge.
Ticket information: Admission is $5
per day. Tickets may be obtained at the
gate or in advance.

NEBRASKA

Crawford Fiddle Contest

Crawford City Park Pavilion, Crawford, Nebr. 69339
Fiddle contest
One day in late July
The Park Pavillion in Crawford, which seats 500 people, is the setting for this fiddler's contest and old settlers' reunion
Director: Ellis "Peabody" Hale
Sponsor: Old Settlers' Assn.
Accommodations: Hilltop and Townline motels in Crawford can provide accommodations. Camping in the rough is available at the site.
Ticket information: Tickets are free

NEW JERSEY

June Day Festival

Eagle Rock Reservation, West Orange, N.J.
Folk
Second weekend in June
From a family day for members of the Folk Music Society of Northern New Jersey in 1970, June Day has grown to be a weekend festival of stature. The Festival includes singing, dancing, children's activities, crafts, concerts, workshops, and jams. Such performers as David Bromberg, Pat Sky, Oscar Brand, Pete Seeger, Lew Killen, and Tahuantinsuyo have participated. There are both coverd and uncovered stages, while all audience seating is uncovered.
Director: Jeff Heilbrun
Sponsors: Folk Music Society of Northern New Jersey and Essex County Park Commission
Accommodations/other items of interest in area: Two motels in the area are the Turtlebrook Inn, and Town & Campus in West Orange.
New York City is 15 miles away.
Ticket information: Free ($1 donation requested)
How to get there: Leave I-280 at Exit 8-B, go N. ¾ mile, turn right onto Eagle Rock Ave

New Jersey Folk Festival

c/o American Studies Dept.
Douglass College, New Brunswick, N.J. 08903
Folk and bluegrass
A 1-day festival, usually held the last weekend in April
The 5-year-old New Jersey Folk Festival features many different types of folk music, such as banjo player Ola Belle Reed, British Isle balladeer Murray Callahan, Irish fiddler Ed McDermott, and the Molehill Mountain Boys, a bluegrass jug band; other performers have included Kathy D and the Lentil Soup Boys, Just Plain Folk, and the Pineconers, from the Pine Barrens. The Festival includes a juried crafts show and a children's play area.
During the day the music is played outdoors, and in the evening it is indoors at 138 Hickman Hall, Douglass College

Director: Dr. Angus Gillespie
Sponsor: American Studies Association,
American Studies Department, Douglass
College
Accommodations: The Ramada Inn and
the Sheraton Inn are both in East
Brunswick. Camping is not allowed. Pic-
nicking is permitted, and food is avail-
able at the Festival.
Ticket information: Admission is free
How to get there: Take Route 18 to
George Street in New Brunswick

NEW YORK

Fox Hollow Festival of Traditional Music and Arts

R.D. 1, Fox Hollow, Petersburg, N.Y.
12138
Folk and traditional
Early August
The Fox Hollow Festival, among the
best-loved of its kind, features traditional
folk artists and some contemporary ones
as well. All music is acoustical. Concerts
are held throughout the day and in the
evening. There are also such activities as
concert workshops, storytelling, dance
workshops, demonstrations of traditional
crafts, and a dance each night in the town
hall. There are food booths on the
grounds. Patrons should come prepared
for some rain and should bring warm
sweaters and folding chairs.
The 3-day festival is held outdoors in a
natural amphitheater.
Director: Evelyne C. Burnstine
Accommodations: There are 3 campgrounds in the area. Bus transportation
is provided between the campgrounds
and the festival. For a list of the campgrounds and motels in the area, write to
Fox Hollow, R.D. 1, Petersburg, N.Y.
12138
Ticket information: Admission is $7.50
per day in advance, $8.50 at the gate.
For ticket information and brochure,
send a stamped, self-addressed envelope
to the Fox Hollow Festival.
How to get there: Fox Hollow is located
at the junction of routes 2 and 22 in
Petersburg, N.Y., about 30 miles E. of
Troy, N.Y.

Long Island Bluegrass and Old Time Country Music Band Contest

Sunrise Mall, Massapequa, L.I., N.Y.
Bluegrass and old time
April
This is Long Island's largest country
music show. During the 2-day festival,
22 amateur and semi-professional bands
compete for prizes.
The event is held indoors and can accom-
modate several thousand spectators.
Director: Douglas Tuchman
Sponsors: Bluegrass Club of New York
and Sunrise Mall Merchants' Association
Accommodations: Lodging is readily

available in the area. There is no camping or picnicking.
Ticket information: Admission is free
How to get there: To get to Massapequa, take Southern State Parkway to Route 110, then go S. to the mall. Massapequa can also be reached by the Long Island Railroad (LIRR).

Mockingbird Bluegrass Festival
R.R. 1, Box 171, Arcade, N.Y. 14009
Bluegrass and old-time music
Last or next-to-last weekend in July
This festival takes place at a privately owned 235-acre campground during a 3-day weekend. There is a best band competition with a $100 prize. Participants have included Jim and Jesse, Virginia Boys, Lewis Family, Grand Ole Opry stars, and New York and Pennsylvania groups. Chicken barbecues and parachute jumping are additional events. Foul weather clothing is recommended.
Director: Walter Mattson
Accommodations: Basic camping fee is $4.50 for 4 people. Electricity, sewer, and water are available. There are trailer facilities. Lodging is available at the Arcade Hotel and Johnny's Motel in Arcade.
Ticket information: Weekend tickets are $13 in advance, $14 at the gate. For tickets, write to Mockingbird Park, R.R. 1, Box 171, Arcade, N.Y. 14009.
How to get there: Travel 2 miles N. of Arcade on Route 98-N

New York City Bluegrass and Old-Time Country Music Band Contest & Crafts Fair
South Street Seaport, Fulton St. and East River, New York, N.Y.
Bluegrass and country music
Early August
This is the largest annual country music festival in New York City. Amateur and semi-professional bands from all over the northeastern U.S. come to play and compete for prizes over a 2-day weekend. The Crafts Fair is usually completely sold out. Up to 20,000 people attend and enjoy music outdoors on the pier of a historic maritime museum. Seating provided by the audience.
Director: Douglas Tuchman
Sponsors: Douglas Tuchman and Gail Schiller
Other items of interest in area: The South Street Seaport is the permanent

berth of several "tall ships."
Ticket information: Tickets for the contests on Saturday and Sunday nights are $4 each. The Crafts Fair is free.

Smokey Greene's Annual Bluegrass Festival
Box 71, Schuylerville, N.Y. 12871
Bluegrass
Second week in August
Initiated in 1972, this festival was the first major bluegrass festival held in N.Y. State. It takes place for 4 days in an open field near Saratoga, N.Y., and has attracted in recent years musicians such as Lester Flatt, Ralph Stanley, Charlie Moore, the Lewis Family, and Red Allen.
Director: Smokey Greene
Accommodations: Camping is available free at the site. Water and restrooms are provided. Trailers are welcome.
Ticket information: Tickets cost $5 per day, $12.50 for all 4 days
How to get there: Festival site is at Bishop Farm, Porter Corners, off Route 9 N., 8 miles from Saratoga, N.Y.

WCNY-Cato Masons' Bluegrass Ramble Picnic
c/o Bill Knowlton, WCNY, Liverpool, N.Y. 13088
Traditional (bluegrass and old-time country)
Early August (1 day)
This annual picnic was begun in 1973 as a meeting of listeners to the "Bluegrass Ramble," over WCNY-FM from central New York. Bluegrass and old-time country music are performed outdoors, on a covered stage, and shows are taped for broadcast over several Eastern Educational Network stations. Performers include many bands from central New York, as well as Canada. About 8,000 people attend the picnic. There is parking for 3,000 cars. Food and crafts are offered for sale on the picnic grounds.
Director: Bill Knowlton
Sponsors: Cato Lodge 141 F & A Masons and WCNY-FM/TV, Syracuse, N.Y.
Accommodations/other items of interest in area: There is camping in the rough and trailer camping at the Festival for a modest fee. Motels in the area are located in Auburn, Weedsport, and Baldwinsville, New York.
Items of interest in the area include the

Finger Lakes and Lake Ontario, as well as numerous state parks.
Ticket information: There is a modest price for admission. Tickets are available at the gate.
How to get there: The picnic is held 25 miles northwest of Syracuse at the Frank Saplin Farm (1 mile N. of Meridian, off Route 370)

NORTH CAROLINA

Bascom Lamar Lunsford's Mountain Music and Dance Festival
Mars Hill College, Mars Hill, N.C. 28754
Mountain music, dance, bluegrass
First weekend in October
Named after its founder, who helped to preserve many of the traditions of the Appalachian mountain people, the Festival has grown from a one-night affair in 1968 to a 3-day-long celebration of old-time mountain music and dancing. Everything from clawhammer banjo and flat-pick guitar playing to old-time fiddling and dulcimer playing to folk songs and mountain clog dancing takes place on the campus of Mars Hill Coll. during the day and in Moore Auditorium (capacity of 2,000) at night. Related events include demonstrations by weavers, whittlers, quiltmakers, spinners, and woodworkers.
Director: Harold Herzog
Sponsor: Southern Appalachian Center
Accommodations: Lodging is available at the Holiday Inn in Asheville, N.C.
Ticket information: Tickets are $1.50 for evening performances

Bluegrass and Old Time Fiddler's Convention
Veterans Memorial Park, West Lebanon St., Mt. Airy, N.C. 27030
Traditional (bluegrass and old time)
First weekend in June
This bluegrass and old-time music contest features 2 days of individual and band competition, in which only string instruments are judged. There is a dance competition as well.
The event is held outdoors, if weather permits, with grandstand seating. There are concession stands, as well as picnic sheds, and there is parking for 3,000 cars.
Director: G. F. Collins
Sponsors: American Legion and V.F.W.
Accommodations: There are ten acres of shady woods for camping and picnicking at the Veterans Memorial Park, where the contest is held. Camping is $5 per day. There are several motels in

the immediate area of the Park.
Ticket information: Admission is $3
per day, $5 for a two-day ticket.
Tickets are available at the gate.

Byard Ray Folk Festival

Route 1, Box 88, Hurdle Mills, N.C.
27541
Folk
Last weekend in June
This festival is for folk music only—
featuring the traditional music and
dance of the Southern Appalachians.
Performers are local artists who have
learned their music from their fore-
fathers. The Festival, now in its 3rd
year, is held at the Thomas Wolfe
Auditorium of the Asheville, N.C., Civic
Center, which seats 2,500.
Director: Betty Sue Johnson
Sponsor: National Endowment for the
Arts
Accommodations: Hotels in Asheville
include the Hilton, the Sheraton, the Inn
on the Plaza, and the Ramada Inn.
There are many campgrounds in the
Asheville area.
Ticket information: Admission is $3.
Tickets are available at the box office.

Coats Annual Bluegrass Festival

Coats Fairgrounds Park, Coats, N.C.
27521
Bluegrass
Second week in June
This annual 3-day bluegrass festival is
now in its 8th year. Performers at past
festivals have included Knoxville Grass,
Blue Denim, Grass Strings, McRay
Gardner, and the Blue Valley Boys.
The Festival is held on the grounds of
a large park.
Seating is outdoors, on a well-shaded
sloping hill.
Director: J. D. Norris
Accommodations: The following hotels
and motels are in the area: Howard
Johnson's, the Holiday Inn, Ramada Inn,
Days Inn, and Dutch Inn. Camping is
available in the area, with facilities for
trailers.
Ticket information: Prices are $3 to $5.
For tickets, write to Jr. Council 17,
Coats, N.C. 27521.
How to get there: The fairgrounds are
S. of Coats on Highway 55

Fiddlers' Convention

Oak Ridge Public School, Oak Ridge,
N.C.
Folk and bluegrass (no electric instru-
ments)
Easter Monday evening
The Oak Ridge Fiddlers' Convention has
been bringing old-time and bluegrass
music to its loyal fans for 35 years.
Amateur musicians from within a 75-
mile radius of Oak Ridge compete for
cash prizes in a 700-seat indoor facility.
The convention is held in conjunction
with an annual horse show.
Director: Bob Benbow
Sponsor: Oak Ridge P.T.A.
Accommodations: Accommodations in
the area include The Albert Pick and a
Holiday Inn, both on I-40 in Greensboro,
N.C. Picnicking and camping are not
allowed.
Ticket information: Tickets are $3 each
and are available from Bob Benbow,
Box 5130, Greensboro, N.C. 27403.

Mountain Dance and Folk Festival

Asheville Civic Center, Asheville, N.C.
Traditional Southern Appalachian
mountain music and dance
The 1st Thursday, Friday, and Saturday
in August
It began with folklorist Bascom Lamar
Lunsford, who rode the Great Smokies
and the Blue Ridge by muleback to
record and preserve the music he loved.
It began on a wooden dancing platform
on a knoll overlooking his home in
South Turkey Creek. Here his neighbors
would come to dance and make their
music. In 1927 Bascom Lunsford
brought his dancing platform and his
"neighbors" to the square in Asheville,
with the blessing of the city fathers.
Each year since, mountain fiddlers,
banjo pickers, dulcimer sweepers, tune
bow and mouth harp players have come
to enjoy themselves along about sundown the 1st weekend in August.
The Festival, held in the auditorium of
the Asheville Civic Center, presents
regional amateur talent, some of whom
have become widely known through the
years.
Director: Mrs. Jackie Ward
Sponsor: Folk Heritage Committee of the
Asheville Area Chamber of Commerce
Accommodations: There are Sheraton,
Hilton, and Downtowner inns on the

plaza in Asheville and picnicking, camping, and trailer facilities within 5 miles.
Ticket information: Admission is $3 and
$4, with a $10 package admission for all
three nights. For tickets, write to
Asheville Area Chamber of Commerce,
P.O. Box 1011, Asheville, N.C. 28802.
tel. (704)254-1981.
How to get there: The civic center is in
downtown Asheville

Mt. Pleasant Jaycee Fiddlers' Convention
Mt. Pleasant, N.C. 28124
Old-time country music
Last Saturday in July
Performers of old-time country music
from North Carolina and neighboring
states have been getting together for this
convention annually since 1964.
Performances take place outisde for 4
hours in the early evening in the Mt.
Pleasant High School Stadium. In case
of rain everything will move indoors
into an auditorium.
Director: William Ewdy
Sponsor: Mt. Pleasant Jaycees
Accommodations: No camping available
Ticket information: Ticket prices are
$3 for adults, $2 for students. Write to
P.O. Box 536, Mt. Pleasant, N.C. 28124.
How to get there: The stadium is located
on Highway 49, 9 miles E. of Concord

Old-Time Fiddlers' Convention
P.O. Box 38, Union Grove, N.C. 28689
Folk
The Thursday, Friday and Saturday
before Easter
The Old-Time Fiddlers' Convention had
its beginning in 1924 with not quite
200 fans in a little tin-roofed school-
house. It rained that 1st night, making
a racket on the roof that the music
couldn't compete with. But when the
rain stopped, the music was so good
that the convention eventually grew
to need the 12,000-seat coliseum that
now houses it, 55 years later. Founder
H.P. VanHoy, the father of the current
director, attributed the success of the
Festival at least in part to the fact that
the musicians reaching the finals have
always shared in the proceeds. Authentic, old-time string music is the major
reason, of course.
Director: J. Pierce VanHoy
Accommodations: There are many

motels within a half-hour's drive of
the Festival, in Statesville, Hampton-
ville, and in other nearby towns. Camping sites and parking are available on a
first-come, first-served basis without
additional charge.
Ticket information: Tickets, available
at the gate, cost $25 for all 3 days,
$20 for Friday and Saturday, and $10
for Saturday only. There is a $4 per
day charge for early arrivals.
How to get there: The convention is
held on the VanHoy farm, just off
I-77 at N. C. 901. Watch for exit 65.

Rockingham Bluegrass Club Festival
c/o Homer V. Wood, 239 N. Main St.,
Eden, N.C. 27286
Bluegrass
June
This is a festival contest—up to 21 bands
have performed at previous festivals.
Seating is outdoors—bring lawn chairs
and rain gear.
Director: Homer V. Wood
Accommodations: There is an Innkeeper
Motel and primitive camping is available.
Trailers are welcome and picnicking is
allowed.
Ticket information: $4 at the gate

Smoky Mountain Folk Festival
117 Piegon St., Waynesville, N.C. 28786
Traditional southern Appalachian music
and dance
Last Thursday, Friday, and Saturday in
July
The Festival started in 1971 as a centennial celebration of the founding of
Waynesville. Traditional mountain
music and dance of all kinds—smooth
and clog dance teams as well as individual buck dancing—take place each night.
On Saturday night there is a special
old-time fiddle, banjo and stringband
contest with $500 in cash prizes. There
are also dance contests. Other events
include a traditional crafts and antiques
fair, a street dance, and the Smoky
Mountain Muzzel Loaders' Beef Shoot.
The main events take place in the gym
at Waynesville Junior High, which has a
2,000-seat capacity.
Director: Joe Sam Queen
Sponsor: Waynesville Parks and Recreation Dept.
Accommodations/other items of interest
in area: There are many motels in the
area. For information, write to Haywood

County Chamber of Commerce, Waynesville, N.C. 38786. There are also many
camping sites available in the area.
Regional points of interest include
Smoky Mountain National Park and
"Unto These Hills," an outdoor drama
in Cherokee, N.C.
Ticket information: Tickets are $3 per
day, available only at the gate
How to get there: Just off I-40 on the
way to Smoky Mountain National Park

NORTH DAKOTA

**Irrigation Days Old-Time Fiddling
Contest**
Oakes Armory, Oakes, N.D.
Fiddling contest
Early June
This event brings together 60 to 70
fiddlers for a day of competitive musi-
cianship. In addition there is a steam-
threshing bee, an art show, and a turkey
barbecue. It all takes place near or at
the 900-seat Oakes Armory in downtown Oakes.
Sponsor: Oakes Chamber of Commerce
Accommodations: Accommodations are
available at the A-1 Motel, E & I Motel,
and Star Hotel in Oakes
Ticket information: Afternoon tickets
cost $1, evening tickets cost $2 (available only at the door)

OHIO

Appalachian Festival
c/o 1015 Vine St., Room 304,
Cincinnati, Ohio 45202
Traditional and gospel
Mid-May (for 5 days)
The Appalachian Festival was begun in
1970 to provide a marketing outlet for
Appalachian regional craftsmen. Over
the years the music program has
expanded greatly, partly as the result
of a National Endowment for the Arts
grant. The music is traditional Appala-
chian, bluegrass, blues, and gospel.
Performers at past festivals have in-
cluded the Katie Lauer Band, Larry
Sparks and the Lonesome Ramblers,
Wrystraw, and Martin, Bogan and Arm-
strong. The Festival, which is held at the
Cincinnati Convention Center, includes
crafts exhibits and sales, crafts demonstrations, and music workshops.
The concert area seats several hundred.
Sponsor: Appalachian Community
Development Association (ACDA)
Accommodations: Hotels in the im-
mediate area include Stouffer's, 141
W. 6th; and the Netherland-Hilton,
5th and Race, Cincinnati, Ohio 45202
Ticket information: Admission to the
Festival is $2. Tickets are available at
the door.
How to get there: The convention center
is in downtown Cincinnati, at Sixth and
Plum Streets, 2 blocks from both I-75
and I-71

Bluegrass Music Festival
State Route 64, Swanton, Ohio
Bluegrass and country
Mid-June
Started in 1972, this festival has a "blue-
grass campground" and a hall that seats
approximately 1,500 people. Events
take place over a 3-day weekend and in
recent years have featured performers
like Hylo Brown, L. B. Siler and the
Round Mountain Boys, and Carl Story.
There is usually a square dance on both
Friday and Saturday nights.
Director: Dick Sulewski
Sponsors: Dick Sulewski, L. B. Siler,
Rita Sulewski
Accommodations: Camping is available,
at $2 per day, with all facilities. Trailers
are welcome.
There are picnicking and playground
areas, and hiking trails.
Ticket information: Tickets are $15 in
advance or $18 at the gate. Call Dick
Sulewski, Swanton, Ohio, at
(419) 875-5110.
How to get there: On Route 64, 3 miles
S. of Airport Highway in Swanton

Foxfire International Bluegrass Festival
Foxfire Campgrounds, Ottawa, Ohio
Bluegrass
Third weekend in July
This festival provides a 3-day weekend of
bluegrass music by well-known U.S. and
Canadian entertainers—Bill Monroe and
the Blue Grass Boys, Lilli Mae and the
Dixie Gospel Aires Quartet, James
Monroe and the Midnight Ramblers,
and Cody have all appeared in past
years. In addition there is a Sunday morn-
ing church service.
Performances take place outdoors; in
case of rain, a tent is available. Seating
provided by the audience.
Director: Lilli Mae
Accommodations: In nearby Lima, Ohio,
accommodations are available from
Howard Johnson's, Days Inn, Ramada
Inn, and others. Camping is available
on the Festival site free with a 3-day
ticket. Electricity hook-ups are $4 extra
for the weekend. Trailers are welcome.
Ticket information: Tickets are $6 for
Friday, $7 for Saturday, and $6 for
Sunday. Tickets for all 3 days are $15.
All tickets are available only at the gate.
How to get there: Foxfire campgrounds is
2 miles N. of Ottawa on State Route 15

Ohio National Bluegrass Festival;
October Bluegrass Reunion;
Spring Bluegrass Reunion
Hillbrook Recreation Area, P.O. Box
257, Ottawa, Ohio 45875
Bluegrass
National: early August (3 days);
October: early October (3 days);
Spring: early May (3 days)
The Hillbrook Recreation Area, N. of
Ottawa, is home to these 3 bluegrass
festivals. Concerts are held on indoor
and outdoor stages in the recreation
area, which is a vacation spot with
facilities for camping, swimming, fishing,
paddle boating, and even banquets.
The 3 music events are different each

year, but the locale remains the same.
For information about those appearing
at the Festival and the Reunions, write
to the sponsor at the address given
above.
Director: Henry J. Verhoff
Sponsor: Hillbrook Recreation
Accommodations: This recreation area
has everything for camping: electric
hook-ups, ice, a laundry, and there are
facilities for swimming, fishing and boating. For information about prices, write
to the Festival.
How to get there: Four miles northwest of Ottawa on Route 15

Yankee Peddler Festival
Clay's Park Resort, Canal Fulton, Ohio
Folk
Three weekends in September
Fiddle, banjo, and dulcimer contests
involving local musicians make up the
musical portion of this pioneer festival.
It also features a crafts show with 150
participants, a pioneer foods festival,
and a variety of entertainments ranging
from a hot-air balloon to a medicine
show.
All activities are outdoors in an un-
covered area during each day of the
Festival.
Director: F. R. Cajka
Sponsor: Yankee Peddler Festival Assn.
Accommodations/other items of interest
in area: Camping is available at the site.
Also occurring nearby in late September
is the Marietta College Indian Summer
Arts & Crafts Festival, at the Washington
County Fairgrounds in Marietta, Ohio.
Ticket information: Tickets are $3 for
adults. For tickets, write to Yankee
Peddler Festival Association, 4046
State Road, Medina, Ohio 44256. Dead-
line for advance sale tickets is August
31. Send self-addressed, stamped
envelope.

**Zane's Trace Festival of Traditional
Music**
c/o David Taylor, Ohio Univ., Zanesville, Ohio 43701
Folk, bluegrass
Third weekend in June
This outdoor festival of traditional music
features folk, old-time country, and
bluegrass. The performers are groups
from the Zanesville area. Included in
the Festival are fiddle and banjo

contests.
Director: David Taylor
Sponsor: Zanesville Area Chamber of
Commerce
Accommodations: There are various
hotels and motels in the area and camping
facilities as well
Ticket information: Admission is free
How to get there: The Festival is held
in the Putnam Historic District in
Zanesville

OKLAHOMA

Davis Bluegrass Festival

Davis City Park, Davis, Okla.
Bluegrass
A weekend in late June
This festival was started in 1973 and features an old-time fiddle contest. It takes place for 2 days in an uncovered outdoor area in Davis City Park. Light clothing is recommended.
Director: Helen Webber
Sponsor: Davis Chamber of Commerce
Accommodations: The Sundown Motel and Roy Motel can provide accommodations in Davis. Camping is permitted at the site for $3 per day, with electricity available. Trailers are welcome.
Ticket information: Tickets cost $5 per day. For tickets, write to Helen Webber, 405 S.D. St., Davis, Okla. 73030.

Grant's Bluegrass and Old Time Music Festival

Salt Creek Park, Hugo, Okla. 74743
Bluegrass
Early August
This annual festival of wholesome family entertainment features 5 days of bluegrass music concerts, as well as contests on all bluegrass instruments, including band contests. All major bluegrass artists have performed at the Festival during its 11 years.
The Festival is held outdoors, with seating on tree-shaded benches. Patrons are welcome to bring their own lawn chairs. There is a pit barbecue concession on the grounds for meals and sandwiches. Parking on the grounds is unlimited.
Directors: Juarez and Bill Grant, Route 2, Box 11-K, Hugo, Okla. 74743
Accommodations: Salt Creek Park is open free of charge to festival campers. Electrical hook-ups are available at $3 per day. Motels in Hugo include the Village Inn, the Karriage House, the A OK Motel, and the Tower Motel.
Ticket information: Admission ranges from $5 to $7 per day. A 5-day ticket is $22.
How to get there: Hugo is in the southeast Oklahoma area known as Kiamichi County. Salt Creek Park is located 1 mile E. and 1½ miles N. of Hugo.

Powderhorn Pack

Langley, Okla.
Bluegrass
Early July
This family-oriented 4-day festival features well-known performers such as Lester Flatt, Merle Haggard, Ralph Stanley, and many more fine country groups. Gospel and bluegrass all day Sunday is a tradition of the Festival. All the music is acoustical. The Festival has been filmed for educational television.
The Festival is held in an 8,000 capacity outdoor amphitheater; all seating is shaded.
Director: Joe J. Hutchison
Sponsor: Pepsi Cola
Accommodations/other items of interest in area: Motel accommodations are available at Grand Motel, Ketchum, Okla., or Rocky Rest Motel, Langley, Okla. Camping, at $1 per day, with electric hook-up for $3, is available, with shower and restroom facilities. Trailers are allowed, and there is picnicking.
The Festival is near Grand Lake o' the Cherokees and state parks.
Ticket information: Admission is $5 per day, or 4 days for $17. For tickets, send a check or money order to Joe J. Hutchison, Star Route 1, Spavinaw, Okla. 74366.
How to get there: The Festival is on State Highway 82, 17 miles southeast of I-44 (Will Rogers Turnpike) at Vinita, Okla., 50 miles E. of Tulsa

Sanders Family Bluegrass Festival

Route 6, Box 15, McAlester, Okla. 74051
Bluegrass and folk
Four days during the 2nd or 3rd week of June
In 1979, the 3rd year of the Sanders Family Bluegrass Festival, about 6,000 people attended. They gathered to hear such performers as Lester Flatt, Mac Wiseman, the Lewis Family, Jim and Jesse, Harold Morrison, the Pinnacle Boys, the Sullivan Family, and the Tennessee Gentlemen. On Sunday morning a prayer service with gospel and bluegrass is held.
Director: Freddie Sanders
Sponsor: The Sanders Family
Accommodations: Hotels and motels in the area include a Holiday Inn

(Highway 69 Bypass S.); McAlester Motor Inn Motel (700 N. Main); McHoma Lodge (southeast of McAlester); and Hiway Lodge (southeast of McAlester). Camping, including trailers, hook-ups, modern restrooms and hot showers, is free.

Ticket information: Tickets are $5 a day and $17 for a 4-day ticket. To obtain tickets call (918) 423-4891 or write to Freddie Sanders, Route 6, Box 15, McAlester, Okla. 74501.

How to get there: Location is 5 miles W. of McAlester on Highway 270

OREGON

Annual Willamette Valley Folk Festival
Suite 2, E.M.U., Univ. of Oregon,
Eugene, Ore. 97403
Folk and blues
Mid-May
The Festival was begun in 1970 by a group of Univ. of Oregon students (known as the Cultural Forum) who program special events of social, educational and cultural merit for the university. The focus of the Folk Festival is to capture and present traditional styles of the American folk-music heritage. For 3 days, concerts and workshops take place on campus at an uncovered lawn area or at a 1,000-seat indoor ballroom. Performers who have participated over the years include Woody Harris, Sunnyland Slim, Tracy Schwartz, the Robert Gray Band, the Flying Karamazov Brothers, and many local groups. Bring your own seating for outside events. In case of rain, performances are moved indoors, but it is advisable to bring rain gear to this festival.

Sponsor: E.M.U. Cultural Forum
Accommodations/other items of interest in area: Within walking distance of campus are 4 motels on Franklin Boulevard: Best Western New Oregon Motel, Green Tree Motel/Best Western, Angus Inn Motel, and Maverick Motel. Camping is available in the area, although not on campus.

The City of Eugene has many art galleries, public markets, rose gardens, and other items of interest.

Ticket information: Day-time performances and workshops are free. Evening concerts are $4.50 for non-students. For tickets, write to E.M.U. Main Desk, Univ. of Oregon, Eugene, Oregon 97403

Canyonville Pioneer Days
c/o Gynn O. Deaton, P.O. Box 487,
Canyonville, Ore.
Old-time fiddle
August
For over 12 years an annual fiddle contest has been held in Canyonville. In addition to the contestants, state and regional fiddle champions perform. Pioneer Days offers many events—something for everyone, young, old,

and in between.

The fiddle contest is held in a gymnasium which can accommodate an audience of 1,000.

Director: Gynn O. Deaton

Accommodations: Lodging in Canyonville is available at Riverview Motel, Valley View Motel, and Evergreen Motel on Old Highway 99, and Nendels Motel on Fifth St. There is free camping on the school grounds. Camping facilities, and facilities for trailers, are available in Stanton Park, N. of Canyonville.

Ticket information: Admission is $2 at the door

PENNSYL-VANIA

Appalachian Fiddle and Bluegrass Assn.
176 East Moorestown Road, Wind Gap, Pa. 18091
Bluegrass
Early August
This 3-day family festival is held at Klein's Grove in Bath, Pa. Past performers have included Lester Flatt, Country Ham, Mac Wiseman, Jimmy Martin, the Lewis Family , the Country Gentlemen, Osborne Brothers, Bill Harrow, the McLain Family, the McPiak Brothers, the Spirits of Bluegrass and many others. The Festival is held in a 1-acre wooded grove.
Sponsor: Appalachian Fiddle and Bluegrass Assn.
Accommodations: Accommodations are available at the Holiday Inn, Routes 512 and 22, and the Melody Motel, Wind Gap, Pa. Camping, in the rough, is free. There are hot showers. Trailers are allowed, and there is picnicking.
Ticket information: Admission for 3 days is $12 in advance or $15 at the gate
How to get there: Follow Route 22 to exit 512. Go N. to Bath, Pa., and follow the signs.

Brandywine Mountain Music Convention
Newlin Grist Mill, Concordville, Pa.
Folk and country
One weekend at the end of July
The Brandywine Mountain Music Convention, in its 7th year, is dedicated to preserving traditional country music. It features a different theme each year; the theme for 1979 was early country radio. Performers have included the New Lost City Ramblers, Wade Mainer, Hank Williams Original Drifting Cowboys, the Bailer Brothers, the Highwoods String Band, Tommy Jarrell, and Ola Belle Reed.
Director: Carl Goldstein
Sponsor: Brandywine Friends of Old Time Music
Accommodations/other items of interest in area: There is a Ramada Inn in the area. Camping is available at a nominal fee; there are no facilities for

trailers.
The Brandywine Historical Area is nearby.
Ticket information: Tickets are $6 per day, available at the Festival. Information may be obtained by writing to Brandywine Mountain Music Convention, Box 3504, Greenville, Del. 19807.
How to get there: The Festival is on Route 1, Concordville, Pa., 2 miles N. of Route 203 between Media and Chaddsford

Eagles Peak Bluegrass Festival
Robesonia, Pa.
Bluegrass
Mid-June
Fine bluegrass bands offer entertainment for 3 days at Eagles Peak Campground in the South Mountains. Additional events include arts and crafts displays, a 10,000 meter run, and clogging workshops.
Performances are on a covered stage on "Uncle Sam's Campground."
Director: Stephen P. Corvair
Accommodations/other items of interest in area: Camping is $2 per day, or $3.50 with hook-ups. Trailers are welcome. There is picnicking. Lodging is available at Lantern Lodge in Myerstown and at Deska Motel in Robesonia.
The campgrounds are in a Pennsylvania Dutch area.
Ticket information: A weekend ticket is $14; day tickets range from $5 to $8. Prices are higher at the gate. Tickets can be ordered in advance from Corvair-Huntzinger Productions, 12 W. Lancaster Ave., Shillington, Pa.
How to get there: From exit 21 of Turnpike 76 take Highway 272 N. to Route 897; go left at the light. From Route 78 or US 422, take Route 419 S. Turn left at the light in Newmanstown.

Luzerne County Folk Festival
301 Market St., Kingston, Pa. 18704
Folk (ethnic)
Mid-September
This 4-day folk and ethnic festival presents music, song, and dancing by Polish, Latin American, Lithuanian, Ukranian, and many other groups. There are also films, an exhibition and demonstration area, and an ethnic food area. Children's events are part of the program.
If you like to polka, this is the place to be. The Festival is held in the 109th Artillery Armory in Kingston, with a capacity of 5,000.
Director: Paul Lauer
Sponsor: Luzerne County Tourist Agency
Accommodations/other items of interest in area: There are camping facilities within 10 miles of the Festival site, and motel accommodations are available. For information write to Luzerne County Tourist Promotion Agency, 301 Market Street, Kingston, Pa. 18704.
This mountainous area has superb fishing and fine camping. Golf and swimming are favorite activities. There are also good restaurants and nightclubs in the area.
Ticket information: Admission is about $2. Tickets can be obtained at the door or in advance from Luzerne County Tourist Promotion Agency.
How to get there: Take I-80 and I-81 and the northeast extension of the Pennsylvania Turnpike to Luzerne County

Penn State Annual Fiddlers' Competition
c/o Bob Doyle, 708 South Pugh St., State College, Pa., 16801
Fiddlers' competition
One weekend day in mid-July
Founded in 1975 by Matthew Guntharp and Bob Doyle, the competition has grown to become one of the premier events of the Central Pennsylvania Festival of the Arts. The Buffalo Chip-Kickers give an annual concert at the competition, which is held in an outdoor facility that seats several thousand people.
Director: Bob Doyle
Sponsors: Central Pennsylvania Festival of the Arts, the Pennsylvania Council on the Arts, and the Bob Doyle Agency.
Accommodations/other items of interest in area: Some of the hotels in State College, Pa., are the Holiday Inn, Penn State Sheraton, Nittany Lion Inn (on PSU campus). There is no camping allowed at the competition, but there is a KOA and other campgrounds off I-80 at Exits 23 and 24. Food concessions are part of the Festival, and there are numerous restaurants in the area.
Other points of interest nearby are Penn State University, the Pennsylvania Military Museum, the Boal Mansion, a Pennsylvania Dutch auction in Belleville,

KATE WOLF AND FRIEND AT THE PHILADELPHIA FOLK FESTIVAL (PHOTO PREVIOUS PAGE)

and several recreational areas.
Ticket information: Admission is free
How to get there: The Festival is located
in downtown State College, Pa., approxi-
mately 12 miles from Exits 23 and 24 on
I-80

Philadelphia Folk Festival
Old Poole Farm, Schwenksville, Pa.
Folk, bluegrass, old timey, traditional
Late August
For over 18 years this festival has been
held the weekend before Labor Day.
It features 3 evening concerts, daily
workshops, afternoon concerts, jam-
ming, and crafts displays and demon-
strations. Past performers have included
Pete Seeger, Tom Rush, Odetta, Arlo
Guthrie and many more.
The main stage is outdoors on a big
hillside. There is some reserved seating
on chairs.
Sponsor: Philadelphia Folk Song Society
Accommodations/other items of interest
in area: Lodging is available at Sheraton
Valley Forge Motel and Budget Valley
Motel. Camping on the Festival grounds
costs $8 above the price of a weekend
ticket. Trailers are allowed. There is picnicking, and some campfires will be
allowed.
Ticket information: A 3-day ticket is
$30. Evening tickets are $10 and day
tickets $8. For tickets, write to PFF,
7113 Emlen St., Philadelphia, Pa. 19119.
How to get there: Take Pennsylvania
76 to Truck Route 202 S. Follow this
to Route 73 W., and follow this to
Route 29. Then follow the Festival
signs.

Press Old Newsboys Benefit Bluegrass Concert
Children's Hospital of Pittsburgh, Pa.
15213
Bluegrass
Late March or early April
Bluegrass, with its driving, unamplified
banjo, guitar, mandolin, fiddle, dobro
and bass, has a distinctive and unified
sound which can vary in texture from
rough and rural to quite smooth and contemporary. Leaders in the Pittsburgh
bluegrass movement from its earliest
years, and others from the second generation whose parents played bluegrass
or who have come to the music from
other musical forms, join for this fine
1-day bluegrass festival, whose profits
go to Children's Hospital of Pittsburgh.
The concerts are indoors.
Director: Thomas P. Foley, Jr.
Sponsor: Press-Old-Newsboy Andy
Russell and the students of Carlow
College
Accommodations: Lodging is available
at Cross Keys Motor Inn on Forbes Ave.
in Oakland section, and Howard Johnson's Motor Inn, also in Oakland section.
There is no camping or picnicking.
Ticket information: Tickets are $5.
Send a self-addressed, stamped envelope.

Susquehanna
Route 147, Halifax, Pa. 17032
Bluegrass and country rock
July
Performers such as John Hartford,
II Generation, Charlie Moore, Lester
Flatt, Wilma Lee Cooper, the Osborne
Brothers, and Harold Morrison are
featured in this 3-day festival held the
2nd weekend in July. The Festival also
sponsors contests for amateurs.
There is camping and picnicking on the
Festival grounds. Guests should bring
jackets or raincoats, and lawn chairs.
Director: Alma Heyne
Sponsor: Halifax Hotel, Inc.
Other items of interest in area: The
grounds of the Festival are along a
river. Hiking, caves, fishing and boating
are available.
Ticket information: Festival tickets are
$12 in advance, $15 at the gate. For
advance tickets write to Alma Heyne,
P.O. Box K, Halifax, Pa. 17032.
How to get there: The Festival is on
Route 147 in Halifax, 23 miles north-
west of Harrisburg

White Oak Bluegrass Festival
Route 3, Quarryville, Pa. 17566
Bluegrass, gospel, and country
Early June
This 3-day festival features mostly local
singers and musicians. Past performers
have included Stella Parton, Five Strings,
Joyful Strings, High Ridge Mountain
Boys, the Bailey Brothers, and others.
The Festival is held outdoors, but in
case of rain it will move inside.
Accommodations/other items of interest
in area: Camping is allowed; the cost
is $6. Facilities include electricity,
water, and sewage disposal. Trailers
are also allowed. There is picnicking.
Of interest in the area are the Penn-

sylvania Dutch country, Strasburg Railroad, Dutch Wonderland, Amish farms, and farm animals at the campground. Ticket information: Admission is $3 and $4. Write to Bessie Wise, White Oak Campground, Quarryville, Pa. 17566. How to get there: From Route 30 E. of Lancaster, Pa., go S. on 896 to Strasburg, straight through at light for 4 miles

York County Fiddlers' Convention

Brogue, Pa., 17309 (York County)
Country and old time
Late August
Local talent keeps feet tapping during this 1-day festival of country and old-time music held the 4th Saturday in August. The Festival has become a York County tradition since it began in 1960. The event is held on an outside stage and in an indoor dance hall.
Sponsor: York County Fiddlers' Association
Accommodations: There are hotels and motels around York, Pa. Camping is allowed; facilities include toilets and food but no hook-ups. Trailers and campers are welcome. There is picnicking.
Ticket information: Admission is $2 at the gate
How to get there: The Festival is 15 miles S. of York on Route 74

TENNESSEE

Bluegrass Ramp Tramp Festival Seminar Week

Box 189, Benton, Tenn.
Bluegrass
Mid-April
This week-long festival at Linsdale School features clogging contests, gospel singing, bluegrass shows, hikes, election of a ramp tramp queen, and a variety of other events. One purpose of the festival is to bring together area talent and impressarios from the entertainment field. Events are held indoors and outdoors. Patrons are advised to bring lawn chairs.
Director: Emmitt S. Adams
Sponsor: Polk County Ramp Tramp Club
Accommodations: Motel accommodations are available at the Etowah Tenn. Motel in Etowah, and the Holiday Inn in Cleveland, Tenn. Camping is free, but there are no hook-ups. Trailers are okay.
Ticket information: Tickets are $2 and $3, obtainable at the gate only. Under 12 admitted free.
How to get there: Linsdale School in N. Benton, Tenn., is on US 163 near US 411 and US 11

Country Music Fan Fair

2804 Opryland Drive, Nashville, Tenn. 37214
Country
June
This musical extravaganza enables participants to see and hear the music industry's greatest country music stars. The week-long festival presents over 30 hours of stage shows, a bluegrass concert, a fiddling contest, Opryland U.S.A., a square dance and tape sessions. Non-musical events include autograph parties, a softball tournament, and exhibitions.
Events are held in Municipal Auditorium in downtown Nashville which can seat about 10,000 people.
Director: Jerry Steobel
Sponsor: Country Music Assn. and Grand Ole Opry
Accommodations/other items of interest in area: For information on lodging and on points of interest in the area, write Chamber of Commerce, 161 4th Ave. N.,

Nashville, Tenn. 37219.
Ticket information: Registration for the week is about $30 per person. Tickets for the Grand Ole Opry are an additional $6.

Dulcimer Convention

Cosby, Tenn.
Folk
Mid-June
This 3-day event provides an opportunity for makers, players, and lovers of hammer and mountain dulcimers to get together and explore the possibilities of the instrument through workshops and evening concerts.
The gathering takes place in an outdoor uncovered amphitheater atop a hill where the usual access is only by foot. Sturdy shoes, flashlight, chairs, blankets, and trash bags are recommended. For the elderly and infirm only, a shuttle bus service is provided along an access road to the convention site.
Directors: Jean and Lee Schilling
Sponsor: Folk Life Center of the Smokies
Accommodations/other items of interest in area: L. Ranch Motel, on Highway 73, and Cub Motel and Restaurant, Highway 32, both near Cosby, can provide lodging. Camping in the rough at the Festival site is available free with weekend admission. Trailer space is available, but without hook-ups.
Great Smoky Mountain National Park is a nearby point of interest.
Ticket information: Weekend tickets (3 days) cost $12; daily tickets, $5. Write to Folk Life Center of the Smokies, P.O. Box 8, Cosby, Tenn. 37722
How to get there: The site is located on Roostertown Road, off Highway 32, S. of Cosby.

Fall Color Cruise and Folk Festival

c/o Chattanooga Area Convention and Visitors Bureau, Market at 10th, Chattanooga, Tenn. 37402
Bluegrass and folk
October
The folk festival features a bluegrass contest; categories include band, banjo, guitar, mandolin, fiddle and buck dancing. There is also square dancing, free entertainment from the Nashville Jubilee, working artists and craftspeople,

boat rides, and more. Many national and regional bluegrass musicians perform.
The Festival began as a small local boating event and is now one of the largest boating events in the South.
Director: W. Camp Turner
Sponsors: Area Shrine Clubs, Mid-South Arts and Crafts Assn., area boat clubs, U.S. Coast Guard Auxiliary, Chattanooga Convention and Visitors Bureau
Accommodations/other items of interest in area: For information on lodging contact the Festival at the address above. There are campgrounds nearby, and there is picnicking.
Many of the most popular attractions of the mid-South are in the Chattanooga area.
Ticket information: Admission is free. Bus tickets from Chattanooga to the Festival are $1. Riverboat tickets from Chattanooga through the Grand Canyon of the Tennessee River are $10 downstream to the site, $5 upstream.
How to get there: From Chattanooga take US 41 N. (the Scenic Highway) to Hales Bar Dam ; by boat cruise, through the Grand Canyon to river mile 431

Mountain Music Festival

Mountain Music Shows, Box 131, Reliance, Tenn. 37369
Traditional bluegrass
Summer
Mountain Music Shows sponsors festivals of traditional music on the 4th weekend of June, the 2nd weekend of July and the 4th weekend of August. A variety of groups perform bluegrass, mountain, gospel, and old-time folk music.
The Festivals take place at Maggie Mountain Campground, which offers swimming, boating, fishing, and river floating. Patrons are advised to bring lawn chairs.
Director: Emmitt Adam
Sponsor: Mountain Music Shows
Accommodations: Rough camping at $2 per day is available on Maggie Mountain; showers and rest rooms are available.
Ticket information: Admission ranges from $1 to $3
How to get there: Maggie Mountain Campground is 3½ miles N. of Reliance, Tenn. Take US-30, which leads from US 411 through the Cherokee National Forest to US 64, and turn N. at Reliance

(crossing the Hiwassee River)—then follow Campground signs.

Smithville Fiddlers' Jamboree and Crafts Festival

On the Public Square, Smithville, Tenn.
Traditional
Friday and Saturday nearest the Fourth of July
The Smithville Festival began in 1972, originally as a Fourth of July celebration to present Smithville's new facilities provided by the Model Cities program. It has grown over the years to an estimated 50,000 spectators. The Friday evening and all-day Saturday contest presents traditional music in various categories, including gospel and folk singing, fiddle, banjo, harmonica, band competitions, square dancing, and buckdancing. The Smithville Festival was the subject of a 1-hour documentary film that was shown over the educational television network.
Sponsors: Smithville Merchants Assn.; Chamber of Commerce; Jaycees; Rotary Club
Accommodations: For information about accommodations, write or call the Chamber of Commerce, P.O. Box 64, Smithville, Tenn. 37166; tel. (615)597-4163
Ticket information: Admission is free
How to get there: Smithville is 66 miles E. of Nashville on US 70

State of Tennessee Old-Time Fiddlers' Championships

Austin Peay State University, Clarksville, Tenn. 37040
Traditional
First weekend in April
Held annually for the past 6 years, this festival features old-time country music contests and jam sessions. There are contests for fiddle, banjo, mandolin, old-time string band, old-time singing, harmonica, and "no-holds-barred flatfoot dancing." The event is held in the Winfield Dunn Center, which seats 9,000. Proceeds from the event benefit the APSU scholarship fund.
Director: Dr. Steve Davis
Sponsor: Austin Peay State University
Accommodations: In Clarksville there is the Holiday Inn (Highway 41-A North), the Midtowner Motel (Kraft St.), and Motel 6 (Kraft St.). Camping is available at no cost, but there are no trailer hook-ups.
Ticket information: Admission is $2 per day. Tickets are available at the door.
How to get there: Clarksville is located 47 miles northwest of Nashville, just off I-47. The Festival is on the campus of Austin Peay State University.

TEXAS

Athens Old Fiddlers' Reunion
P.O. Box 1441, Athens, Tex. 75751
Fiddling
Late May
For more than 40 years the Athens
Old Fiddlers' Reunion has taken place,
rain or shine, on the last Friday of
May, and each year there have been
more people than the year before. This
event is the oldest one of its kind and
is known nationwide. The big event,
the Fiddlers' Contest, has 4 divisions:
over 65, under 65, under 18, and ladies.
Entertainment is also provided by guest
bands. A carnival offers additional
diversion.
The event is outdoors, with unlimited
seating. Foul-weather clothing is
recommended.
Director: Bob McGee
Sponsor: Texas Fiddlers' Assn., Inc.
Accommodations: Lodging in Athens
is available at Spanish Trace Inn, 716
East Tyler St.; Andrews Motel, 611 West
Corsicana St.; and Flame Motel, Dallas
Highway. Camping is allowed at no cost,
and there is picnicking at Lake Athens,
3 miles E. of Athens.
Ticket information: Admission is free
How to get there: The Festival is at
Courthouse Square in Athens

Belton Rodeo and Celebration
P.O. Box 659, Belton, Tex. 76513
Country-and-Western and bluegrass
Early July
Belton's July 4th celebration includes
a rodeo, a carnival, the Independence
Day Parade, a band concert and
patriotic program, and a God and
Country concert. The celebration has a
history going back over 100 years, and
the rodeo, the main event of the weekend, began in 1924. The music is by
local groups and others from all over
Texas.
Concerts are held outdoors under large
pecan trees. Lawn chairs are
recommended.
Director: Clarence Griggs
Sponsor: Chamber of Commerce
Accommodations: Lodging is available
at River Forest Motel on I-35 and 6th
Ave., and at Inn 7 at 1102 E. 2nd Ave.,
both in Belton, Texas. There are camping
sites in the area. Picnicking is permitted.
Nestled between 2 lakes, Belton offers
fishing, swimming, golf, tennis, and a
warm-hearted atmosphere.
Ticket information: The music is free.
Rodeo tickets can be ordered in advance
from the Chamber of Commerce at the
address shown above.
How to get there: Contact the Chamber
of Commerce for directions

Bluegrass and Old-Time Music Festival
Bronson, Tex.
Bluegrass, gospel, and old-time
Mid-May, mid-June, and mid-September
These three 2-day festivals feature a
variety of bluegrass, gospel, and old-time
music groups. The festivals also sponsor
such entertainment as a hog calling con-
test, watermelon eating contest, and
spitting contest, as well as the more
familiar clogging and band contest.
The Festival is outdoors.
Directors: Edy and Matt Mathews,
Norma and Bob Smith
Sponsor: Southeast Texas Bluegrass
Music Assn.
Accommodations/other items of interest
in area: Lodging is available at the
Holiday Inn in San Augustine, Tex.
There is camping at the Festival grounds;
rough camping is free, hook-ups are $3
per day. There is plenty of running
water.
Good fishing places are located within
16 to 20 miles of the Festival grounds.
Ticket information: Day tickets are
$3 to $4. They may be obtained from
Edy and Matt Mathews, 7110 Lewis
Drive, Beaumont, Tex. 77708; or Norma
and Bob Smith, Box 264, Sulphur, La.
70663.
How to get there: The Festival is 29 miles
N. of Jasper, Tex., and 16 miles S. of
San Augustine

Buffalo Gap Bluegrass Jamboree
Box 454, Hawley, Tex. 79525
Bluegrass
Mid-June
This 3-day bluegrass festival has featured
such performers as Wendy Holcombe,
Scotty Ousley and the Texas Travelers,
Cloggers and a number of Texas blue-
grass bands. It also presents band and
banjo contests and a gospel show. Events
are held outdoors, with seating for
6,000. Those attending should bring

lawn chairs and a light raincoat.
The proceeds of this festival go to the
West Texas Rehab Center.
Sponsor: West Texas Rehab Center
Accommodations/other items of interest
in area: Lodging in the area is available
at the Holiday Inn and American Royal
Inn. Camping in the rough is free; facil-
ities are available at a charge. Trailers
are welcome. There is picnicking, and a
chuck wagon barbecue will be part of
the celebration.
Buffalo Gap is a very scenic small town.
A nearby State Park has a swimming
pool.
Ticket information: Day tickets range
from $3 to $6. A 3-day ticket is $10.
Tickets can be obtained from Robert
Boyd, in care of the Festival.
How to get there: The Festival is 13
miles S. of Abilene, Tex., and 1 mile
W. of Buffalo Gap on the Perini Ranch

Chamizal Fiesta of the Arts; Border Folk Festival
800 S. San Marcial, El Paso, Tex. 79903
Folk, ethnic, blues, bluegrass, traditional,
jazz
Early July and late September
The Chamizal Fiesta of the Arts occurs
on the week ending with the Fourth of
July celebration. All styles of music,
dance and the arts are presented, both indoors and outdoors, in pavilion tents and at
an open-air stage. The traditional emphasis and the variety of cultures and groups
represented make this a lively and colorful festival.
The 3-day Border Folk Festival includes
country and western, bluegrass, jazz,
mariachi, nortena, black blues singers,
East Texas music, black gospel. Appalachian music with traditional instruments,
and old-time fiddling. Other events include ethnic dances, Native American
dances, charreada (Mexican rodeo), mime,
puppets, and arts and crafts displays.
Events are held both indoors and outdoors.
Director: Carlos Chavez
Sponsors: National Park Service and
National Council for the Traditional Arts
Accommodations/other items of interest
in area: Lodging is available at the Holiday
Inn at I-10 and Raynolds; and at the
Plaza Hotel, Del Norte Hotel, Travellodge,
and the Holiday Inn in the center of town
about 3 miles from the Festival area.
There is no camping.

The Festival is 50 yards from Juarez,
Mexico.
Ticket information: Admission to all
events is free
How to get there: Get off I-10 at the
Juarez exit. Keep going until you reach
Paisano, turn right at the traffic light
and go to the next traffic light; the
Festival should then be visible. The
address is 800 S. San Marcial, opposite
Bowie High School.

Country Music Festival and Fiddle Contest
New Boden, Tex.
Folk (country, bluegrass, and old-time
fiddling)
Early October, and once a month
The 1st Saturday of October each year,
all day until midnight, this festival pre-
sents band music and a fiddle contest.
The Festival is in the auditorium of the
Community Center of New Boden,
which seats 325, and throughout the
building. Barbecue plates, sold to hungry
listeners, are a festival tradition.
On the 1st Saturday night in every month
there is country music in the Community
Center, with an open door to musicians
and guests.
This festival has been in existence for
over 22 years, and is well known in
Texas and Louisiana.
Director: Hardy Ellison
Accommodations/other items of interest
in area: Lodging is available in the area.
Camping and trailers are allowed.
Of interest in the area are the General
Mercantile Store, operating since 1886,
and the Franklin Cemetery, resting
ground of Tex Owens, author of Cattle
Call, and Texas Ruby, wife of Kurley
Fox.
Ticket information: Admission is free
How to get there: New Boden is 15
miles N. of Hearne on Highway 79

East Texas Yamboree Fiddlers' Contest
Courthouse Square, Gilmer, Tex.
Old-time country
Last Saturday in October
Started in 1932, this contest is the 2nd
oldest fiddlers' contest in Texas, and
one of the most prestigious to win.
The Yamboree itself is a harvest festival
and attracts crowds of 25,000 to the
small East Texas town of Gilmer each
fall.

In addition to the fiddlers' competition there is a street dance, country and western dance, square dance, livestock and food exhibits, a marching band contest, gold tournament, beauty pageant, and carnival. Most events take place outdoors. Seating to be brought by the audience.
Director: Richard Harrison
Sponsor: East Texas Yamboree Committee
Accommodations: Lodging can be obtained at the Holiday Inn, Ramada Inn, and Contessa Inn in Longview. No camping is available.
Ticket information: Fiddlers' contest is free, as are most exhibits and the street dance; there is a small charge for indoor dances and the carnival

Kerrville Folk Festival; Kerrville Gospel Jubilee; Kerrville Blueglass Festival
P.O. Box 1466, Kerrville, Tex. 78028
Folk and regional; Gospel (traditional and contemporary); Bluegrass
Late May; late July; early September
The *Kerrville Folk Festival* is held over Memorial Day Weekend and includes country and bluegrass concerts and gospel singers and musicians. It also sponsors horse races, a parade, mule races, and a country auction. Jimmy Driftwood and other fine folk artists have been featured. The program includes the Great Texas Harmonica Blow-off, ballad-tree sessions, arts and crafts displays, workshops, and informal concerts. A ticket for the entire festival is $20.
Kerrville resounds with gospel music for three days in late July during the *Gospel Jubilee.* There is Saturday-afternoon gospel singing in the town square and a sunrise service on Sunday morning. Many fine gospel singers and musicians perform in the Festival's outdoor theater. A weekend ticket is $10.
The *Kerrville Bluegrass Festival* is held over Labor Day Weekend. It offers over 40 hours of bluegrass music and has featured such performers as the Country Gentlemen and Lester Flatt. The Buck White International Mandolin Championship is a special event, along with bluegrass-banjo and band championships. There are crafts displays and a Sunday morning gospel sing. Four-day tickets are $16.
The Festivals are held in an outdoor theater with a capacity of 4,800. There is bench seating for 1,500. Patrons are advised to bring lawn chairs and rain gear. The theater is uncovered, and the concerts are held rain or shine.
Director: Rod Kennedy
Sponsor: Kerrville Festivals, Inc.
Accommodations: Lodging is available at the Holiday Inn, Budget Inn, Inn of the Hills, and Sands Motel. Early reservations are advised. Complete camping facilities are available; their cost is included with festival tickets. Trailers are permitted, but there are no hook-ups.
Ticket information: Tickets can be obtained by mail or at the gate.
How to get there: The Festival site is 9 miles S. of Kerrville, on Highway 16

National Collegists' Fiddlers' Festival
East Texas State Univ., Commerce, Tex.
Old-time country music
Mid-June
This 1-day event was begun in 1973 to preserve the traditional Texas-style fiddling, and it has become the most popular event on the East Texas State campus during the summer months, attracting as many as 3,000. Regional old-time fiddlers take part, including in recent years musicians like 3-time world champions Terry Morris and Jim Chancellor, and 7-time world champion Louis Franklin. There is also a fiddlers' accompanist contest.
The Festival takes place outdoors on the campus. The audience brings seating.
Director: Richard Harrison
Sponsor: East Texas State Univ.
Accommodations: The Holiday Inn and Ramada Inn in Greenville and the University Inn in Commerce can provide accommodations. No camping is available.
Ticket information: Admission is free

Oakdale Park's Bluegrass Reunion, Bluegrass Jamboree, Country Gospel Jubilee, and Bluegrass Picnic
Box 548, Glen Rose, Tex. 76043
Bluegrass and gospel
First weekend in October, Memorial Day weekend, 1st weekend in November, and 1st weekend in April, respectively.
Festivals take place at a privately owned vacation park near the Paluxy River in central Texas. Musicians like Grandpa Jones, Lester Flatt, the Osborne Brothers, and the Lewis Family perform

in an outdoor stage area for the Bluegrass Reunion and Jamboree. The Country Gospel Jubilee has featured such performers as the Florida Boys. The Bluegrass Picnic has no planned program, but has jam sessions all over the park.

Foul weather clothing is recommended. Patrons may bring lawn chairs.

Directors: Whimp and Pete May

Accommodations/other items of interest in area: Camping is available at $4 per night per unit ($5 for Bluegrass Picnic). Facilities at park include 200 full hookups, swimming pool, hot showers, laundry, ice, propane, and mail service. Nearby is Dinosaur Valley State Park.

Ticket information: Three-day tickets for the Bluegrass Reunion and Bluegrass Jamboree are $15. Two-day Gospel Jubilee tickets are $8. The Bluegrass Picnic is free. Write for tickets.

How to get there: Oakdale Park is on Highway 144 S. in Glen Rose

Red River Valley Exposition Fiddlers' Contest

Paris Fairgrounds, Paris, Texas

Old-time country music

First Saturday in August

Besides the old-time fiddlers' contest, this event also includes livestock exhibits, food exhibits, and a fair and carnival. The contest, involving regional competitors, takes place outdoors.

The audience should bring their own seating. An auditorium is available in case of rain.

Director: Richard Harrison

Sponsor: Red River Valley Exposition and Fair

Accommodations: Accommodations are available in Paris from Ramada Inn, the Holiday Inn, and Nicholson House. No camping is available.

Ticket information: Fiddlers' contest and exhibits are free; the carnival has small daily prices

Harry C. Smith Fiddlers' Contest

Harry C. Smith home, Powderly, Tex.

Old-time country music

Last Saturday in July

Harry C. Smith sponsors this old-time fiddlers' contest, providing the prize money from his own pocket since the contest began in 1971. He enjoys hearing the music and having the fiddlers

in his home, and he says he will hold the contest as long as he lives.

The contest takes place outside and lawn chairs or blankets are brought by the audience.

Director: Richard Harrison

Sponsor: Harry C. Smith

Accommodations: Motels such as the Holiday Inn, Ramada Inn, and Nicholson House in nearby Paris can provide accommodations

Ticket information: Admission is free

How to get there: Powderly is 9 miles N. of Paris

Southwest Bluegrass Club Bluegrass Festival

Mitchell Park, Perrin, Tex.

Bluegrass

Mid-July

This 3-day festival features groups such as Lost and Found, Buck White and the Downhome Folks, and Lonnie Glosson, as well as many semi-pro regional bluegrass groups. A bluegrass band contest is a festival highlight.

Events are held in Mitchell Park in an outdoor wooded area. There is a shaded stage area with stump seats for some, and room for everyone. Guests should bring lawn chairs.

Director: Anne Uhr

Sponsor: Southwest Bluegrass Club

Accommodations: Lodging is available in Jackson and Mineral Wells. There is camping in Mitchell Park, with a $3 hook-up charge daily. There is picnicking, and homemade food will also be available.

Ticket information: A 3-day ticket is $12. Day tickets range from $4 to $6. They are available at the gate.

How to get there: Mitchell Park in Perrin is between Jacksboro and Mineral Wells, on Farm to Market Road 2210

Texas State Championship Fiddlers' Frolics

K of C Hall, Highway 77 South, P.O. Box 46, Hallettsville, Tex.

Bluegrass, Western, swing

Fourth weekend in April

Since 1971, this festival in the small town of Hallettsville has provided a prestigious competition and friendly gathering for Texas and regional fiddlers and spectators. In addition to the championship, there is a Nashville Night with a

dance and stage show and induction of a top fiddler into the Fiddlers Hall of Fame.
Activities take place in the K of C Hall which seats 1,350.
Directors: Clifford Fryer, Frank Zaruba, Kenneth Henneke
Sponsor: Hallettsville Knights of Columbus
Accommodations: Accommodations are available at Cloud Nine Motel on Highway 90-A and the Bel-Air Motel at Highway 77 and 90-A in Hallettsville. Camping is available at the Festival grounds and also at the city park. Trailer hook-ups are $5 per day.
Ticket information: For information write to Texas State Championship Fiddler's Frolics, P.O. Box 250, Hallettsville, Tex. 77964

VERMONT

Brattleboro Folk Festival and Traditional Craft Fair
Box 1057, Brattleboro, Vt. 05301
Folk
The weekend on or immediately following the Fourth of July
The Chelsea House Folklore Center, which presents this festival each year, is dedicated to the preservation and perpetuation of traditional music and dance, folklore, and the folk arts as individual activities. Concerts are held on Friday and Saturday evening the weekend of the Festival; there are workshops throughout the day on Saturday and Sunday, on traditional instruments and folk singing and dancing, and such topics as pocket instruments and cowboy and gospel singing. The Sunday evening event is a contradance.
All events are held outdoors.
Director: Carol Levin
Sponsors: Chelsea House Folklore Center
Accommodations: For a list of accommodations, write to the Festival director. There is a campground near the Festival site.
Ticket information: Admission is $20 for the entire weekend. Individual day and evening tickets are also available. Get tickets at Chelsea House, at ticket outlets, or by mail from the Chelsea House Folklore Center.
How to get there: The Festival is located on Route 9, 4 miles W. of Brattleboro

Old-Time Fiddling
Box 206, Chelsea, Vt. 05038
Old-time fiddling
Second Saturday in August
Fiddlers from all over the northeastern United States and from Quebec in Canada compete at this annual gathering in Chelsea, in E. central Vermont. Begun in 1969, the event takes place in the Chelsea High School gym which seats 500.
Director: W. S. Gilman
Sponsor: Chelsea Historical Society, Inc.
Accommodations/other items of interest in area: There are motels nearby at White River Junction and Barre, Vt. No camping is available.
Of interest in the are are the Mormon monument at Sharon, granite quarries in

Barre, and the marble museum in Proctor.
Ticket information: Tickets are $2.50
and are available only at the door
How to get there: Chelsea is on Route
110 in E. central Vermont

VIRGINIA

Appalachian Music Days
Box 1039, Bristol, Va. 24201
Bluegrass and old time
Early May
On the 1st weekend in May each year,
Bristol celebrates spring with bluegrass,
country and western, gospel and old-
time music. Entertainment is provided
by such performers as Jim and Jesse,
Johnnie Cash, and Ralph Stanley and the
Clinch Mountain Boys. The Festival
also features bluegrass and old-time
band contests. Bristol's main street is
converted into a mall for the Festival.
There are arts and crafts displays.
Concerts are held in an outdoor arena
which is partly covered. Guests are advised to bring foul-weather clothing.
Sponsors: Bristol Chamber of Commerce
and Bristol Country Music Foundation
Accommodations/other items of interest
in area: Lodging in Bristol (on the Tennessee side of this town which spans
2 states) is available at the Holiday Inn
and Bristol Motor Inn. There is free
camping; trailers are welcome, and picnicking is allowed.
Of interest in the area is a bluegrass
museum.
Ticket information: Day tickets are
$3 to $4, available at the gate

Blue Ridge Folklife Festival
Ferrum College, Ferrum, Va. 24088
Folk (traditional)
October
The music in this 1-day festival goes on
simultaneously in 3 different areas. It includes old-time string bands, religious
songs, blues, ballad singing, and fiddle,
banjo, and dulcimer playing. There are
also workshops in music and dance, and
music for children.
The Festival presents demonstrations of
outdoor crafts (e.g., blacksmithing and
beekeeping), indoor crafts (e.g., fiddle
and banjo making, quilting), food pre-
paration, and preservation, and farm
equipment demonstrations (e.g., steam
sawmilling, hand-tie baling).
The Festival is at Ferrum Coll., located
in the heart of the Blue Ridge Mountains,
and it is committed to the preservation of
the heritage of the home craftsman.
Director: Roddy Moore

Sponsor: Blue Ridge Institute
Accommodations: Motel accommodations are available; for a listing write to the Festival. There is no camping in October. There is picnicking, and home-style meals will be sold.
Ticket information: Admission is free
How to get there: To get to Ferrum take Route 40 W. at Rocky Mount

A. P., Sara, and Maybelle Carter Memorial Festival
Hilton's, Va.
Folk and bluegrass
Early August
Founded in 1974 to honor A. P., Sara, and Maybelle Carter, this weekend festival features strictly old-time music—no amplification allowed. Performances by musicians such as the McLain Family, Hotmud Family, and Lost and Found take place in a partially covered area that seats 1,000. There is also a crafts show.
Director: Janette Carter
Accommodations: The Scott Motel, in Gate City, Va., can provide lodging. Camping in the rough is available. There is a field for trailers.
Ticket information: Tickets for 2 days cost $11. Write to Janette Carter, Hilton's, Va. 24258
How to get there: Hilton's is 20 miles from Bristol, Va.

Cherokee Ole Time Bluegrass Music Festival
540 New Bethal Road, Bristol, Va. 24201
Bluegrass and old time
First weekend in August
Good amateur and professional bands come the 1st weekend in August every year to perform and compete at this well-established festival. All the music is acoustical. There are competitions for dulcimer, old-time fiddle, claw-hammer banjo, and clog and flat-foot dancing. The Festival takes place on 155 acres of shady, wooded land. There is seating for 2,000 around the stage. Picnicking is allowed. Foul weather clothing may be necessary.
Director: Carl N. Pennington
Sponsor: Cherokee Promotions
Accommodations/other items of interest in area: Lodging is available at the Holiday Inn, the Downtowner, the Briscoe Inn, and the Twin City Motel.

There are areas for camping in the rough at no cost, and hook-ups for $2. Of interest in the area are the S. Holsten Dam, Rocky Mount, the Appalachian Bluegrass Museum, and Barter Theater.
Ticket information: Admission is $3 to $5 per day at the gate
How to get there: The Festival is near the Bristol Country Club; take exit 7 on US 81

Lake Whippoorwill Bluegrass Festival
Warrenton, Va. 22186
Bluegrass
Mid-June
Every year since 1970 this festival has brought together for a weekend bluegrass players and bands from all over Virginia and beyond, such as Jimmy Martin, J. D. Crowe and the New South, and the Fifth Street Symphony.
The setting is outdoors and unsheltered.
Sponsor: Warrenton-Fauquier Jaycees
Accommodations: Weekend camping fee is $5. Fresh water and dumping station are available, but no electricity is provided.
Ticket information: Up to $20 for 3 days. For tickets, write to Warrenton-Fauquier Jaycees, P.O. Box 508, Warrenton, Va. 22186
How to get there: Just off Route 29-211, 1 mile N. of Warrenton

Mountain Music Festival
Route 1, Box 57, Elk Creek, Va. 24326
Old-time and bluegrass
Second weekend in June
As many as 15 bands—mostly local, with some from North Carolina, Tennessee, and West Virginia—participate in this 2-day gathering. Events take place outside in a partly shaded area. Bring your own lawn chair. Foul weather clothing is recommended.
Director: Reid Robertson
Accommodations: Camping in the rough is available at the Festival site. Motels in the area include the Rose Lane in Galax, and the Black Rock in Independence.
Ticket information: Tickets are $3, and available only at the gate
How to get there: Located on Route 805 between Fries, Va., and US 21

The National Folk Festival
Wolf Trap Farm Park, Vienna, Va.
Folk
One weekend in late July, early August
The Festival, sponsored by the National
Council for the Performing Arts, was first
held in St. Louis in 1934. During the following years it moved to various cities
until it finally settled in Vienna, near
Washington, D.C. in 1970. Its distinctive
feature is the performers—basic, everyday
people who are generally unknown outside their own locality, rather than being
commercial professional folksingers. They
are farmers, shop owners, housewives and
cowboys who perform music from many
ethnic traditions: bluegrass, blues, Cajun,
Native American, Irish ballads, old-time
country have been included. In addition
during the 3 days of the Festival there
are afternoon workshops in such diverse
areas as Highland harp, uillean pipe,
Depression songs, hammered dulcimer,
and Yaqui religious music and expression.
Evening performances are in a 6,500-seat
covered hall, while during the day, 5 outdoor uncovered stages operate continu-
ously and can accommodate 25,000.
Director: Joe Wilson
Sponsor: National Council for the Performing Arts
Accommodations/other items of interest
in area: There are many hotels and
motels in the Vienna, Arlington, and
Falls Church area. There is no camping
on the Wolf Trap grounds but camping
sites are available nearby. For information, write to Fairfax County Park
Authority, Box 236, Annandale, Va.
22003 or call (703)941-5000.
Many historic sites of interest are nearby,
including Arlington Cemetary, Mt. Vernon, and Washington, D.C.
Ticket information: Tickets cost from
$4 to $7 daytime and evening. They
should be obtained in advance, especially
before driving long distances, as the event
is often sold out before the Festival
occurs. For tickets, write to Wolf Trap
Box Office, 1624 Trap Road, Vienna,
Virginia 22180.
How to get there: Follow signs to Wolf
Trap from the Capital Beltway around
Washington, D.C.

Old-Time Fiddlers' Convention
P.O. Box 655, Galax, Va. 24333
Old-time and bluegrass
Mid-August
This week-long convention was started
in 1935 by a few Moose members and has
grown by leaps and bounds ever since.
The central features of the Festival are
the competitions for bluegrass and old-
time fiddle, guitar, bluegrass and claw-
hammer banjo, mandolin, dulcimer,
dobro, bands, dance and folk song.
There are also special attractions and
square dancing.
The Festival is held outdoors. There
are covered stands which seat 5,000
and plenty of room on the grounds
for blankets and chairs.
Sponsor: Galax Moose Lodge 733
Accommodations: Lodging in Galax
is available at Rose Lane and Midtowner.
Camping outside the Festival grounds is
free; within the park where the Festival
is held, camping is $5 per space per day
on a first-come, first-served basis.
Ticket information: Admission is $3
to $4 at the gate
How to get there: The Festival is 80
miles southwest of Roanoke. Take
I-81 to I-77.

Ole Time Fiddlers Convention and Bluegrass Memorial Weekend
Lithia, Va.
Bluegrass and old-time
Late May
In addition to performances by bluegrass
and old-time bands, this 3-day festival
sponsors contests for bands, vocalists,
and instrumentalists ranging from old-
time and bluegrass fiddlers to bass fiddle,
dobro, and dulcimer players. There are
also prizes for the best flatfoot and clog
dancers.
The Festival is outdoors at Fringers
Farm, but in case of rain a large tent
will be set up and the show will go on.
Patrons are advised to bring lawn chairs.
Director: Charlie Cox
Sponsor: Botetourt Jaycees
Accommodations: Accommodations are
available at Ramada Inn on Plantation
Road in Roanoke, Va., and at Howard
Johnson's in Daleville, Va. There is
camping at no cost. Some electric hook-
ups are available on a first-come, first-
served basis.
Ticket information: A 3-day ticket, in

advance, is about $15. Tickets can be ordered from Botetourt Jaycees, P.O. Box 157, Daleville, Va. 24083.
How to get there: From I-81 take exit 45 or 46, then follow the signs. The Festival is 15 miles N. of Roanoke.

Orange Blossom Park Bluegrass Fest
2487 Calf Mountain Road, Waynesboro, Va.
Traditional and bluegrass
Four weekends a year: the 2nd weekend of June, July, and August, and the 1st weekend in October
In its 8th year, this traditional bluegrass festival is held outdoors 4 times each year. Past performers have included Bill Monroe, Ralph Stanley, the Lewis Family, Carl Story, Don Reno, and Bill Harrell. Patrons are asked to bring lawn chairs.
Sponsor: Orange Blossom Entertainment
Accommodations: Camping is allowed and is included in the price of the tickets
Ticket information: Tickets are available at the gate only: Friday, $5; Saturday, $7; Sunday, $5; all 3 days, $14

Shenandoah Valley Farm Craft Days
Belle Grove, Box 137, Middletown, Va. 22645
Folk and bluegrass
Third weekend in July
Farm Craft Days is a folk-craft festival featuring bluegrass music, traditional and rural craft demonstrations, and craft and food sales. Performers in previous years have included John Jackson, Madelaine McNeil, Phil Mason, Herb Smoke, and many local folk singers. The event is held at Belle Grove, a working farm built in 1794, that has been designated a national historic landmark. Belle Grove is in the heart of the Shenandoah Valley on the Civil War site of the Battle of Cedar Creek.
The stage is outdoors with some seating available. Patrons are encouraged to bring blankets or folding chairs.
Sponsor: Belle Grove National Trust for Historic Preservation
Accommodations/other items of interest in area: Accommodations include the Wayside Inn, Middletown, Va. 22645; the Newcomer Motel, Strasburg, Va. 22657; the Hamilton Motel, Woodstock, Va. 22664. Camping facilities for both tents and trailers are available at the

Cedar Creek Campground, which is 500 yards from the entrance to Belle Grove. Picnicking is allowed on the Belle Grove property.
There are many places of historic interest in the area, including the headquarters of Stonewall Jackson and George Washington.
Ticket information: Admission is $2.
Tickets are available at the gate.
How to get there: Belle Grove is located on US 11, one mile S. of Middletown. It is approximately 90 minutes from Washington, D.C.

Shriner's Bluegrass Festival
Wise County Fairgrounds, Wise, Va.
Bluegrass
Late June (4 days)
The annual Shriner's Bluegrass Festival features continuous music for 4 straight days, rain or shine. The Country Gentlemen, Jim and Jesse, the Hotmud Family, Larry Sparks, the Lewis Family, and Ralph Stanley are among those who have performed at recent festivals. Concerts are held in a covered grandstand which seats 5,000.
No alcoholic beverages are permitted in the concert area.
Director: Glenn Roberts, Jr.
Sponsor: Wise County Shrine Club
Accommodations: Camping is permitted and is included in the cost of the ticket; there are limited electric hook-ups. Motels in Wise include The Inn and Carriage Hill. There are also motels in nearby Norton and Pound.
Ticket information: Tickets can be ordered by contacting Mr. Glenn Roberts, Jr., 921 Park Ave., Norton, Va. 24273. In 1979, the price was $27 for the entire 4-day event; $6 for Thursday; $10 each for Friday and Saturday; or $4 for Sunday.
How to get there: The Wise County Fairgrounds are in Wise, Va., on Route 23, 20 miles from the Kentucky state line

Smith Mt. Moto Cross Bluegrass Festival
Intersection 670 and 834, Wirtz, Va.
Bluegrass
Early July
This 2-day festival presents such groups as the Country Gentlemen, the Seldom Scene, Mac Wiseman, Ralph Stanley, Marshall Family Gospel, Lost and Found, and the Osborne Brothers. The concerts

are outdoors, but there is a big tent in case of rain.

There will be concessions, and picnicking is allowed.

Director: Hillard Jones
Sponsor: Dick Robertson
Accommodations: Lodging is available at Franklin Motel on Route 220. There is free camping, but without facilities.
Ticket information: 2-day tickets are $10 and 1-day tickets are $6, at the gate.
How to get there: Take I-181 to 581, proceed to Roanoke, then go S. to 220, turn right at Route 40 to Route 122, then go 8 miles to 670 and 4 miles more to the festival

Southwest Virginia Bluegrass and Country Music Festival
Route 3, Box 41A, Lebanon, Va.
Bluegrass and country music
Late August and early September
With 5 days of music in a picturesque mountain setting, this festival brings together as many as 25 bluegrass and country groups. Virtually unlimited seating is available outdoors in front of a covered stage. The O'Roark Brothers Band, Whetstone Run, Don Williams, Connie Cato, the Seldom Scene, and J. D. Crowe and the New South have performed in recent years.
Director: Bob Sutherland
Sponsor: Southwest Festivals, Inc.
Accommodations: Free camping in the rough is available. Trailers are welcome.
Ticket information: Tickets available at the gate only
How to get there: Just off US 19 about 17 miles N. of Lebanon

U.S. National Scottish Fiddling Championships
c/o Virginia Scottish Games Association, Box 1338, Alexandria, Va., or Scottish Fire, Ltd., 6365 Lakeview Drive, Falls Church, Va. 22041
Folk (traditional Scottish fiddling)
July
Begun in 1976 as the 1st Scottish fiddling championship competition in the United States, its stated purpose is to stimulate the revival of the art of Scottish fiddling in this country. The fiddling championship is held in conjunction with the Scottish games (piping, drumming, Highland dancing, athletics). Scottish and American foods are available on the grounds. Foul-weather clothing is recommended. The kilt is the preferred attire for Scottish festivals. The Festival is held outdoors if possible, but an indoor location will be arranged in case of rain.
Director: Paul R. Brockman
Accommodations: Contact the Alexandria Tourist Council. For camping, write to the Virginia State Travel service, Richmond, Va.
Ticket information: Tickets are $3 in advance and $4 at the gate (available in May)
How to get there: Directions to the Festival are provided with tickets purchased in advance

WASHINGTON

Northwest Regional Fiddle Contest
Central Valley High School
South 821 Sullivan Road
Spokane, Wash. 99206
Folk (fiddle contest)
Early April
Contestants from 2 Canadian provinces
and 9 northwestern states compete for
awards and cash prizes in this annual 2-
day fiddle contest, the 2nd largest in the
U.S. Fiddlers range in age from 6 to 90.
Additional events include jam sessions,
a hoedown and dance, and a potluck
supper. There are bluegrass bands and
other music in addition to the fiddle
contest. The main hall provides seating
for 2,000.
Director: Dee Pollett
Sponsor: Spokane Chapter of the Washington Old-Time Fiddlers Association
Accommodations: There is ample hotel
and motel space in the area. Camping is
free of charge. Trailers must be self-
contained.
Ticket information: Admission is $2

Northwest Regional Folklife Festival
Seattle Center House, 305 Harrison St.,
Seattle, Wash. 98109
Folk
Memorial Day weekend
This is a festival of traditional folk music,
arts, and crafts. Musicians and performers
usually number almost 700 for this 4-day
event. Festival attendance in 1978 was
100,000 with admission free for all. Additional events include workshops in folk
dance and music and the Northwest Coast
Native American Pow Wow.
The Festival takes place at Seattle Center,
which is a 74-acre entertainment park
containing an Opera House (3,200 seats),
Playhouse (900), Arena (6,000), Coliseum (15,000), numerous outdoor stages,
conference rooms for workshops, and exhibition halls and rooms for other performances and exhibitions.
Director: Jim Royce
Sponsors: City of Seattle, Seattle Folklore Society, National Park Service
Accommodations/other items of interest
in area: Many hotels are within walking
distance.
The Space Needle Restaurant (600 ft.
high), Pacific Science Center, and the
Seattle Art Museum are other attractions in the vicinity.
Ticket information: Admission is free
of charge, except for some Opera House
events for which a $1 donation is re-
quested

WEST VIRGINIA

Annual Bluefield Old-Time & Bluegrass Fiddlers Convention

New Glenwood Park, W. Va.
Old-time country and bluegrass
Late July
This 2-day annual event, begun in 1972, features competitions in everything from bluegrass fiddle to dobro, as well as dances on both Friday and Saturday nights. Contests have over $2,000 in prizes.
Performances are by regional musicians and take place in a country park outdoors on a covered stage. Seating brought by audience. There is a playground for children nearby.
Director: J. C. Parks
Sponsor: New Glenwood Park
Accommodations: There are hotels and motels in Princeton and Bluefield, W. Va. Camping is available at the convention site free with admission. Trailers are welcome.
Ticket information: Ticket prices are not yet set; tickets will be available at the gate only.
How to get there: New Glenwood Park is on Route 20, between Bluefield and Princeton, W. Va.

Bunner Ridge Bluegrass Festival

509 Deveny Building, Fairmont, W. Va. 26554
Bluegrass and old time
Mid-June
This 2-day festival grew from local groups performing together on Sunday afternoons. Now, local talent is just one aspect of things, with outside groups invited in, and workshops offered in banjo, fiddle, mandolin, and old-time music.
Events are held in an outdoor amphitheater which can accommodate 3,000.
Director: Tom Arnold
Sponsor: Marion County Parks and Recreation Commission
Accommodations: Lodging is available at Ramada Inn in Morgantown or at Holiday Inns in Morgantown or Fairmont. Primitive camping is free. Trailers are welcome, but there are no hook-ups. There is

picnicking.
Ticket information: Day tickets are $5 or $6; weekend tickets $10, if purchased in advance from Marion County Parks and Recreation Commission, 509 Deveny Bldg., Fairmont, W. Va., 26554. At the gate, tickets are $1 more per day.
How to get there: The Festival is 6 miles E. off the East Fairmont exit of I-79 South

Mountain Heritage Arts & Crafts Festival

Near Harpers Ferry, West Va., 25425
Folk
Early June and late September (2 weekends)
This old-time festival of Appalachian folk music and crafts takes place during 2 weekends annually. There is continuous entertainment, featuring folk dancing and singing, in addition to 125 craftspeople, selected for the high quality of their products, demonstrating and selling their crafts. The festival takes place in an open field, in a quiet country atmosphere. There are food concessions on the Festival grounds.
Director: George E. Vickers
Sponsor: Jefferson County Chamber of Commerce
Accommodations: Motels in Jefferson County include Cliffside Motor Inn and Hilltop House Hotel in Harpers Ferry; Turf Motel, Shenandoah Motel, and Town House Motor Lodge in Charles Town
Ticket information: Admission is $2. Tickets are available at the gate

Mountain State Art and Craft Fair

Cedar Lakes, Ripley, West Va., 25271
Traditional Appalachian to contemporary bluegrass (also arts, crafts, and dancing)
5 days around July 4
Each year since 1963, over 100 of the best West Virginia artists and craftsmen meet at the Cedar Lakes Fairgrounds for this fair. Here the heritage crafts of Appalachia blend with the contemporary trends of modern craftsmanship, and mountain music plays throughout the 5-day event. Eight groups play at three spots on the fairgrounds from 10 A.M. until 8 P.M. each day. In addition, on Sunday there is a special gospel sing. Appalachian heritage is featured through Appalachian folk dancing, native musical instruments, and pure traditional hill

music. Recent guest performers have included Roger Bryant, Aunt Jenny Wilson, Putnam County Pickers, Trapezoid, and Bill Miller.
Sponsors: Board of Trustees, Mountain State Art and Craft Fair, several West Virginia state agencies
Accommodations: There are 12 campgrounds in the area surrounding Ripley, and most have trailer facilities; the highest price is $6 per night. There are also many motels in the vicinity.
Ticket information: Tickets can only be brought at the gate; admission is $2.50 for adults and $.50 for children
How to get there: Cedar Lakes is N. of Charleston on I-77

Mountain State Bluegrass Festival
Mountain State Park, W. Va.
Bluegrass
Mid-August
This is a weekend of outdoor bluegrass music on the 147-acre site of a State Park. Performers in recent years have included the Lewis Family, the Marshall Family, Grandpa Jones, and the Bluegrass Tarheels.
Patrons are encouraged to bring lawn chairs.
Sponsor: Diana Volunteer Fire Department
Accommodations: Camping is free (no electricity). Other accommodations include the Webster Springs Hotel and the Motor Lodge Hotel in Webster Springs, and the William and Mary Motel in Mineral Springs.
Ticket information: Advance tickets for 3 days are $12; at the gate, $14. Write to Eddie Arbogast, 209 W. McCutcheon St., Webster Springs, W.Va., 26288, or Dwayne Fisher, 600 Elk St., Webster Springs, W.Va., 26288.
How to get there: State Route 15, 18 miles E. of Webster Springs

Mountain State Forest Festival
P.O. Box 369, Elkins, W. Va. 26241
Bluegrass and old-time
Early October
Mountain State Forest Festival was begun in 1930 as a homecoming for people of Elkins, and has been continuous except for an interruption during World War II. The Festival includes fiddle and banjo, woodchopping, and sawing contests. It also features parades,

square dancing, dance band contests, turkey calling, hang gliding, and many more events during 5 busy days.
Director: E. Clifton Hyre, O.D.
Sponsor: Mountain State Forest Festival Assn.

Parkersburg Community College Heritage Days
Parkersburg Community College, Box 167-A, Route 5, Parkersburg, W. Va. 26101
Folk and bluegrass music
Mid-April
Since it began in 1973, this festival has grown to include numerous concerts and workshops and as many as 50 craftsmen demonstrating traditional arts and crafts. Fiddle and banjo-playing contests are also scheduled during the Festival's 3 days.
Performers who have participated recently include Trapezoid, the Green Grass Cloggers, the Booger Hole Revival, and Lennie Moore and the West Virginians.
Director: Nancy Pansing
Sponsor: Parkersburg Community Coll.
Accommodations: Lodging can be obtained at the Holiday Inn, Red Roof Inn, and Best Western Green Acres, all on Route 50, one mile from campus. No camping.
Ticket information: Admission is free

Pipestem Folk Music, Arts, and Crafts Festival
Pipestem, W. Va. 25979
Folk
A weekend in mid-July
Appalachian mountain musicians have been making music at Pipestem for 14 years, Merle Travis, Hedy West, and George Tucker among them.
Bring foul weather clothing, just in case (the theater is not covered).
Director: Don West
Sponsor: Appalachian South Folklife Center
Accommodations/other items of interest in the area: The Mt. Lion Motel is in nearby Athens, and the Coast to Coast Motel is in Hinton. Camping is included in the ticket price, and picnic facilities are available. Trailers cannot be accommodated.
A nearby state park offers swimming, fishing, and boating.

Ticket information: Tickets are $10 per day or $20 for the weekend, including camping. They are sold at the gate or by mail from Don West, P.O. Box 5, Pipestem, W. Va., 25979

How to get there: One mile off State Route 20 in Pipestem

Potomac Highlands Park Bluegrass Festival

Box 302, Moorefield, W. Va. 26836
Bluegrass
Mid-August (3 days)
This annual 3-day bluegrass festival is held at Potomac Highlands Park, on the banks of the Potomac River, each August. Guest performers in recent years have included Jimmy Manton, the Seldom Scene, Dixie Grass, Raymond Fairchild, and Ralph Stanley and the Clinch Mountain Boys.
There is no limit to the number of people the park can hold, but patrons are asked to bring their own lawn chairs. Also, they are advised that no motorcycles or alcoholic beverages are allowed in the park. However, rain or shine, the concert will go on!
Director: Genny Milliman, Manager
Accommodations: The Evans Motel in Moorefield can provide lodging. Camping is permitted in Highlands Park. There are electrical hook-ups for $2 per night.
Ticket information: Tickets can only be bought at the gate; the cost is $10 for adults for the entire weekend, $1 per day for children ages 6 to 12. Children under 6 are admitted free.
How to get there: One hundred feet N. of the Moorefield city limits, off Route 220

Skyline Bluegrass Festival

Box 6, Ronceverte, W. Va. 24970
Bluegrass
Early June (3 days)
In its 5th year, this annual bluegrass festival is held on a mountain overlooking a lake in Ronceverte, West Virginia. For three days each June, patrons camp in the rough and hear continuous music from the likes of John Hartford, Bill Monroe and the Bluegrass Boys, Norman Blake, Bill Harrell and the Virginians, the Katie Laur Band, and the McPeak Brothers.
Jackets and raincoats are recommended at that time of year in Ronceverte, and patrons are advised that no alcoholic beverages are allowed at the Festival site.
Director: William R. Simms
Sponsors: William B. Blake and William R. Simms
Accommodations: Camping is included in the price of the ticket. There are porta-johns and a water truck, but no electrical hook-ups. Also, the Fort Savannah Inn and Old Colony Inn are in nearby Lewisburg.
Ticket information: Admission for the entire 3 days is $18 if tickets are bought at the gate; if bought in advance, the cost is $13.50. To obtain advance tickets, write to Skyline Productions, Box 6, Ronceverte, W. Va., 24970, or call (304) 645-6500. Children under 12 are admitted free.
How to get there: 2 miles S. of Ronceverte, on the Alta Vista Road

West Virginia Bluegrass Festival

Route 1, Walker, W. Va. (Cox's Field)
Bluegrass
Late August
This 3-day festival offers the best in bluegrass music. Past performers have included Ralph Stanley and the Clinch Mountain Boys, the Boys from Indiana, the Hillsiders, the Black Mountain Boys, Frog and the Greenhorns, and East Ohio Grass.
The Festival is held outdoors; the stage area is shaded. Patrons are advised to bring lawn chairs.
Director: John Cox
Accommodations: Lodging is available at the Holiday Inn and Best Western in Parkersburg, W. Va. There is plenty of space for camping and trailers.
Ticket information: Admission is $15 for 3 days. Tickets are available at the gate.
How to get there: Cox's Field is located 9 miles E. of Parkersburg on Route 47 and Walker Road

WISCONSIN

Great River Festival of Traditional Music and Crafts

Pump House, 119 King, La Crosse, Wis. 54601
Folk (traditional)
Late August or early September
This 2-day festival emphasizes authenticity. Individual musicians and groups perform. There are many music workshops: Medieval roots of folk music, women's music, unusual musical instruments, ballad singing, and songs of work and technology are only a few which have been offered in recent years. Other events include storytelling, ethnic dance, and many intriguing children's events. Traditional crafts are demonstrated and displayed and ethnic food is available.
The Festival is held outdoors on the Univ. of Wisconsin campus. In case of rain it moves into the student center.
Director: Fred Starner
Sponsors: Univ. of Wisconsin; Great River Festival of the Arts, Inc.; National Endowment for the Arts; State Arts Boon
Accommodations/other items of interest in area: Lodging is available in the area. Nearby camping costs $4 for facilities; trailers are allowed. There are picnic areas in the vicinity.
La Crosse is a scenic bluff area on the Mississippi River. There is much good fishing around.
Ticket information: Day tickets are $2 at the gate

WYOMING

Annual Festival of Strings

Wyoming Fiddlers' Assn. District 2
P.O. Box 1124, Cody, Wyo. 82414
Folk (fiddle)
Late November
This annual 1-day event was founded in 1975 to promote old-time fiddle music. It is open to all members of District 2 of the Wyoming fiddlers who have played at least 3 jams during the course of the preceding year. Except for the bass guitar, the sponsors encourage the use of only acoustical instruments. The Festival also features one guest artist each year from outside Wyoming. In past years these have included Jeff Pritchart from Kansas and Junior Daugherty from New Mexico. The event is held in an indoor hall with a seating capacity of 1,000.
Directors: Carl Wendvott; Leonard Foxworth
Sponsor: Wyoming Fiddlers' Association District 2
Accommodations: There are many motels in Cody
Ticket information: Admission is $2, and tickets are sold only at the door

MISCELLANEOUS

ALABAMA

Birmingham Festival of the Arts
Suite 910, Commerce Center, 2027
1st Ave. N., Birmingham, Ala. 35203
Music and art from a different country
each year; the range includes classical,
folk, and more depending on the
country
Spring
The purpose of the Birmingham Festival
of the Arts is to honor a different country each year and to promote international understanding through cultural,
artistic, educational and industrial ex-
changes with the honored country. As
well as a range of musical performances
by guest artists and ensembles from the
honored country, there are craft displays, films, art exhibits, sports events
and theater.
Events are held in halls, theaters and
churches throughout Birmingham.
Patrons can expect to enjoy the balmy
weather of a Southern spring.
Director: Sara C. Crowder
Accommodations: Birmingham, a major
Southern city, has many hotels and
motels including Holiday Inn, Hilton,
Sheraton, Ramada and Hyatt House
Ticket information: Prices of ticketed
events range from $1 to $10

CALIFORNIA

Concord Pavilion
2000 Kirker Pass Road, Concord, Calif.
94523
All types of musical and theatrical events
May to October (evenings)
It started in 1969 in a local park with
the Concord Summer Jazz Festival,
which sponsored 6 shows. Today it is a
65-show season held at the Concord
Pavilion, which seats 8,500—3,555 under
its acre-square roof, and another 5,000
on the lawn surrounding the Pavilion on
3 sides. In recent years, the Pavilion
concerts have featured pop and rock
stars such as Boz Scaggs, Barry Manilow,
Abba, and Kenny Rogers; comedians
Bob Hope and Bill Cosby; and classical
conductors such as Seiji Ozawa.
Director: John Toffoli, Jr.
Sponsor: City of Concord
Accommodations/other items of interest
in area: There are many motels in the
Concord area; no camping is permitted
near the Festival site.
Concord is 40 miles from the Napa
Valley wine country.
Ticket information: Tickets range in
price from $5 to $8.50 and may be pur-
chased in advance from the Concord
Pavilion Box Office, P.O. Box 6166,
Concord, Calif. 94524; they are also
available through Ticketron outlets and
at Macy's in New York City.
How to get there: Concord is 40 miles
from the Napa Valley wine country.

Midsummer Music Festival
P.O. Box 3250, San Francisco, Calif.
94119
Classical, folk, jazz, dance
Mid-June to mid-August
Since its first summer in 1938, the
Festival has provided classical, folk, and
jazz concerts for audiences of up to
25,000 music lovers in Stern Grove—an
uncovered natural amphitheater surrounded by eucalyptus and redwood trees.
This is the nation's oldest continuous
free midsummer music festival. Performers such as Arthur Fiedler and the
San Francisco Symphony, the Preservation Hall Jazz Band, the San Francisco
Ballet, and Pete Seeger have taken part
over the years.
Director: James M. Friedman

Sponsors: Stern Grove Festival Association, San Francisco Recreation and Park Dept.
Accommodations: Many motels and hotels in San Francisco provide accommodations.
Ticket information: Free
How to get there: Concerts in Stern Grove are near both Golden Gate Park and the San Francisco Zoo.

Music in the Garden
Montalvo Center for the Arts, Villa Montalvo, Saratoga, Calif. 95070
Opera, New Orleans jazz, and classical music
Concerts from June to August
Every summer since 1954 this festival has brought together distinguished artists and promising young performers for concerts throughout the season. Performers in recent years include Jorg Demus, the Kronos Quartet, Turk Murphy Jazz Band, and Fernando Valenti. The grounds of Villa Montalvo, where the concerts are held, include formal gardens and trails to hillside vantage points. The Villa itself, converted into a center for creative activities in the arts, offers monthly exhibitions in 3 galleries in addition to art classes throughout the year.
Seating in the Garden Theatre—uncovered but sheltered—is more than 700, and the Carriage House Theatre seats 300.
Director: Harriet Lundquist
Sponsor: Montalvo Music Committee
Accommodations: In Saratoga there is the Hacienda Inn, and in nearby Los Gatos, the Los Gatos Lodge
Ticket information: General admission is $6. For tickets, write to Montalvo Association, P.O. Box 158, Saratoga, Calif. 95070
How to get there: Entrance gates are ½ mile from the center of Saratoga on the Los Gatos Road

CANADA

Banff Festival of the Arts
Box 1020, Banff, Alberta TOL OCO, Canada
Classical, jazz, dance, theater
August
The performers at this 3-week festival at the Banff Centre, School of Fine Arts, are students of the school; many past performers are now internationally known. The Festival features over 60 productions in opera, ballet, drama, music, readings, and more—not only in the principal theaters but in churches, schools, and the out-of-doors in and around Banff. There are a number of free concerts, recitals and workshops in ballet, drama, musical theater, opera and play-writing, as well as readings and art exhibitions.
Director: Thomas M. Kouk
Accommodations/other items of interest in area: For information on hotel and motel accommodations write to the Banff Chamber of Commerce, Box 1298, Banff, Alberta TOL OCO, Canada.
Camping is allowed at a cost of $3 Canadian per night. There are facilities for trailers. Picnicking is allowed.
This is a good area for hiking and mountain climbing. Lake Louise offers boating, swimming, and other sports.
Ticket information: Admission ranges from $5 to $7.

COLORADO

Aspen Music Festival
Box AA, Aspen, Colo. 81611
Classical, choral, opera, jazz
Late June to late August
For 9 weeks every summer musicians from all over the country and beyond gather at the bottom of Aspen's ski slopes, 8,000 ft. high in the Rockies, to study, teach, and make music at this festival which first began in 1949. The Aspen Amphitheater, a 1,600-seat-capacity tent, is one of several sites for music ranging from early Renaissance to contemporary, opera, and choral works to jazz-rock. The concert-goer has a choice of full-sized orchestras, chamber orchestras, chamber ensembles and soloists. Five regularly scheduled concerts are offered weekly, while many other performances take place throughout the summer, making a total of over 150. There are also master classes, seminars, lectures, and films available to the public. In addition, the Conference on Contemporary Music takes place during the Festival.
Recent performers include Itzhak Perlman, Pinchas Zukerman, Misha Dichter, Juilliard String Quartet, and many others of note.
Directors: Gordon Hardy and Jorge Mester
Sponsor: Music Associates of Aspen
Accommodations/other items of interest in area: For accommodations write to the Aspen Chamber of Commerce, Aspen, Colo. 81611.
The area is one of great natural beauty, with many opportunities for hiking, fishing, rafting, horseback riding, tennis, and other sports.
Ticket information: Tickets for orchestral concerts are $10, chamber music, $9, and jazz-rock, $5. For tickets, write to Music Associates of Aspen, Box AA, Aspen, Colo. 81611, Attn: Ticket Sales.
How to get there: Take I-70 from Denver to Glenwood Springs, S. on Route 82 to Aspen

Mozart Festival
Pueblo Symphony Association, 1117 Lake Ave., Pueblo, Colo. 81004
Classical and folk
Late January

This festival, held annually the last 2 weeks of January, includes various kinds of music, ranging from folk and band concerts to classical with an emphasis on Mozart. A central feature of the Festival is the Young Artists Competition. There is also a Mozart poster competition and various exhibits.
Events are held in Memorial Hall which seats 1,675, Sangre de Cristo Arts Center, seating 500, and Hoag Recital Hall which seats 700.
Director: Gerhard Track, Music Director
Sponsor: Pueblo Symphony Association, Inc.
Accommodations/other items of interest in area: For information on accommodations write to the Festival.
Of interest in the area are an ice skating rink, several museums, art centers and galleries, the Royal Gorge and Bent's Fort.
Ticket information: Admission ranges from $1 to $6.50
How to get there: Pueblo is on I-25, exits 91 through 99B

Summer Symphony
P.O. Box 1692, Colorado Springs, Colo.
Classical, folk, jazz, dance, children's theater
Mid-June to July 4
Five concerts by the Colorado Springs Symphony take place in different uncovered parks in Colorado Springs. As part of pre-concert entertainment, jazz, folk, mime, and dance (ballet, folk, and ethnic) groups perform. Recent performers of note are Bob Wilber (jazz clarinetist), Larry Trujillo Dancers (Mexican and Spanish), John Bayley (Calypso), and Sensorium (children's experiential art).
On July 4 additional events include fireworks and parachute drops.
Director: Charles Ansbacher
Sponsors: Park and Recreation Department of the City of Colorado Springs and the Colorado Springs Symphony
Ticket information: Admission is free

REV. ROBERT WILKINS (LEFT) AND DAVID "HONEYBOY" EDWARDS (PHOTO PREVIOUS PAGE)

CONNECTICUT

Greater Hartford Civic and Arts Festival

250 Convention Plaza, Hartford, Conn.
06103
Classical, jazz, folk, dance, theater
Early June
This comprehensive festival presents more
than 150 events. The range is from opera
and symphony concerts to folk music
and jazz. There is also dance and theater.
Special children's programs are scheduled
as well.
Events take place in Constitution Plaza
in downtown Hartford. At main events
there is seating for 1,000 and standing
room for 1,000. Smaller indoor and outdoor theater spaces are also used.
Director: Evelyn R. Warner
Sponsors: Greater Hartford Arts Council,
Downtown Council, and Chamber of
Commerce
Accommodations: Lodging is readily
available in downtown Hartford. There
is picnicking but no camping.
Ticket information: Admission is free

Starlight Festival of Music

Yale Law School Courtyard—Wall St.
between York and High Sts., New
Haven, Conn.
Classical, folk, jazz
Late June through late July
Held outdoors in a magnificent Gothic
courtyard, this annual festival features
chamber music, as well as some folk
music and jazz in a series of 5 weekly
concerts. The performers include the
teaching and performing artists at Yale
Univ., those in the New Haven community, and internationally famous artists.
In past years these have included Charlie
Byrd, Carlos Montoya, the Eastern
Brass Quintet, the Dave Brubeck Quartet, and the Paul Winter Consort.
There is seating for 1,200 in the courtyard. In case of foul weather, concerts
are held in the Yale Law School Auditorium.
Director: Julius E. Scheir
Accommodations: There are many
hotels and motels in the New Haven
area
Ticket information: Admission is $3.50-
$5.50 per concert. For reservations,
call (203)624-6405.

FLORIDA

Palm Beach Festival

P.O. Box 3511, West Palm Beach, Fla.
33402
Classical, theater, ballet, modern dance,
jazz
Late March to mid-April
The Festival began in 1978 and featured
the New York City Ballet. Its success in-
spired the Festival's continuation with
Ballet Galaxie '79 featuring stars such as
Gelsey Kirkland and John Meehan. The
other fine arts were represented by Orpheus, a chamber orchestra whose members are all virtuoso musicians; Edward
Albee directing his own plays; the Juil-
liard Theater Center; Pilobolus, a modern
dance company; and John Houseman's
The Acting Company.
Performances take place at the West
Palm Beach Auditorium (2,500 seat
capacity) and the Poinciana Playhouse
(850).
Director: Dale Heapps
Accommodations/other items of interest
in area: Hotel, motel, and camping information can be obtained from the
Chambers of Commerce in West Palm
Beach, Fla. 33401 and Palm Beach, Fla.
33480.
The Norton Gallery of Art and the Four
Arts Museum are additional points of
interest.
Ticket information: Ticket prices range
from $6 to $10 for each performance.

Seven Lively Arts Festival

Young Circle Bandshell, Federal Highway
1 and Hollywood Blvd., Hollywood, Fla.
Opera, classical, dance, contemporary,
popular
March or April
It is possible in 2 days at this festival to
hear great operas, the works of classical
and contemporary composers played by
the Hollywood Philharmonic Orchestra
with renowned guest soloists, musical
comedy and jazz which share the spot-
light with folk, ethnic, country and
western, patriotic, and "top 40." And
not only that, but a range of dance from
classical through jazz ballet is presented.
There are also art exhibitions and crafts
displays.
Events occur outdoors in the Young
Circle Bandshell which seats 2,200.

Director: Pat Mascola
Sponsor: Seven Lively Arts Festival, Inc.
Accommodations: For information contact the Festival at P.O. Box 737, Hollywood, Fla. 33020
Ticket information: Admission is free

ILLINOIS

Mississippi River Festival
Southern Illinois University, Edwardsville, Ill. 62026
Rock, folk, jazz
Evenings throughout the summer
This annual, summer-long festival features rock, folk, jazz, and pop groups, who perform on weekend evenings from June through September. Concerts are held outdoors on the campus of Southern Illinois University—Edwardsville. Artists have included Meat Loaf, Andy Gibb, George Benson, Dave Manson, and Marshall Tucker Band.
A pavilion seats 2,400, and an additional 13,000 people can be accommodated on the lawn. No bottles, glass containers, alcoholic beverages, recording devices, or cameras are permitted.
Director: R. Wayne Nederlander
Sponsor: Nederlander Organization
Accommodations: Hotels in the area include the Holiday Inn in Edwardsville and Round Table Motor Lodge and the Holiday Inn in Collinsville.
Ticket information: Tickets range in price from $6 to $9.50 and may be ordered by mail by sending a stamped, self-addressed envelope to the address given above
How to get there: Twenty-five minutes from downtown St. Louis, 35 minutes from the St. Louis airport

National Women's Music Festival
Box 2721, Station A, Champaign, Ill. 61820. Tel. (217)333-6443
Varied
Late May to early June
This week-long festival was born in 1974 and has become an annual event, attended by women from all over the U.S. and Canada. This festival embraces a little bit of every kind of music, and past performers have included Victoria Spivey, Dr. Antonia Brico, Margie Adam, Holly Neare, Malvina Reynolds, and Suni Paz. Festival events include workshops, jam sessions, open mikes, and dance.
Except for outdoor jam sessions, all events are held indoors at the University of Illinois, either in the campus auditorium (2,000 seats) or Smith Music Hall (600 seats).
Sponsor: National Women's Music

Festival Collective

Accommodations: Arrangements for housing are made through the Festival directors. There is also camping available at $2 to $3 per day.

Ticket information: Admission is $30 for the full week; $21 for the weekend; and $6 for individual concerts. Tickets may be obtained by mail, or at the door at a slightly higher cost.

How to get there: Take I-57, I-72, or I-74 to the University of Illinois campus.

IOWA

Spring Music Festival
Cornell College, Mt. Vernon, Iowa 52314
Classical and jazz
May
The Spring Music Festival is in its 82nd year in 1980. Sonny Rollins, the St. Paul Chamber Orchestra, the Bill Evans Trio, Joe Pass, Phil Woods, the Chicago Symphony, and the Minneapolis Orchestra are among past participants.
Director: Dr. Jesse G. Evans
Ticket information: Tickets cost from $3 to $8 and are available from the Business Office, Cornell College, Mt. Vernon, Iowa 52314

LOUISIANA

Festival of the Fine Arts Foundation of Lafayette

P.O. Box 53320, Lafayette, La. 70505
Tel. (318)233-2045
Classical and jazz
September
This annual festival, which began with only one performance in July 1973, has grown into a month-long celebration during September involving concerts—classical and jazz—master classes, workshops, lecture-demonstrations, art exhibitions and seminars. Concerts are given in an auditorium which seats 2,300, a ballroom which seats 900, and a church which seats 250. Featured performers at recent festivals include pianist Boris Block, cellist Robert Cohen, violinist Hiroko Yajima, jazz musicians Al Beletto, the Rusty Mayne Trio, the Skyliners, the New Orleans Philharmonic, and the Stuttgart Piano Trio.
Director: Michael Curry
Sponsor: The Fine Arts Foundation of Lafayette
Accommodations/other items of interest in area: There are many hotels and motels in the area.
There are many places of historical interest in this French-speaking area of Louisiana.
Ticket information: Ticket prices have not yet been determined; for information, contact the Fine Arts Foundation at the address given above
How to get there: Lafayette is located midway between New Orleans and Houston, on I-10, Highway 1

New Orleans Jazz and Heritage Festival

P.O. Box 2530, New Orleans, La. 70176
Largely jazz; also, rhythm and blues, gospel, Cajun, blues, folk, Latin, country and western, and bluegrass.
End of April
The jazz portion of this festival features evening concerts at Municipal Auditorium, an international jam session at a grand hotel ballroom until the wee hours, and concerts on the Steamer *Admiral* as the boat makes its way up and down the Mississippi River. Musicians who have participated in the years since 1969 when the Festival was inaugurated include Doug Kershaw, B.B. King, Doc

Watson, Onward Brass Band, Muddy Waters, Odetta, Dave Brubeck, James Booker, New Orleans Bluegrass All Stars, and many others. The Festival has as many as 200 craftsmen displaying, demonstrating and selling their work, whether it be wooden toys, stained glass, blown glass, or blacksmithing, to name only a few examples.
The Heritage Fair portion takes place on the infield of the Fairgrounds Race Track. It has 10 stages of simultaneous music—one is a gigantic gospel tent, another is a jazz tent, and a third is a special performance tent.
Director: Quint Davis
Sponsor: Jos. Schlitz Brewing Co.
Accommodations: Hotel accommodation is plentiful in New Orleans. The Festival's official hotel is the Hyatt Regency New Orleans. There are camping facilities in the city but not at the Festival itself.
Ticket information: Tickets range in price from $3 to $12.50. For tickets, write to Werlein's Ticket Office, P.O. Box 2500, New Orleans, La. 70176, or tel. (504)522-6522.

MAINE

The Maine Festival
Bowdoin College Campus, Brunswick, Me.
Classical, rock, folk, jazz, dance, theater
Late July/early August
The Festival gathers together a broad
spectrum of Maine artists, craftsmen, and
interested audiences for creative collabo-
ration over a 3-day weekend.
Besides musical events, there are exhibitions and demonstrations of the visual
arts, folklore, building, literature, applied
arts, children's arts, magic, film and
vaudeville.
Evening concerts are held indoors in a
hall with 2,400 seats; all other events are
held outdoors or under tents. In case of
rain daytime concerts move indoors.
Director: Linda Bliss, Executive Director
Sponsors: The Maine Festival of the Arts,
Inc., and Maine-based businesses.
Accommodations/other items of interest
in area: Lodging reservations are recom-
mended. For information, write to the
Brunswick Chamber of Commerce, 59
Pleasant St., Brunswick, Me. 04011.
A point of interest nearby is the Bath
Marine Museum in Bath, Me.
Ticket information: Ticket prices range
from $3 to $5 per day or portion thereof.
For tickets, write to The Maine Festival,
P.O. Box 192, Brunswick, Me. 04011.

Saco River Festival
RFD, Kezar Falls, Me. 04047
Classical, jazz, folk
July and August
The Saco River Festival Association was
formed in 1976 to present concerts, support programming in schools, and stimulate arts activity in the community. Its
summer festival includes orchestral,
choral and chamber works, and jazz and
folk concerts. There are exhibitions of
both art (painting, drawing and sculpture) and fine crafts. Workshops for
children are offered in art and in body
movement with music. A special feature
of this festival is 4 informal coffee talks
with musical illustrations by musicians.
Events are held in Sacopee Valley Regional High School, S. Hiram, which seats
over 1,000, and Cornish Elementary
School Auditorium, seating 260.
Director: Ruth G. Glazer
Accommodations/other items of interest

in area: Lodging is available at Midway
Motel, Cornish, Maine. There is a camping park in the area.
The Festival is near Sebago Lake in the
foothills of the White Mountains. Scenic
drives and athletic and arts activities
may be of interest to festival guests.
Ticket information: Single admission is
$3 and series tickets are about $12. They
can be obtained at the gate or by mail.
How to get there: The Festival is 40
miles W. of Portland on Route 25.

MASSACHU - SETTS

Summerthing
Boston, Mass.
Popular, jazz, swing, dance, theater
Early July to end of August
Summerthing is a summer-long, city-wide festival that tours parks, playgrounds, street corners, community centers and nursing homes with everything from street discotheques to classical dance. Major national performers such as Taj Mahal, David Bromberg, New Riders of the Purple Sage, and Joan Baez, all of whom have played in recent years, may perform.
A major aspect of Summerthing is Bravo Boston, which highlights a different
art form every night of the week (except Mondays). Tuesdays is folk dancing, Wednesday is dance, Thursday and Friday are theater, Saturday is big bands, and Sunday is jazz.
Director: Helen Rees
Sponsor: The Mayor's Office of Cultural Affairs
Ticket information: Free admission except for benefit concerts

MICHIGAN

Meadow Brook Music Festival
Oakland University, Rochester, Mich. 48063
Classical, folk, jazz, ballet
Late June to late August
Situated on the campus of Oakland University, this festival was founded in 1964 and has grown to become a major 10-week music festival of international reputation. In 1978, for example, 185,000 people attended. The summer home of the Detroit Symphony Orchestra, the Festival has also sponsored summer institutes with master classes directed by Vladimir Ashkenazy and Itzhak Perlman and has acted as a showcase for pre-concert chamber music, operatic concerts, open-air art exhibits, and ballet and modern dance rehearsals.
Concerts take place at an outdoor pavilion; its roof, open on the sides, covers some 2,200 seats. It is surrounded by trees and a sloping lawn to accommodate an additional 5,000 concert-goers. The natural amphitheater and fiber-glass shell eliminate any need for sound reinforcement. Many patrons picnic at the Festival site before each concert.
Director: Stuart C. Hyke
Sponsor: Oakland University
Accommodations: Northfield Hilton Inn and Somerset Inn in Troy, Mich., Sheraton Motor Inn in Pontiac, Mich., and Spartan Motel in Rochester can provide accommodation near the Festival. No camping available.
Ticket information: Ticket prices range from $4 to $11
How to get there: Go N. of Detroit on I-75, then take University Drive exit

EIGHTEENTH-CENTURY GATES AT THE ENTRANCE TO THE CARAMOOR FESTIVAL (PHOTO PREVIOUS PAGE)

MISSOURI

St. Louis County Pops
Queeny Park, 550 Weidman Road,
Manchester, Mo.
Pops
Late June through mid-August
For over 5 years "Pops Goes the Summer" has been the word in Manchester's Queeny Park. On Wednesday through Saturday, concerts called "Disco Party," "Wide World of Sports," "America the Beautiful," "Big Band Night," "Down Memory Lane," and many more are conducted by Richard Hayman, or guest conductors such as Mitch Miller. Guest performers Roger Williams, Gordon MacRae, the Modernaires with Paula Kelly, Jr., and Ferrante and Teicher, have also been featured.
Concerts take place in Greensfelder Recreational Complex which is air conditioned and seats 3,000.
Director: Richard Hayman
Sponsor: St. Louis County
Accommodations: There is picnicking in Queeny Park, but no camping
Ticket information: Admission ranges from $3 to $7. Series ticket range from $8 to $35.
How to get there: Write to the Festival for a map included in their brochure

NEW JERSEY

Annual Choir Festival
Ocean Grove Camp Meeting Association,
Ocean Grove, N.J. 07756
Sacred choral
Second Sunday in July
Choirs and individuals from the surrounding cities and states come together for a massed rehearsal Sunday afternoon under the leadership of ten guest conductors, and the concert is given that evening at 7:30 P.M. Anyone capable of learning the music on their own is invited to attend. The purchase and learning of the music is up to the individual or group. The Festival began over 25 years ago with a handful of interested choirs and individuals and has grown to almost 100 choirs and individuals, numbering 1,000 singers in the Festival. The program is recorded and records and tapes may be purchased.
The concert is held in the Great Auditorium which seats 7,000.
Director: Lewis A. Daniels
Sponsor: Ocean Grove Camp Meeting Association
Accommodations/other items of interest in area: Accommodations are available at Shawmont Hotel, 17 Ocean Ave., Ocean Grove, N.J. There is no camping. Ocean Grove is a historic town with Victorian architecture. It is near Allaire State Park, Atlantic Highlands, and Twin Lighthouses.
Ticket information: There is no admission charge; an offering is taken during the program
How to get there: Ocean Grove is next to Asbury Park. No cars are allowed in Ocean Grove on Sunday; park in the surrounding area and walk a few short blocks into town to the auditorium.

Fair Lawn Summer Music Festival
Memorial Park, Fair Lawn, N.J.
Classical and jazz
End of June through the beginning of September
Since 1960 free Sunday evening concerts at Memorial Park have been a summer tradition of Fair Lawn, N.J. The program is usually classical, but jazz and big bands are occasionally featured. Vocalists from major opera companies, instrumental soloists, and top jazz names

have appeared at the Festival. Seating is outdoors and patrons are advised to bring folding chairs. In the event of inclement weather, concerts move indoors.

Director: Isadore Freeman

Sponsor: Borough of Fair Lawn, N.J.

Accommodations/other items of interest in area: There are many motels in the area. No camping or picnicking is allowed. Passaic Falls in nearby Paterson, N.J., the home of poet William Carlos Williams, is the second largest falls east of the Mississippi River.

Ticket information: All concerts are free

How to get there: Fair Lawn is 10 miles W. of the George Washington Bridge, on the New Jersey side

NEW YORK

Guggenheim Concerts by the Goldman Band

300 Madison Avenue, New York, N.Y.

Band concerts

Mid-June through mid-August

For over 60 years the Goldman Band has been giving free summer concerts for the enjoyment of the people of the City of New York, and now on Long Island as well. Concerts are given at the Guggenheim Memorial Band Shell in Damrosch Park (near Lincoln Center) on Wednesday, Friday, and Sunday evenings; at Seaside Park, Brooklyn, on Saturday evenings; and at Christopher Morley Park, Roslyn, Long Island, on Thursday evenings. The Goldman Band is noted for the scope and quality of its repertoire. In addition to works dating from the 18th and 19th centuries, a large number of 20th century works for band, many of them written for the Goldman Band, are performed.

Director: Dr. Richard Franko Goldman

Sponsor: Daniel and Florence Guggenheim Foundation

Ticket information: Concerts are free

Morgan Park Summer Music Festival

Box 296, Glen Cove, N.Y. 11542

Classical and other

July through August

For over 20 years, Morgan Park, on Long Island Sound, has offered free Sunday evening concerts in July and August. Band concerts, operettas, ballet, folk, brass, and jazz have all been presented. Performers have included Shirley Verrett, Virgil Fox, Jean Kraft, Manhatten Savoyards, George Seaffert, the N.Y. Brass Choir, Gospel groups, and many others. Concerts are held in a covered gazebo. There is seating for 100 in chairs and for 10,000 more on the grass.

Accommodations/other items of interest in area: No camping is allowed in the park.

The park offers swimming, all sports, and an Indian museum.

Ticket information: Admission is free

How to get there: Take the L.I. Expressway to Glen Cove Road, go N. to Glen Cove. Turn left after the Fire House to the park.

NORTH DAKOTA

International Festival of the Arts
Bottineau, N.D. 58318
Classical, dance, theater, and jazz
Early June to late July
The Festival is part of the summer program at the International Music Camp which draws as many as 2,200 students from North and South America, Europe, Asia, and the Middle East.
The Camp, which includes instruction, performance, and exhibitions in all areas of the fine arts for both students and adults, takes place at the International Peace Garden. The International Oldtime Fiddlers Contest is an additional attraction.
The concerts are performed in a new auditorium which seats 2,000. Evenings are cool; warm jackets are recommended.
Director: Dr. Merton Utgaard
Sponsor: International Music Camp
Accommodations: Camping is available at the site for $5 per night. There are electrical hook-ups and central restrooms. Trailers are welcome.
Ticket information: Tickets for each concert cost $3. Write to International Festival of the Arts, International Music Camp, Bottineau, N.D. 58318.
How to get there: The International Peace Garden is 10 miles N. of Dunseith

OHIO

Blossom Music Center
1145 W. Steels Corners Rd., Cuyahoga Falls, Ohio 44223
Classical, dance, jazz, rock, folk
Mid-June through mid-September
Blossom Music Center is on 800 acres of natural wooded land. Concerts take place at Blossom Pavilion, an architecturally sophisticated structure seating 4,640; lawns sloping up from the Pavilion can accommodate 13,500 more. The Center is the summer home of the Cleveland Orchestra. The diverse summer program includes, as well as fine classical music, jazz, ballet, country and folk music, and more. Well-known artists in all these genres are featured at Blossom.
Patrons are advised to bring rain gear.
Director: J. Christopher Fahlman
Sponsor: Musical Arts Association of Cleveland
Accommodations/other items of interest in area: A list of motels and hotels is available: contact Blossom Music Center, P.O. Box 1000, Cuyahoga Falls, Ohio 44223. Camping facilities are located in Cuyahoga Valley National Park. There is an abundance of picnic facilities on the Blossom grounds.
Of interest in the area are museums and historical sites and the National Football League Hall of Fame.
Ticket information: Ticket prices vary . For information write to Blossom Music Center, Box 1000, Cuyahoga Falls, Ohio 44223
How to get there: Blossom Music Center is in Northampton between Cleveland and Akron. It is a few miles S. of exit 12 on the Ohio Turnpike and 2 miles W. of Ohio Route 8. It is also accessible from I-71 and I-77.

Square Fair/Ethnic Fest
P.O. Box 1124, Lima, Ohio 45802
Folk, jazz, ethnic
Early August
There is all-day entertainment at this 2-day outdoor festival. As well as jazz and folk music performances, ethnic music and dance is featured. The Festival is held on the public square in downtown Lima, where visual artists and craftspersons in all fields will be demonstrating their work. There will be mime, theater

and workshops for children, hot air balloon ascension and refreshments, including ethnic food.
Director: Dean R. Gladden
Accommodations: For information on lodging write to Lima Area Chamber of Commerce, Lima Ohio
Ticket information: Admission is free

OKLAHOMA

Tri-State Music Festival
Drawer 2127, University Station P.O.,
Enid, Okla. 73701
Classical and jazz
Early May
Primarily a festival for secondary school groups, the Tri-State Music Festival takes place during 4 days in Enid, Oklahoma. Concert and marching bands, choruses, orchestras, jazz vocal groups, large and small ensembles, and drum corps participate. Since it began in 1932, Tri-State has attracted almost a half million participants.
Events take place at a convention center (seating capacity 2,500), Plainsmen Field (10,000) and 12 other auditoriums in the city (1,000 to 1,500).
Director: Milburn Carey
Sponsors: Phillips University and Citizens of Enid, Oklahoma
Accommodations: Midwestern Inn, Ramada Inn, Holiday Inn, and Hotel Youngblood can provide accommodations in Enid. Camping and picnicking are also available in the area.
Ticket information: Tickets are $3.50 or less depending on the event and seat location, and are available only at the box office

PENNSYL-VANIA

Central Pennsylvania Festival of the Arts

Box 1023, State College, Pa. 16801
Classical and other
Mid-July
This 5-day festival on the campus of
State College presents a variety of events
including many concerts, ranging from
classical to bluegrass. There are theater
performances, films, storytelling, and a
range of workshops. There are also dances
and competitions. A popular attraction is
the Annual Sidewalk Art Sale and Exhibition; 400 artists and craftspeople are
selected to participate from across the
country. Most events are held outdoors,
but the concert halls of State College
and local galleries are also used.
Director: Lurene Frantz
Accommodations/other items of interest
in area: For a hotel/motel list write:
State College Area Chamber of Commerce, 131 Sowers St., State College, Pa.
16801. For camping information write:
Bellefonte KOA Kampground, Box 303,
R.D. 2, Bellefonte, Pa. 16823. Another
source of information on accommodation is: Lion Country Visitors and Convention Bureau, Train Station, Bellefonte,
Pa. 16823.
There are golf courses, fishing streams,
limestone caves, and state parks within
easy traveling distance of the Festival.
Ticket information: All events are free
How to get there: For a map of the
area write to Lion Country Visitors and
Convention Bureau and for a map of
State College write to State College
Area Chamber of Commerce, at the
addresses given above

Temple University Music Festival

Festival site: Meetinghouse Road and
Butler Pike, Ambler, Pa. 19002
Mailing address: TUMF, Philadelphia,
Pa. 19002; Tel. (215)CE5-4600
Classical, rock, folk, jazz, modern dance
July and August
From the beginning of July through the
end of August each year, the sponsors
offer a different musical or modern dance
event every night. The Festival site is a
covered theater with open sides which
seats 3,000; canvas walls can be hung in
case of rain. In addition to the Pittsburgh
Symphony Orchestra, with André Previn
conducting (in residence for a 6-week
period each year), the Festival has in
recent years been host to Johnny Cash,
Ella Fitzgerald, David Bromberg, Bonnie
Raitt, the Alvin Ailey American Dance
Theater, and McCoy Tyner.
Director: Samuel K. Wolfgang
Sponsor: Temple University
Accommodations/other items of interest
in area: In nearby Fort Washington are
the Sheraton, the Holiday Inn and
Ramada Inn. There is no camping permitted in the area.
Historic Valley Forge is nearby.
Ticket information: Admission ranges
from $5 to $12 for individual events;
the theater box office is open from
10 A.M. to 9 P.M. daily from June 1
to August 31.
How to get there: To get to the theater,
take exit 26 (Fort Washington) on the
Pennsylvania Turnpike; from there,
head N. on Route 309 and get off at
the Susquehanna exit, then follow the
"Festival" signs.

SOUTH CAROLINA

Ticket information: For program and ticket information, write to Spoleto Festival U.S.A., P.O. Box 704, Charleston, S.C. 29402

Spoleto Festival U.S.A.
P.O. Box 157, Charleston, S.C. 29402
Classical, opera, dance (modern and ballet), theater, jazz, symphonic, chamber music
Late May to early June
Up to 18 days long and covering 3 weekends, this is the American counterpart of the Spoleto Festival in Italy founded by Gian Carlo Menotti in 1957. Charleston was chosen in 1976 to be the American setting for this "Festival of Two Worlds" because of its rich musical heritage and its well preserved 18th-century beauty. Many days begin with lectures by artists and participants in the Festival. There are art exhibits in museums, galleries, and parks on a daily basis as well. At noon each day a chamber music concert is held at the historic Dock Street Theatre, originally built in 1736. Afternoons are often filled with mini-festivals featuring storytellers, instant theater, gospel music, puppets, and mime. On many afternoons there are matinee performances of plays, operas and ballets. In late afternoons there are church concerts and recitals. In the evenings, operas, plays, and dance programs are presented at the Dock Street Theatre and the Gaillard Municipal Auditorium.
Artists of note in recent years include the Westminster Choir, Martine van Hamel, Tennessee Williams, Ella Fitzgerald, and the Netherlands Dance Theatre, to mention only a few.
Directors: James T. Kearney, General Manager; Gian Carlo Menotti, Artistic Director; Christopher Keene, Music Director
Accommodations/other items of interest in area: For accommodations information write to the Chamber of Commerce, Visitor Information Center, 85 Calhoun St., Charleston, S.C. 29401.
Charleston and the surrounding area have many historic points of interest including the Citadel, Cabbage Row, Boone Hall Plantation, and Charlestowne Landing.

TENNESSEE

Memphis Music Heritage Festival
Mid-America Mall, Memphis, Tenn.
Blues, jazz, gospel, rock, soul
Early September
The Memphis Music Heritage Festival, held on Labor Day weekend, gives an authentic taste of a musical legacy which began with work chants, gospel singing, and parlor pianos, and is associated with artists such as B.B. King and Elvis Presley. The Festival offers "a mile of Music" outdoors on a pedestrian mall in downtown Memphis. Past performers have included Muddy Waters and Asleep at the Wheel. The Festival includes a crafts fair, food, and a fireworks display.
Director: Quint Davis
Sponsor: Jos. Schlitz Brewing Co.
Accommodations: Hotel and motel accommodations are available in Memphis
Ticket information: Admission is free

TEXAS

Texas Folklife Festival
801 S. Bowie at Durango Boulevard, San Antonio, Tex. 78205
Folk, ethnic, jazz, and blues
Early August
The 4-day Texas Folklife Festival is an occasion for musicians, singers, dancers, craftspeople and cooks from 30 ethnic, national, and cultural groups in Texas to present their traditional music, dance, crafts, and food to Festival guests. The Festival prides itself on its authenticity; it presents folklife, not just a folksy atmosphere. This colorful celebration of Texas diversity is spread across the 15-acre grounds of the Institute of Texan Cultures located in downtown San Antonio.
It is an open air festival with plenty of shade. Approximately 100,000 visitors are expected each year.
Director: Claudia Ball
Sponsor: Institute of Texan Cultures
Accommodations: For a lodging guide, write: San Antonio Convention and Visitors Bureau, P.O. Box 2277, San Antonio, Tex. 78298. There is no camping.
Ticket information: Tickets, which must be purchased in advance, are $3

VIRGINIA

Festival of Arts

900 E. Broad St., Room 825, Richmond, Va. 23219

Classical, modern, and jazz

Mid-June to mid-August

For over 20 years this festival has been offering a varied program of music, theater, dance, and art, primarily by Richmond-area artists. Events take place at Dogwood Dell in Byrd Park in an outdoor uncovered amphitheater which seats 2,000 people.

A Sunday supper series is usually held on the Carillon Mall in the park; bring blankets, chairs and picnic suppers.

Director: Agnes Cain

Sponsor: The Richmond Department of Recreation and Parks

Accommodations/other items of interest in area: Accommodations are available in Richmond at the Sheraton Motor Inn, Holiday Inn, and Howard Johnson's.

The city of Richmond also features the state capitol building, several museums, and the White House of the Confederacy.

Ticket information: No charge

WASHINGTON

Seattle Arts Festival: Bumbershoot

Seattle Center, 305 Harrison St., Seattle, Wash. 98109

Jazz, popular, and classical

Labor Day weekend

Begun in 1971, Bumbershoot is an annual celebration of the arts in the Pacific Northwest which focuses primarily on music while also featuring visual arts and crafts, theater, dance, film, literature, and other performing special projects. The music section is oriented toward jazz and classical music with some popular fusion forms. Overall, some 50 events are jazz, 20 classical, 15 popular, with about 100 additional events. Oscar Peterson, Vassar Clements, Pat Metheny, Jimmy Buffet, the Northwest Chamber Orchestra, and the Seattle Symphony are among those who have performed in recent years.

Events take place at Seattle Center, 1 mile from downtown Seattle. There are 4 covered halls: Opera House (3,200 seats), Playhouse (900), Arena (6,000), and Coliseum (15,000). Outdoor stages include the Mural Amphitheater (3,000) with other smaller stages around this urban park. Other indoor stages are set up in multipurpose halls and rooms.

Director: Jim Royce

Sponsors: City of Seattle, Seattle Center, Seattle Arts Commission, and the Seattle Parks Dept.

Accommodations: Dozens of hotels are within walking distance.

Other points of interest include the Space Needle restaurant (600 feet high), Pacific Science Center, and the Seattle Art Museum.

Ticket information: Tickets costs from $1 to $7. For tickets, write to Bumbershoot, 305 Harrison St., Seattle, Wash. 98109

WISCONSIN

Equinox Festival
Capital Concourse, Madison, Wis.
Music, dance, theater
Mid-September
This extravagant 3-day festival features
more than 200 performers on 5 stages
set up in the State Capital Square in the
middle of Madison. Local and regional
musicians, dancers, thespians and mime
performers participate. Nationally known
artists and groups are also brought in.
The Festival presents workshops, and a
number of open-mike sessions. There is
a lively children's area. Of special note is
the ethnic food fair which accompanies
the Festival.
Director: Charles Moore
Sponsor: University YMCA
Accommodations/other items of interest
in area: There are many hotels and motels
in Madison and the surrounding areas.
There is no camping at the Festival, but
there are nearby parks where it is allowed.
Madison is on an isthmus. There are 4
lakes with small-craft sailing. There are
many bike routes, large parks and sites
of historical interest. Indian summers in
Madison are beautiful.
Ticket information: Admission is free

Summerfest
200 N. Harbor Dr., Milwaukee, Wisc.
53202
Varied program
Late June through early July
This large and varied festival is 11-12
days long and 50 acres wide. Among the
3 largest festivals in the nation, it draws
over ½ million visitors each year. On 5
stages, nearly 150 bands perform in a
wide variety of musical styles. Extra-
musical events include a circus, zoo,
comedy tent, bike and canoe races and
children's theater, to name only a few.
The Festival boasts 25 places to eat.
Director: James T. Butler
Sponsors: Milwaukee civic, corporate,
and private organizations
Accommodations: All major motels and
hotels have branches in Milwaukee. There
is no camping on the Festival grounds,
but there is picnicking.
Ticket information: Admission is $2.50
in advance or $3 at the gate. For tickets,
write to the Festival at the above address
with a check and self-addressed stamped
envelope.
How to get there: The Festival is on
Milwaukee's Lakefront, 2 blocks E. of
downtown.

INTERNATIONAL

CLASSICAL

AUSTRALIA

North Queensland Festival of Arts and Opera
Box 882, Innisfail, North Queensland 4860, Australia
Classical (opera, dance, theater)
First 3 weeks in December
This annual performing arts festival was founded in 1967 and sponsors a series of performances in classical music, opera, dance, and theater over a 3-week period. Artists who have performed at past festivals include Ron Maconaghie, Lorraine Davies-Griffiths, Phyllis Ball, Catherine Duval, and John Curro. Performances take place in 2 indoor facilities: City Hall, with a capacity of 100, and the Conservatorium Theatrette, which seats 220.
Director: A. L. Martinuzzi
Sponsor: North Queensland Conservatorium of Music
Accommodations: There are many hotels and motels in Innisfail
Ticket information: Tickets cost from 5 to 7.80 Australian dollars

AUSTRIA

Bregenz Festival
A 6900 Bregenz, Kornmarkstrasse 6, Austria
Classical
Mid-July through mid-August
This annual event has been held since 1946 in the Austrian town of Bregenz, which is on Lake Constance at the edge of the Alps, and 1,300 ft. above sea level. Concerts are held on the world's largest aquatic stage, an uncovered facility which seats 4,300. The Festival extends over a 1-month period and also includes the presentation of operas and plays, performed in an indoor hall with a seating capacity of 640. The Vienna Symphony Orchestra is the resident orchestra at the event. Performers at past concerts have included André Bernard, Jorg Demus, Wilhelm Kempff, the Budapest Madrigal Ensemble, and the Chorus of the Vienna State Opera. In 1979, *Tartuffe* was produced at the Festival by Ingmar Bergman.
Director: Professor Ernst Bär
Accommodations/other items of interest in area: For information about accommodations, write to Bregenz Tourist Office, Inselstrasse 15/Seestrasse, A-6900, Bregenz, Austria (tel. 05574-23391/92).
Since Bregenz lies in the intersection of 4 countries, it is well suited to sightseeing. The tropical island of Mainau is nearby as well.
Ticket information: For tickets, write to Bregenzer Festspiele, A 6901 Bregenz, Postfach 119, Austria; or in the U.S., Mrs. Rosemarie Fliegel, Suite 207, 545 Fifth Ave., New York, N.Y. Tickets range in price from 150 to 550 schillings.

Bürgenländische Festspiele
A-7072 Mörbisch am See, Austria
Classical (operetta) and theater
May to August
The Bürgenländische Festspiele are:
(1) the Burgspiele Forchtenstein, which consists of plays and is given from the end of May to the end of June; and
(2) the Seespiele Mörbisch, which takes place from the end of July to the end of August. Operettas are presented.
Director: Prof. Fred Liewehr

Carinthian Summer Music Festival
During festival: Sekretariat
Carinthischer Sommer, A-9570 Ossiach,
Austria (tel. 04243-510 or 502)
Until end of May: Franz-Josefs-Kai 65,
A-1010 Vienna, Austria (tel. 0222-
311292)
Classical (ballet and theater)
June to August
In addition to the concert and stage
events the Festival presents seminars,
courses, lectures, and workshops
Director: Professor Helmut Wobisch

Mozart Festival Week
Internationale Stiftung Mozarteum,
Postfach 34, A-5024 Salzburg, Austria
Classical
January to February

Operetta Weeks
Herrengasse 32, A-4820 Bad Ischl,
Austria
Operettas
July to September
Director: Eduard Macku
Ticket information: Write to Operetten-
gemeinde, Herrengasse 32, A-4820
Bad Ischl, Austria (tel. 06132-3839)

Osterfestspiele (Easter Festival)
Festspielhaus, A-5010 Salzburg, Austria
Classical and opera
Week before Easter (8 days)
Founded in 1961 by Herbert von
Karajan, this 8-day festival takes place
in Salzburg each year during the week
before Easter. Held indoors in a concert
hall with a seating capacity of 2,170,
this event always features Herbert von
Karajan. In 1979, he conducted the
Berlin Philharmonic in Wagner's
Parsifal as well as in Mozart's *Requiem*
(KV 626), among other classical works.
Winter lasts a long time in Salzburg, and
patrons are advised to bring along suit-
able clothing.
Director: Herbert von Karajan
Sponsor: City of Salzburg
Accommodations: There are many
hotels in Salzburg, ranging from first-
class to pensions
Ticket information: Tickets may be purchased in advance by writing. They are
to be purchased for a set of 3 concerts
and range in price from 1,900 to 5,000
schillings.

Salzburg Festival
Hofstallgasse 1, 5010 Salzburg, Austria
Classical (orchestral and chamber) and
opera
Late July to late August
The 1st opera was performed in Salzburg
in 1616, and since that time, the city has
grown to have a cultural tradition in
music unequaled in Europe. Annual
Mozart music festivals began here in
1842, and in 1877 the Vienna Philharmonic started to visit this city. The
Salzburg Festival as it is known today
was founded in 1919, and has taken
place annually since then. Today, the
Festival consists of a series of concerts,
operas, solo recitals, and plays that take
place each night over the 1-month
period from the end of July to the end
of August. Over the years the Festival
has been host to the best-known artists
and performers of the world, recently
including Herbert von Karajan, the
Berlin Philharmonic, the Vienna Philharmonic, Leonard Bernstein, Sviatoslav
Richter, and Maximilian Schell.
As the Festival grew in size and reputation, the city of Salzburg erected concert halls specifically for these events;
the large Festival House and the small
Festival House, to name a few. Together,
these seat 3,500 people. In addition,
there is an open-air facility in the
Cathedral Square, which has a seating
capacity of 2,100. Evening dress is required at all performances.
Directors: Josef Kaut, President; Otto
Sertl, Director
Sponsor: Austrian government
Accommodations: There are many
hotels and pensions in Salzburg. Camping is permitted in designated areas on
the outskirts of the city; trailer facilities are available.
Ticket information: Prices are as follows
for performances: operas, 400 to 1800
schillings; concerts, 200 to 900 schillings; and plays, 100 to 600 schillings.
Tickets may be ordered until January
8, by writing to Salzburger Festspiele,
Ticket Office, Hofstallgasse 1, 5010
Salzburg, Austria.
How to get there: All concert halls are
located in the center of the city

**Schubertiade Hohenems (Hohenems
Schubert Festival)**
A-6845 Hohenems, Schlossplatz 8, P.O.
Box 61, Austria (tel. 05576-2091)

Classical (Schubert)
Mid- to late June (2 weeks)
This annual 2-week festival was founded in 1977 with the intention of presenting, over a ten-year period, all the works of Schubert, in roughly chronological order. The Schubertiade takes place in the Palace of Hohenems, a building of the early 17th century. Concerts are held in 2 small indoor rooms, one which seats 350 and the other 700, and in the courtyard of the palace, which can be covered by canvas in the event of rain. Those who have performed at the lieder recitals, choir concerts, piano recitals, chamber concerts, and orchestra concerts in the past include the Vienna Philharmonic, Sviatoslav Richter, Elizabeth Schwartzkopf, Karl Böhm, and the Melos-Quartet.
Director: Hermann Prey, Artistic
Accommodations: For information regarding accommodations, contact the Festival Office, A-6845 Hohenems, P.O. Box 61, Austria.
Ticket information: Tickets range in price from 100 to 500 schillings. They can be obtained at the Hohenems Palace Box Office starting in mid-May or by mail through the Festival Office.

Styrian Autumn
Mandellstrasse 38, A-8010 Graz, Austria
Classical and theater
September to November
The Festival originated in 1968 and features avant-garde music and drama
Director: Dr. Paul Kaufmann
Ticket information: Write to Zentralkartenburo, Herrengasse 7, A-8010 Graz, Austria; or, Tageskasse der Vereinigten Buhnen, Landhausgasse 7, A-8010 Graz, Austria

BELGIUM

Festival de Wallonie (Festival of Wallonia)
12 rue Saintraint, 5000 Namur, Belgium (tel. 081-712700)
Classical
Mid-June to mid-October
Classical music is celebrated at this festival each year from June to October in the many concert halls, churches, and abbeys in the Walloon region of Belgium. Eight major organizations sponsor this event, which features concerts in nine different towns and cities of Belgium—including Brussels, Liege, Chimay, and Stavelot—almost every night during the course of the Festival. There is equal emphasis here on symphonic and chamber orchestra music. Among those who have participated at recent festivals are Jean-Pierre Rampal, the Medici String Quartet, the Ensemble Suzuki of London, the National Orchestra of Belgium, the Scottish Baroque Ensemble, and Munich's Orchestra Pro Arte.
Director: Gouverneur Vars
Sponsors: Bell Telephone, Belgian Shell S.A., IBM, Groupe Bruxelles Lambert, Sabena, Loterie National, C.G.E.R., Ciment d'Obourg
Accommodations: For information about accommodations in Belgium, contact 1000 Bruxelles, Tourisme-Information-Bruxelles, rue Marché-aux-Herbes 61, Belgium (tel. (02)513-8940)
Ticket information: Admission ranges from 100 to 350 francs; for information regarding advance tickets, contact Tourisme-Information-Bruxelles, rue de la Montagne, 1000 Bruxelles, Belgium

BRAZIL

Festival Villa-Lobos
Museu Villa-Lobos, rua da Imprensa 16,
Rio de Janeiro 20.030, Brazil
Classical
November
This festival includes concerts, recitals,
lectures, and an international choral
contest. Past performances have been
by the Orquestra Sinfonica Brasileira,
Orquestra Sinfonica Nacional and Choral
of Municipal Theater, with guest soloists.
Events are held at the Municipal Theater,
which seats 4,000; and at Sala Cecilia
Meireles, which seats 1,000. The Festival
is in November, which is summer in
Brazil.
Director: Arminda Villa-Lobos
Sponsor: FUNARTE (Ministerio de
Educacao e Cultura)
Accommodations: Lodging is available
at Hotel Argentina
Ticket information: Admission is free

BULGARIA

International Festival of Chamber Music
Boris Dischlier St., 4000 Plovdiv,
Bulgaria
Classical
September
The Festival in Plovdiv was founded in
1964
Director: Angel Christov

CZECHOSLO-VAKIA

Bratislava Music Festival
c/o Secretariate of the Bratislava Music Festival, Palackeho 2, 89820 Bratislava, Czechoslovakia (tel. 33-72-52 or 33-10-64)
Classical
October
Concerts are given in a number of locations: the concert hall of the Slovak Philharmonic (700 seats), the Slovak National Theater (500 seats), the concert hall of the Czechoslovak Radio (200 seats), Mirror Hall of the Principal Palace (120 seats), the concert hall of Bratislava Castle (100 seats), and the concert hall in Clarist Church (100 seats).
Bratislava has temperate weather in fall.
Director: Dr. L. Mokry
Accommodations: Reservations at hotels can be made through the Czechoslovak travel agencies Cedok, CKM, Slavkoturist, and Tatratour. There is no camping.
Ticket information: For ticket information write to the Secretariate of the Bratislava Music Festival at the above address. Telex 093485.

DENMARK

Bronholm Music Festival
Praestevaenget 1, DK-3720 Akirkeby, Denmark (tel. 03-974103)
Classical (chamber music)
July to August
This festival started 10 years ago and takes place in churches all over Bornholm

Sorø Organ Festival
c/o Sorø Tourist Office
DK-4180 Sorø, Denmark
(tel. 03-630269)
Classical (chamber music, orchestral programs, organ recitals)
June to August (Wednesdays)
The concerts take place in the historic Sorø Church, erected from 1165 to 1200. Many kings and famous people of the Middle Ages are buried here: Bishop Absalon, founder of Copenhagen and the Abbey in Sorø, and Absalon's brother Esbern Snare; Christopher II and his son Valdemar Atterdag (who regained the kingdom which had been pawned by his father); and Ludvig Holberg, the Danish Molière.
The exquisite baroque interior originates from the 17th and 18th centuries. The painting at the altar is Wuchters.
Directors: Asger Larsen, Musical Director (tel. 03-631553); and Knud Vad, Artistic Director

EAST GERMANY

Berliner Festtage
Scharrenstrasse 17, DDR-102 Berlin, East Germany
Classical (concerts and opera), theater, ballet
September to October
Director: Wolfgang Lippert
Ticket information: Prices for tickets range from 2 to 20 marks

ENGLAND

BBC Henry Wood Promenade Concerts
Royal Albert Hall, London, England
Classical
Fifty-six consecutive concerts from mid-July to mid-September
In 1895 the "Proms" began as an impresario's latest scheme for attracting the public. The idea of Proms was not new—the very word is French—and concerts at which a partly strolling audience could come and go had originated in Paris. They were later introduced to England, some 60 years before the 1895 Proms started. The then unknown Henry Wood was chosen as sole conductor of the concerts. The earliest programs deliberately tried to attract audiences with popular concoctions of ballads, arias, light overtures and the like, but these gradually dropped out and the Proms became the way to hear all 9 symphonies by Beethoven in one season; and new music was constantly offered, rehearsed, and performed. Henry Wood introduced works by Sibelius, Rachmaninof, Scriabin, Schoenberg, and many others, for the 1st time in England.
In the early 1960s, when Sir William Glock became Music Controller of the BBC, there was a move to review the Proms to give them a bolder purpose: the repertoire was extended backward and forward in time, complete operas were performed, chamber music was introduced, and the number of guest conductors and orchestras was increased. The Proms are performed in Royal Albert Hall, which seats 7,300.
Sponsor: British Broadcasting Corporation, London
Ticket information: Prices range from £.60 (promenade) to £4. Write to Royal Albert Hall Box Office, London SW7 2AP, England.

Bexhill-On-Sea Festival of Music
De La Warr Pavilion, Marina, Bexhill-On-Sea, East Sussex, England
Classical
Late May
This 3-day festival features 3 concerts by a symphony orchestra. Recent guest orchestras have been the Royal Liverpool Philharmonic Orchestra, Halle

Orchestra, City of Birmingham Orchestra, and Bournemouth Symphony Orchestra. Festival events also include pre-concert dinners, after- concert dancing, and wine tastings.

Performances are held in a concert hall seating 1,100.

Director: David Blake

Sponsor: Rother District Council, East Sussex

Accommodations/other items of interest in area: Hotel and guest house accommodations and camping facilities are all available; for information write Rother District Council, De La Warr Pavilion, Bexhill-On-Sea, Sussex TN40 1DP, England.

Festival patrons may enjoy the beaches and glorious countryside, and may find the area's museums, historic homes, castles, and churches of interest.

Ticket information: Admission ranges from about £1.90 to £3.40

How to get there: Maps are available from Rother District Council

Cheltenham International Festival of Music

Festival Office, Town Hall, Cheltenham, Gloucestershire GL50 1QA, England

Classical

Early July

Started in 1945 to promote contemporary British music, the Festival has grown to become an international event, with world-class artists and an annual audience of over 10,000 for 10 days of concerts, recitals, and opera. Regular festival features are the commissioning and 1st performance of the work of the best modern British composers, the String Quartet series which have recently featured the complete quartets of Beethoven, Mozart and Shostakovich, and Master Classes given by first-rate artists.

Events are held in Town Hall, which seats 1,000; Pittville Pump Room, seating 350; and, for opera, Everyman Theater, which seats 600.

Director: Jaon Manduell, Esq.

Accommodations/other items of interest in area: For information on accommodations and points of interest in the area write to Tourist Information Centre, Municipal Offices, The Promenade, Cheltenham Spa, England.

Cheltenham Spa is one of England's most beautiful inland resorts.

Ticket information: Admission varies according to the event. For information and bookings write to the Festival, enclosing a self-addressed, stamped envelope.

How to get there: Centrally located Cheltenham is 2 hours from Heathrow (London's airport), and 1½ hours from Birmingham and Bristol airports. Routes will be signposted.

Chester Summer Music Festival

6 Northway, Curzon Park, Chester CH4 8BB, England

Classical

July

This 1-week classical music festival has featured such guest artists as Dame Janet Baker, Peter Katin, the Royal Liverpool Philharmonic Orchestra, and the Richard Hickox Orchestra. The Festival was founded in 1978.

Events are held in Chester's cathedral, which seats 1,400, at Town Hall, seating 420, in Gateway Theatre, which seats 450, and at St. John's Church, seating 400.

Director: Martin Merry

Sponsors: Northwest Arts Association and Chester County Council

Accommodations/other items of interest in area: Lodging is available at Grosvenor Hotel, Blossoms Hotel, Queen Hotel, and Chester. There is picnicking.

Chester is a Roman city founded in AD 79. It has a complete circle of Roman walls, a fine cathedral, and unique rows. Chester is very close to North Wales.

Ticket information: Admission ranges from £.80 to £4

Covent Garden Proms

Royal Opera House, Covent Garden, London, England

Opera and ballet

April

This 6-day festival features performances by the Royal Opera and the Royal Ballet at the Royal Opera House in Covent Garden. Recently performed operas include *Parsifal, Il Barbiere di Siviglia,* and *Don Carlos*; recently performed ballets include *Swan Lake, Mayerling,* and a program consisting of *Enigma Variations* and *Symphonic Variations.* There are 700 places available per performance.

Sponsor: Midland Bank

Accommodations: Lodging is readily

available in London
Ticket information: Tickets range from
£1 to £17.50. They are available 1 hour
before performance.

Edington Music Festival
Edington Priory Church, Westbury,
Wiltshire, England
Choral church services
Late August
For one week each August, cathedral
and collegiate choristers come together
to sing choral services in Edington's
priory church. The Festival, held annually since 1956, was founded to give
former choral scholars and choristers
a chance to once again sing daily choral
services. In addition, it raised money for
the restoration of the church, which is
the best example of a 14th-century
collegiate church in southern England.
The scope of the Festival music has
broadened over the years. Many of the
masses, anthems, and services sung
during the past few years are new to
the cathedral repertoire, and the Festival
itself has commissioned new works.
Members of the choirs are drawn from
many different cathedrals and collegiate schools from all over England.
Director: John Hardy
Accommodations/other items of interest
in area: Details of accommodations
and other facilities in the area can be
obtained from the Information Secretary, Gilbert Hardwick, Timber Ridge,
Edington, near Westbury, Wiltshire
BA13 4QW, England (please send postage). Tel. Bratton 430.
There are many interesting places to visit
in the Edington vicinity, including the
Westbury White Horse, the Roman
Baths at Bath, Longleat near Warminster,
Stourhead Gardens, Lacock Abbey, and
Stonehenge.
Ticket information: All the music is
sung in the context of choral church
services, for which there are neither
tickets nor reserved seats
How to get there: Edington is a small
village in Wiltshire. Forty minutes' drive
from Bath or Salisbury, it lies 4 miles
E. of Westbury (the nearest railway station) on the B3098 road.

English Bach Festival
15 South Eaton Place, London SW1,
England
Classical

April and May
The English Bach Festival Trust was
founded in 1962 by harpsichordist
Lina Lalandi; its presidents have been
Albert Schweitzer, Igor Stravinsky, and,
currently, Leonard Bernstein. Each year
the English Bach Festival has definite
themes, chosen and illustrated by means
of research and careful planning, and
organized to the highest international
standards of performance by the best
artists available. The English Bach Festival has been called England's leading
music festival, an event of 1st class
artistic importance.
Concerts take place in Royal Festival
Hall, which seats 2,800; Queen Elizabeth Hall, seating 1,200; and Royal
Albert Hall, which seats 5,500.
Director: Lina Lalandi OBE
Sponsor: Arts Council of Great Britain
Accommodations: Accommodations
are readily available in London
Ticket information: Admission ranges
from £.70 to £4. Tickets can be obtained
from the Royal Festival Hall Box Office,
London SE1, England.

Fakenham Festival of Music and the Arts
Festival Office, Royal Oak House, Oak
St., Fakenham, Norfolk, England
Classical, ballet, choral, theater
May (odd-numbered years)
The small town of Fakenham (population 5,000) prides itself on its 10-day
festival which features 2 orchestral con-
certs, choral works, theater, ballet, an
art lecture, exhibitions, and celebrity
concerts. Events take place at Fakenham
Parish Church, which seats 600; Fakenham Community Centre, which seats
350; and at other sites in the town.
This festival has been growing steadily
since it began in 1963, and is, according
to its many local supporters, the best
value of the year.
Director: D. J. F. Ford
Sponsors: Eastern Arts Association,
Norfolk County Council, others
Accommodations/other items of interest
in area: Hotel accommodations are available at the Crown Hotel on Market
Place, and at the Limes Hotel on Bridge
Street, both in Fakenham. Camping is
allowed at a cost of about £1 per caravan. Trailers are also allowed.
Not far from Fakenham are a sports

THE CHORUS IN WAGNER'S *THE FLYING DUTCHMAN* AT THE BAYREUTH FESTIVAL. (PHOTO PREVIOUS PAGE)

center, the National Hunt Racecourse,
a coastal bird sanctuary, and a number
of stately homes including the Queen's
estate at Sandringham.
Ticket information: The purchase of the
festival brochure for about £3.50 en-
titles the buyer to attend every concert
without further charge
How to get there: Fakenham is in Norfolk 25 miles northwest of Norwich

Glyndebourne Festival Opera
Lewes, Sussex, England
Opera
Late May through early August
The Glyndebourne Festival, founded
in 1934, at first confined its repertoire
to Mozart. It has broadened over the
years, and operas from the earliest
baroque to modern works are now performed. Five operas are presented each
season, in a festival running from the
3rd week of May to the 1st week of
August. The principal artists come from
many different countries and the chorus
is made up of carefully selected young
British singers.
Glyndebourne Opera House seats 830.
Performances begin early, and there is
a long intermission during which dinner
is served in restaurants and patrons
picnic in the gardens. Evening dress is
recommended but not obligatory; dark
suits or velvet jackets for the men and
long or short dresses for the ladies can
always be seen.
Director: Moran Caplat, C.B.E.
Accommodations: Accommodations are
readily available in the area. A special
train and coach service leaves Victoria
Station, returning to London after the
performance. There is no camping.
Ticket information: Admission ranges
from £8 to £17.50. For tickets write to
Box Office, Glyndebourne, Lewes, East
Sussex BN8 5UU, England.

Leeds Musical Festival
40 Park Lane, Leeds 1, England
Classical (choral, orchestral, chamber)
May
Since 1858 this historic 2-week festival
of choral, orchestral, and chamber music
has attracted music lovers to Leeds.
Each year a rich and varied classical pro-
gram is performed by Leeds Festival
Chorus and other Leeds choirs, the BBC
Symphony Orchestra and BBC Northern

Symphony Orchestra, City of Birmingham Symphony Orchestra and Birmingham Chamber Orchestra, and chamber
and other groups such as Medici String
Quartet, Emerson Wind Ensemble, Cam-
bridge Buskers and the Monks of Ample-
forth Abbey.
Concerts are held in Leeds Town Hall,
seating 1,200, Leeds Univ., which seats
450, Leeds Parish Church, seating 1,100,
Leeds Grammar School, which seats
500, and other smaller venues.
Director: H. C. Kendall
Accommodations/other items of interest
in area: A comprehensive listing of
hotels and guest houses is available from
Tourist Information Centre, Central
Library, Leeds LS1 3AB, England.
Bookings at some hotels may be made
through the Tourist Information Centre
for a fee of £.35 per booking.
Leeds Music Library, City Museum, and
points of historical importance may be
of interest to festival patrons.
Ticket information: Admission ranges
from £1 to £5. Tickets can be obtained
from R. Barker and Co., Ltd., Festival
Booking Office, 91 The Headrow, Leeds
1, England. Enclose a stamped, self-
addressed envelope with your inquiry
or order.
How to get there: From London follow
the M1 Motorway. Follow road signs
within the city boundaries.

Three Choirs Festival
25 Castle St., Hereford, England
Classical
Mid- to late August
The oldest musical festival in Europe,
now over 250 years old, the Three
Choirs Festival is held in Gloucester,
Worcester, and Hereford for a week
each year in turn. Primarily an occasion
for the performance of major choral
works, there are also recitals and lectures. Concerts take place in the 3 cities'
cathedrals.
The Festival Chorus of some 280 voices
is drawn from the Choral Societies of
the 3 cities and forms the backbone of
the modern festival.
Director: Donald Hunt
Sponsors: The Arts Council of Great
Britain and others
Ticket information: Series tickets range
from £25 to £35 according to seating

Tilford Bach Festival
Tilford Church (near Farnham), Surrey,
England
Classical
Mid-May for 4 days
In 1953, the Tilford Bach Society was
formed with a view to enlisting 100 sub-
scribing members to provide financial
help in "the annual promotion of a
festival of the music of Bach, his pre-
decessors, contemporaries, and succes-
sors, in a manner most consistent with
the style and demands of the period."
The continuing result is the annual
Tilford Bach Festival, which presents
4 consecutive nightly concerts in the
village church of Tilford. Performers
include the Tilford Bach Choir, Orchestra, and Ensemble, as well as vocal
soloists, all fully professional.
The capacity of the church is 250.
Director: Deny Darlow
Sponsors: Financial support given by the
South East Arts Assn. in conjunction
with the Arts Council of Great Britain;
also, the Waverly District Council
Accommodations/other items of interest
in area: The secretary will gladly supply
details of accommodations on request.
Write to Miss Barbara Gregory, Hon.
Sec., Tilford Bach Society, Ling Lea,
Frensham, Farnham, Surrey GU10 3AZ,
England. Tel. Frensham 2677.
Other items of interest in the area in-
clude Farnham Castle, the towns of
Guilford and Haslemere, and the South
Coast.
Ticket information: Admission ranges
from £1.50 to £2.50. For tickets, write
to the secretary.
How to get there: There is a direct rail
line from Waterloo to Farnham and
there is taxi service from Farnham (3
miles). There is an infrequent bus. Visitors can be met at Farnham Station by
prior arrangement (no charge).

Windsor Festival
Dial House, Englefield Green, Surrey,
England
Classical
Mid- through late September
The 15-day Windsor Festival of classical
music, now in its 10th year, has pre-
sented such artists as Artur Rubenstein,
Yehudi Menuhin, and Janet Baker, in
addition to the London Symphony
Orchestra, the Royal Philharmonic
Orchestra, and the English Chamber
Orchestra. Concerts are held in the
State Apartments of Windsor Castle,
St. George's Chapel, Eton College, and
the Theatre Royal. In addition to the
concerts there are tours of Eton College
and a visual arts exhibition.
Director: Laurence West
Sponsors: Arts Council of Great Bri-
tain, Eastern Authorities Orchestral
Association, Local Councils.
Accommodations: For information on
accommodations, write to Windsor
Tourist Information Centre, Windsor
and Eton Central Station, England
Ticket information: Prices range from
£1 to £7. For tickets, write to Windsor
Festival Box Office, 140 Peascod Street,
Windsor, Berkshire, England (tel. Wind-
sor 51696).

FINLAND

Jyväskylä Arts Festival
Kauppakatu 41 B 11, SF-40100
Jyväskylä, Finland
Classical
June to July
The Festival was begun in 1956. Previous
participants include the Moscow Cham-
ber Orchestra, the New York Pro Arte
Chamber Orchestra, Garrick Ohlsson,
Emil Gillels, Leonid Kogan, John Ogdon,
Kenneth Gilbert, and André Navarra.
Performances take place in the Univer-
sity Hall (seats 755), Musica Chamber
Music Hall (seats 300), Taulumäki
Church (seats 1,000), and the Jyväskylä
City Church (seats 600).
Director: Eeva Kainulainen
Accommodations/other items of interest
in area: Hotels: Raatihotelli, Asemakatu
2, SF-40100 Jyväskylä 10, Finland; and
Cumulus, Väinönkatu 5, SF-40100
Jyväskylä 10, Finland. Camping and
picnicking facilities are available.
Also of interest in the area are numerous
museums (Museum of Central Finland,
Aviation Museum) and Lake Päijänne.
Ticket information: Tickets are 10 to
40 Finnish marks. Write to the above
address or to Lippupalvelu Oy, Manner-
heimintie 5, SF00100 Helsinki 10,
Finland.
How to get there: By air from Helsinki
or by train from Helsinki and Turku

Kuhmo Chamber Music Festival
Kuhmo, Finland
Classical (chamber music)
Late July (1 week)
The Festival is one of those "impossible"
idealistic events that have proved a success. Founded in 1970 by a few young
artists who gathered to play chamber
music in a remote country village deep
in the forests of Finland, it has
developed into an event of international
renown. The concerts are held in the
Kuhmo Church and the concert hall,
with a combined seating capacity of
1,400. Performers at past festivals have
included the Moscow Baroque Quartet,
Alban Berg Quartet, Georgia Quartet,
Edward Auer, and Eli Goren. Featured
at the 10th Festival, in 1980, will be
the contemporary Soviet composer
Arvo Pärt.

An additional offering is a yearly 1-week
Music Course, starting before the Festival and continuing during it. For information and applications, write to
Yoshiko Arai, Toppelundintie 5B9,
02170 Espoo 17, Finland.
Director: Yoshiko Arai, Artistic
Director; Tuulikki Karjalainen, Administrative Director
Accommodations/other items of interest
in area: Camping facilities are available,
both tents (price: 8 to 16 Finnish marks)
and cabins (price: 40 to 50 Finnish
marks). For other accommodations,
write to Kuhmo Travel Service, 88900
Kuhmo, Finland.
Kuhmo, situated deep in the forests of
Kainuu and near the Lentua rapids,
offers many outdoor activities such as
fishing, hunting, and roaming the
wilderness.
Ticket information: Ticket prices range
from 8 to 30 Finnish marks. For advance
booking, write to Ticket Service,
Mannerhiemintie 5, 00100 Helsinki 10,
Finland; or Kuhmo Travel Service,
88900 Kuhmo, Finland.
How to get there: There are flights
from Helsinki to Kajaani, the town
nearest Kuhmo

Lahti Organ Festival
Kirkkokatu 5, SF-151100 Lahti 11,
Finland
Classical
August
In addition to organ concerts, the Festi-
val presents an organ competition for
young organists plus seminars, courses,
and exhibitions.
Concerts take place in churches, mu-
seums, and concert halls.
Director: Aimo Kankanen

Savonlinna Opera Festival
Olavinkatu 35, SF-57130 Savonlinna 13,
Finland
Opera and classical
July
Savonlinna has become internationally
recognized as a lively stage for modern
Finnish opera and unusually fresh productions of world classics. For 3 weeks
in July, operas are performed for audiences of up to 2,000 in the sheltered
courtyard of Olavinlinna, a medieval
castle built in 1475. Other concerts take
place in schools and churches in Savonlinna during the Festival season.

Opera in Olavinlinna, begun in 1912, enjoys the support of the local populace and national Finnish leaders.
For opera performances in the castle, warm clothing is recommended.
Director: Martti Talvela, Artistic Director
Accommodations/other items of interest in area: For information on lodging contact Savonlinna Tourist Office, Olavinkatu 35, SF-57130 Savonlinna 13, Finland. Camping is allowed.
Savonlinna, a spa resort, is in the heart of the Saimaa Region, an undivided lake district and one of the last wilderness areas in Europe. Theater, museums, art exhibitions, and facilities for most sports are offered visitors to the Festival.
Ticket information: Admission is 80 to 100 Finnish marks for opera performances and 10 to 50 Finnish marks for concerts. To obtain tickets contact the Festival at the above address.

FRANCE

Albi Music Festival
Palais de la Berbie, F-81000 Albi, France
Classical
Mid-July through early August
Director: Jean-Pierre Wallez, Artistic Director
Accommodations: For camping information, write to Gîtes Camping à la ferme, Maison des Agriculteurs, B.P. 89, F-81003 Albi, France (tel.543981)
Ticket information: Write to the Palais de la Berbie (during the Festival) or call 542230

Europa Cantat
A Coeur Joie, 8 rue de la Bourse, 69289, Lyon Cedex 1, France
Choral
Late July to early August
This international choral festival is in its 7th year. The Festival site changes each year, and in 1979 it was held in Lucerne, Switzerland. Participants are limited to 3,000, but they come from as many as 20 countries. The program is similar each year: there are the main concerts, which consist of works for choirs a cappella as well as with orchestras; and there are individual concerts given by each participating choir. The Festival takes place over a 10-day period in the summer, and it is sponsored by A Coeur Joie, a European foundation for youth choirs.
Sponsor: A Coeur Joie
Accommodations: Address all inquiries about location and accommodations to A Coeur Joie, at the above address in Lyon.
Ticket information: All information regarding tickets, as well as entry requirements for participants, can be obtained from A Coeur Joie

Festival d'Automne a Paris
156 rue de Rivoli, 75001-Paris, France
Contemporary music, theater, art, dance
End of September to beginning of December
Begun in 1972, at this festival representatives from as many as 30 countries celebrate contemporary arts. Performers in recent years have included Meredith Monk, Charlemagne Palestine, Joan La Barbara, John Adams, Paul Dresher,

TWO YOUNGSTERS GETTING A CLOSE-UP VIEW OF A DOUBLE BASS.

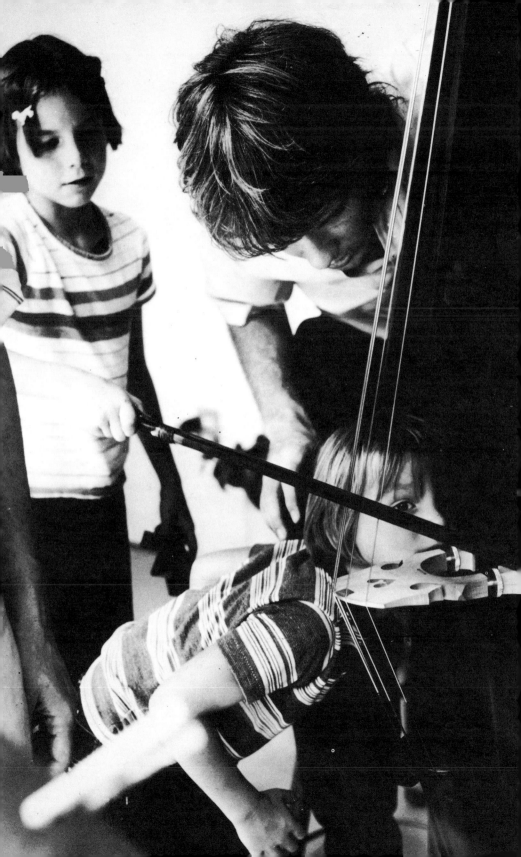

and Merce Cunningham.
The Festival takes place at different
sites throughout Paris.
Director: Michel Guy
Sponsors: City of Paris and others

Festival d'Avignon—Jean Vilar (Avignon Festival—Jean Vilar)
8 bis rue de Mons, 8400 Avignon, France
Sacred music, musical theater, organ,
theater, dance, cinema
Mid-July to early August
This annual festival was founded in
1947, during the French cultural movement that followed the Second World
War. It was created by the stage director Jean Vilar, who headed the program
until his death in 1971. Held over a 3-
week period in the summer, this festival
devotes itself primarily to theater and
musical theater, but is also sponsors
sacred music concerts and organ solos,
held in the Notre Dame des Doms. In
1979, soloists included Francois Delor,
Christopher Stenbridge, and Sergio
Vartolo.
Accommodations: For information
about hotel accommodations and campgrounds in the area, contact Chambre
de Tourisme de Vaucluse, B.P. 147,
84008 Avignon Cedex, France (tel.
90-864342)
Ticket information: Tickets range in
price from 16 to 40 francs. Starting June
1, they can be ordered by mail from
Bureau du Festival, 84000 Avignon,
France, or by calling 90-862443.

Festival J. S. Bach de Mazamet (Bach Festival of Mazamet)
Maison du Tourisme, Square Tournier,
81200 Mazamet, France (tel. 63-612707)
Classical (Bach)
Early September (6 days)
This annual 6-day event features only
the music of Bach. That composer is
honored in a series of organ concerts,
chamber music recitals, and vocal solos
performed by various groups and soloists
of France; recent guests have included
the Chamber Orchestra of Rouen, the
Singers of Saint Eustache, violin soloist
Jean Pierre Berlingen, and soprano
Claudie Saneva, among others.
The Bach Festival was founded in 1965;
concerts are held in churches and con-
cert halls in Mazamet.
Director: R. P. E. Martin, Artistic
Director

Accommodations: For information
about accommodations in the area, contact the Maison du Tourisme
Ticket information: Prices for individual
concerts cost 15 francs for unreserved
seats. Prices for reserved seats range
from 25 to 50 francs; these tickets may
be obtained in advance by writing to the
Maison du Tourisme in Mazamet.
How to get there: The National French
Railroad offers a 20% reduction in the
cost of train tickets to Mazamet on the
presentation of a special festival ticket
that can be obtained from the Maison
du Tourisme in Mazamet

Festival Berlioz
Auditorium Maurice Ravel, 149 Rue
Garibaldi, 69003 Lyon, France
(tel.78-710573)
Classical (Berlioz only)
Mid-September (5 days)
1979 marked the opening of this festival,
which is devoted to the work of Hector
Berlioz. This 5-day event in September
features 5 concerts by the Orchestra of
Lyon, the choir of the Opera of Lyon,
the Royal Society Choir, and French
regional choirs. In future years the
Festival will feature these same performers and will also invite foreign
performers.
Director: Serge Baudo
Sponsor: City of Lyon
Accommodations: There are campgrounds in nearby Dardilly, Meyzieu,
and St.-Genis-Laval; and there are many
hotels in Lyon. For information, contact
Office de Tourisme de Lyon, B.P. 254,
69223 Lyon Cedex 1, France.
Ticket information: Orchestra seats
cost 250 francs, 1st balcony seats cost
120 francs, and 2nd balcony seats cost
80 francs. For information about order-
ing advance tickets, contact Office de
Tourisme de Lyon.

Festival de la Chaise Dieu
Prefecture de la Haute-Loire, F-43012
Le Puy Cedex, France
Classical
Late August to early September
Such musicians as Cziffra, Yehudi
Menuhin, Mstislav Rostropovich and
Marie-Claire Alain have performed at the
Festival de la Chaise Dieu.
Performances include music from the
15th through the 20th centuries.
Director: Guy Ramona

Ticket information: Tickets range from 30 to 160 francs. Write to Agence Velay-Voyages, 37 Place du Breuil, F-43000 Le Puy, France (tel. 71-093888 or 71-092274).

Festival Estival de Paris

5 place des Ternes, 75017, Paris, France (tel. 227-1268)
Classical (orchestral and chamber)
Mid-July to late September
This annual summer-long festival is in its 15th year. The program sponsors symphonic and chamber music concerts every night for the duration of the event, and these performances are held in Paris' most famous churches and historical monuments—the Sainte Chapelle, Saint Sulpice, Saint-Germain-des-Près, and the Conciergerie. A special feature of the Festival is the series it sponsors: every Monday and Tuesday, European vocal and instrumental music in the period of Palladio; every Wednesday, harpsichord and organ music from Europe. The Festival also sponsors workshops, animations, public courses, and exhibitions. In recent years, the Festival was host to Jean-Jacques Grunenwald, Prague's Symposium Musicum, the Sorbonne's Choir, Hopkinson Smith, and Cologne's Musica Antiqua.
Director: Bernard Bonaldi
Sponsors: Radio France, Air France, French Ministery of Culture
Accommodations: There are many hotels in Paris
Ticket information: The regular price of admission is 30 francs; reserved tickets cost 50 francs; those under 25 or over 65 are admitted for 15 francs. Tickets can be purchased at all travel and theater agencies in Paris; they can also be ordered in advance by contacting F.E.P. Office, 4 rue des Prêtres Saint-Séverin, 75005 Paris (tel. (01)633-6177).

Festival de l'Île de France

15 avenue Montaigne, 75008 Paris, France
Chamber music
Early May to early July (1st part) and mid-September to mid-November (2nd part)
Île de France was a former province of north-central France, in the center of the Paris basin, where the Marne and

Ouse rivers join the Seine. Although as a province the area was divided up after the French Revolution, the region boasts a large number of historical monuments, churches, parks and chateaux, in 1975, the French Committee of Tourism came up with the idea of an itinerant music festival to take place in this lush region. During 2 seasons each year, 1 from early May to early July and the other from mid-September to mid-November, the Festival sponsors a series of 5 concerts on a given day in a given location and then moves on to the next location. There are 19 different locations in each season, and they include the Carnavalet Museum in Paris and the Chateau of Fontainebleau, among others.
Many of France's small chamber orchestras provide the music.
Director: Jean Robin
Accommodations: For a program of the Festival with locations and performers, write to Théâtre des Champs-Elysees, 15 Avenue Montaigne, 75008, Paris; or phone 359-7242
Ticket information: Tickets can be obtained at the location of the particular concert. Prices are as follows: 35 francs for all 5 concerts during the day, 20 francs for students and those under 20, and 20 francs for the last concert of the day.
How to get there: Many of the locations are easy to reach from Paris by Metro and train

Festival International d'Art Lyrique et de Musique

Ancien Palais Archeveché, 13100 Aix-en-Provence, France
Classical (opera, symphonic, chamber, recitals)
Mid-July to mid-August (1 month)
This month-long classical music festival celebrated its 30th anniversary in 1978. The program consists of 3 operas, each of which are offered several times during the course of the festival; chamber music concerts, and recitals. Operas are performed in the Theatre of the Archeveché Palace, and the other events are held in the churches, cloisters, abbeys, and châteaux of Aix-en-Provence. Recent guests of the Festival have included the Orchestre du Capitole de Toulouse, the Provence Vocal Ensemble, the Contemporary Choir of the Univ.

of Provence, and soloists Barbara Hendricks, Samuel Ramey, and Michael Devlin.

Also featured during the course of the Festival are lectures, films, expositions, and seminars about music and composers.

Director: Bernard Lefort
Sponsor: Town of Aix-en-Provence
Accommodations: For information about accommodations, write to Office de Tourisme, Place de la Rotande, 13100 Aix-en-provence, France
Ticket information: Admission to operas is from 70 to 220 francs; to concerts, from 25 to 100 francs

Festival International des Milelli (Milelli International Festival)
BP 109, 20177 Ajaccio Cedex, France
Classical (orchestral and opera)
Seven evenings between mid-July and early August
This annual event, a series of 7 concerts and operas, is held on the island of Corsica. Performances are held inside the Milelli Cathedral, which seats 1,000. In 1979, the Festival featured the Orchestra of Provence/Cote d'Azur and a recital by Alexis Weissenberg. Usually there is 1 evening reserved for traditional Corsican music.
Director: Jacques Charpentier
Ticket information: Tickets range in price from 35 to 60 francs

Festival International de Musique de Besançon et de Franche-Comte
Parc des Expositions, B.P. 1913, 25020 Besançon Cedex, France (tel. 81-813532)
Classical (orchestral and chamber music)
Late August to mid-September (2 weeks)
This classical music festival celebrated its 32nd anniversary in 1979. An annual 2-week long event, it features as many as 3 symphonic or chamber music concerts a day. Most concerts are held in indoor halls and churches, with a minimum seating capacity of 1,000; some recitals are held in the Parc des Expositions, an uncovered facility where 500 spectators can be accommodated. In recent years, the Festival has been host to the Boston Symphony Orchestra with Seiji Ozawa, the Paris Orchestra, the Chamber Orchestra of Prague, pianist Michael Rudy, and organist Francis Chapelet. An additional feature of this festival

is its international competition of young conductors, a program instituted in 1951.
Director: M. Jacques Kreisler
Accommodations: Among the hotels in the area are the Frantel, the Novotel, Hotel des Voyageurs, and Hotel du Levant
Ticket information: Admission ranges from 15 to 90 francs

Festival International de Musique Expérimentale de Bourges (Bourges International Festival of Experimental Music)
Groupe de Musique Expérimentale de Bourges, Place André Malraux, 18000 Bourges, France (tel. 36-204187)
Contemporary experimental
Late May to early June (10 days)
This international event was founded in 1971 with the aim of presenting the most advanced forms of today's music. Each year since then, the Festival has featured French and international composers and performers of instrumental, electroacoustic, and mixed music; some recent guests at the event were the Yugoslavian group Interaction and the French Ensemble Asco, from the Pays Bas. In 1979, the Festival opened its program to other artistic domains including experimental cinema, audio-visual shows, and animation. Concerts and film showings are held in the Théâtre Jacques Coeur, and some recitals are held in the outdoor Jardins des Près Fichaux.
Director: F. Barriere
Sponsor: Groupe de Musique Expérimentale de Bourges
Accommodations/other items of interest in area: There are many hotels in Bourges. For information, contact Office de Tourisme, 14 place Etienne-Dolet, Bourges, France (tel. 36-247533). Bourges has many ancient cathedrals and other historical monuments.
Ticket information: For individual music events, the price of a ticket is 18 francs; for film events, 12 francs. For groups, students, and military personnel, 12 and 8 francs respectively. Children under 12 years of age are allowed free entry.
How to get there: By writing to the Groupe de Musique Expérimentale de Bourges, those interested can obtain a special ticket that allows a 20% reduction on the cost of round-trip train

tickets from anywhere in France to Bourges

Festival de Musique en Bourbonnais

Chateloy, 03190 Herisson, France
Chamber music
Late July to mid-August
This annual festival is in its 14th year, and it consists of a series of 6 chamber music concerts given over a 3-week period. Performances are held in 3 different locations—the churches in Chateloy and Saint-Menoux, each of which can accommodate 350 people, and the Chateau de Creux, which seats 500. Featured performers at recent festivals have included the Loewenguth Quartet, the Courmont Trio, the Chamber Orchestra of Versailles, and the Instrumental Ensemble of Provence.
Director: Madame Irmgard Cacheux
Accommodations: The Hotel-Grill Saint-Victor is on Route 144 in Montluçon; there is a campground in Hérisson
Ticket information: Admission prices are 25 francs for unreserved seats and 30 francs for reserved seats; student prices are 15 francs. Tickets can be ordered in advance from Mme Sohier, 03190 Hérisson, France. Tel. 70-068017.
How to get there: All 3 concert locations are situated midway between Bourges and Vichy

Festival de Musique de Chambre de Paris

10, rue de Grenolle, 75006 Paris, France
Classical
Mid- to late September
Works by major classical composers such as Vivaldi, Haydn, Chopin, Beethoven, Mozart, and Schubert are performed by various chamber groups in churches and museums throughout Paris
Director: Bernard Thomas
Sponsor: Geneviève Sego
Ticket information: Tickets cost 30 francs and are available only at the door

Festival de Musique de Menton (Menton Music Festival)

(mailing address): Palais de l'Europe, Avenue Boyer, 06500 Menton, France (tel. 93-358222)
Classical
Ten concerts during August
It all began in 1949, when Andre Borocz was traveling in the south of France with some musician friends. In the old town of Menton, just outside the St. Michel Church, they discovered an old square that overlooks the sea. The acoustics were excellent, and so the Menton Festival began the following year. This annual event, a series of 10 concerts during the month of August, is held outdoors in a facility which seats 900. In recent years, music lovers have had a chance to hear such world-renowned artists as Sviatoslav Richter, Daniel Barenboim, M. Rostropovich, Isaac Stern, and David Oistrakh, among others.
Many young musicians also started their careers at this festival, which also features chamber music.
Director: Andre Borocz
Accommodations/other items of interest in area: There are many hotels in the Menton area. For information, write to Menton Tourisme (F.A.S.T.E.), Palais de l'Europe, Avenue Boyer, 06503, Menton, France.
Menton is situated on the coast of southern France, close to the Italian border. There are many museums and beaches in the area.
Ticket information: Tickets range in price from 10 to 100 francs and can be obtained at the box office, by writing, or by calling
How to get there: To find the square where the concerts are held, follow the stairs that begin at the old port and lead up to the old town

Festival de Musique de Toulon (Music Festival of Toulon)

Palais de la Bourse, Avenue Jean Moulin, 8300, Toulon, France
Classical
June and July
Founded in 1968, this annual classical music festival takes place each year in the French Riviera city of Toulon. The event takes place over a 2-month period, and over the years it has been host to artists such as Artur Rubinstein, Yehudi Menuhin, the London Mozart Players, and Georges Cziffra. Concerts are held in various halls around the city, and patrons are asked to wear evening attire at those taking place at the Opera de Toulon and the Fort de Bregancon. The Festival also sponsors an international competition each year, with

the aim of discovering new talents and encouraging young artists.

Director: M. Henri Tiscornia

Accommodations: There are many hotels in Toulon; for information and reservations, write to Tourist Office, France Welcome, 8 Avenue Colbert, 83000 Toulon, France (or call (94)92-3764)

For information and applications to the international competition, write to Secretariat du Concours International du Festival de Musique de Toulon, Palais de la Bourse, Avenue Jean-Moulin, F-83000 Toulon, France.

Ticket information: Tickets range in price from 15 to 55 francs per concert. They may be ordered by mail through the tourist office in Toulon or by writing directly to the Festival's office.

Festival of Prades
Mairie de Prades, Prades 66500, France
Classical (chamber music)
Late July through early August (2 weeks)

This chamber music festival was founded in 1950 by Pablo Casals and the American violinist Alexander Schneider, and ever since, it has been held for 2 weeks each year. Concerts are held in the Abbey St. Michel de Cuxa, which seats 1,000. In recent years, the Chamber Orchestra of Prague, the Instrumental Ensemble of France, and soloists Eric Heidsieck and Kurt Redel have been among the featured artists.

Director: Mr. Gipolo (mayor of Prades)
Sponsor: Town of Prades

Accommodations/other items of interest in area: Camping, with trailer hook-ups, is allowed. Also, there are 2 hotels in town: Hotel Hostalrich, and Hotel Thermal Molits les Bains.

Prades is close to the sea, and there are many Roman monuments and ruins in the area.

Ticket information: Ticket prices for individual concerts range in price from 10 to 60 francs

Festival of Saint-Denis
Centre Culturel Communal, 61 Boulevard Jules Guesde, Saint-Denis, France (tel. 243-3097)
Classical and dance
Early May to late June

This international festival of classical music and dance takes place over a 2-month period each year and it consists of 10 separate events, many of which are repeated during the course of the Festival. Performances are held in several churches and concert halls in Saint-Denis. In 1979, the Festival was host to the Lar Lubovitch Dance Company, Steve Reich, Sviatoslav Richter, and the English Chamber Chorus.

Sponsor: Centre Culturel Communal de Saint-Denis

Accommodations/other items of interest in area: For information about accommodations, contact Office de Tourisme de Saint-Denis, 2 rue de la Legion d'Honneur, Saint-Denis, France (tel. 243-3355).

Saint-Denis is in metropolitan Paris and abounds with tourist attractions.

Ticket information: There are some free concerts; others range in price from 12 to 35 francs. Tickets can be purchased in ticket outlets in Paris or may be ordered 10 days in advance from the Centre Culturel Communal.

How to get there: There are 2 Metro stops in Saint-Denis: Saint-Denis Basilique and Saint-Denis Porte de Paris. Also, there is a train from the Gare de Nord, and several bus lines have stops in Saint-Denis.

Festival de Sceaux
Festival site: Orangerie of Sceaux
Mailing address: M. Broujean, 5 bis rue Rougemont, 75009 Paris, France (tel. 824-7004)
Classical (chamber) and popular-contemporary
Mid-July to early October (each weekend during this period)

Founded in 1968, the Festival de Sceaux takes place over a 3-month period each summer. Concerts are held each Friday, Saturday, and Sunday night in the Sceaux Orangerie, a building that dates from the 17th century. The Festival concentrates on chamber music, but there are also jazz and popular music concerts. Past performers have included the Quator Parrenin, Gisele Kuhn, the Orchestre Juventia, the duo Leslie and Nadine Wright, and Jean-Louis Haguenauer.

Director: Alfred Loewenguth, Artistic Director
Sponsors: Saison Musicale d'éte de Sceaux and Musée de l'Île de France
Accommodations: For information on

accommodations, contact Saison Musicale d'été de Sceaux, 1 rue des Inbergères, 92330 Sceaux, France
Ticket information: Prices for individual concerts range from 28 to 35 francs. They may be obtained at the Booking Office of the Orangerie starting on July 4 or ordered by mail by contacting S.M.E.S., Chateau de Sceaux, 92330 Sceaux, France
How to get there: The Orangerie is a 10-minute walk from the railroad station Bourg-la-Reine

Festival de Sully Sur Loire (Festival of Sully on the Loire)
94 Route d'Argent, 45620 Cerdon, France
Classical (chamber music and recitals)
Mid-June to mid-July
This chamber music festival celebrated its 6th anniversary in 1979. A series of 10 concerts which take place on weekend evenings during June and July, the event has been host in recent years to Eric Heidsieck, Radu Lupu, Tamas Vasary, Munich's Orchestra Pro Arte, Oscar Caceres, and the Trio Fontanarosa. Performances are held in the Saint-Ythier Church, which seats 700; in the guard room of the Sully Castle, which seats 430; and in the Sully Castle Courtyard, an uncovered area where 1,200 spectators can be accommodated.
Director: Lucien Marois
Accommodations: There is a campsite between the castle and the Loire River and there are trailer facilities. For information about this and the hotels in Sully, contact Tourism Office, Place General de Gaulle, 45600 Sully Sur Loire, France (tel. 38-353221).
Ticket information: Tickets range in price from 30 to 60 francs; they can be ordered in advance by contacting the Tourism office in Sully Sur Loire
How to get there: Sully Sur Loire is located 135 kilometers S. of Paris

Fetes Musicales en Touraine
Hotel de Ville, 37032 Tours Cedex, France (tel. 47-618124)
Classical
End of June through early July
The 1980 season will include performances by pianists Claudio Arrau and Sviatoslav Richter
Director: P. O. Le Chevallier, Artistic Director

Accommodations: Write to Office de Tourisme de Tours, Accueil de France, Place de la Gare, 37042 Tours Cedex, France (tel. 47-055808, telex 750008)

Fetes Romantiques de Nohant (Romantic Festival of Nohant)
B.P. 60, 36400 La Châtre, France (tel. 54-481136)
Classical (romantic)
Two weekends in mid-July
This annual festival of romantic classical music takes place during 2 weekends in June. It consists of a series of 6 concerts, held in a barn on the estate of the Chateau Georges Sand at Nohant. In 1979, Michel Beroff, Claudio Arrau, Christa Ludwig, and Dezso Ranki performed works by Debussy, Brahms, Mendelssohn, and Chopin.
The covered facility can accommodate only 500 people.
Director: M. Belin
Accommodations: For information about accommodations in the area, contact the Hôtel de Ville in La Châtre
Ticket information: Tickets range in price from 15 to 80 francs; they can be bought at the Sous-Préfecture in La Châtre or at the Chateau before the concert; they can also be ordered in advance by writing

Forum des Arts et de la Musique (Forum of Arts and Music): Festival of Music and Choreography
Comité d'Animation Culturelle, Hôtel de Ville, Fréjus, Var, France (tel. 512036)
Chamber music and dance
Mid-July (2 weeks)
The 2nd annual Festival of Music and Choreography of Fréjus took place in 1979. During its 2-week duration, 16 events are presented, including chamber music concerts, recitals, ballet performances, a "Music and the Cinema" series of lectures, and a choral music workshop. Performances are held in an open-air facility which seats 500 and a larger concert hall which seats 1,200.
In 1979, the Festival was host to pianist Gerard Fremy, the French National Balley of Nancy, Arnaud Dumond, and violinist Claire Bernard, among others.
Director: Pierre Costes
Sponsor: Le Comité d'Animation Culturelle de Fréjus
Accommodations/other items of interest

in area: There are many hotels and campgrounds in the vicinity. For information, contact Office de Tourisme, 83600 Frejus, France (tel. 94-515387). The Provence town of Fréjus houses an ancient Roman theater, a cloister, and a large cathedral. Being on the Riviera, Fréjus is an ideal place for outdoor activities.
Ticket information: Admission at individual events ranges from 13 to 26 francs; tickets can be ordered in advance from Agency Var-Voyage, rue Edmond Poupe, 83600 Fréjus, France
How to get there: Fréjus is on the French Riviera, between Cannes and St. Tropez

International Music Festival of Strasbourg
24 rue de la Mesange
F-67011 Strasbourg Cedex, France
Classical (also theater)
June
Previous performers have included Gundula Janovitz, Mignon Dunn, Michel Corboz, Arturo Benedetti-Michelangeli, Montserrat Caballé, and Seiji Ozawa. Seating will be in the following places: the Cathedral, 3,500 seats; the Palais des Congres, 2,000; and the Conservatoire, 600.
Sponsor: Societe des Amis de la Musique (Strasbourg)
Other items of interest in area: Of interest in the area are numerous French vineyards and the Strasbourg Cathedral, as well as the beautiful countryside
Ticket information: Tickets range from 20 to 120 francs. Write to S. Wolf, The Music Shop, 24 rue de la Mesange, F-67081 Strasbourg Cedex, France.

Musique en Morvan a Autun
Mailing address: A Coeur Joie, 8 rue de la Bourse, 69289 Lyon Cedex 1, France
Festival site: Lycee mixte Bonaparte, 71400 Autun, France
Choral
Mid- to late July (1 week)
This annual Singing Week is a presentation of A Coeur Joie, the European Federation of Young Choirs. It features a program of choir concerts given by an international group of choirs that vary each year. The program also includes workshops for participants; in 1979, these included Mozart's *Requiem* and *Nocturnes*. Performances are held in the

Cathedral and Theatre of Autun.
Sponsor: A Coeur Joie and Municipality of Autun
Accommodations: Information about accommodations can be obtained by writing to Semaine Chantante, Lycee mixte Bonaparte, 71400 Autun, France
Ticket information: Information about obtaining advance tickets and entry requirements for participants can be obtained by writing to A Coeur Joie. Admission is from 15 to 30 francs.

Rencontres Internationales d'Art Contemporain de la Rochelle (International Meeting of Contemporary Art in Rochelle)
Hôtel de Ville, 11 rue Chef de Ville, 17000, La Rochelle, France
Contemporary music and theater
Late June to early July (12 days)
The 7th annual Meeting of Contemporary Art took place in La Rochelle in 1979. This 12-day event is held in the summer and features chamber music, musical theater, theater, film retrospectives, and lectures on French culture. A typical day offers no less than 4 different events in each of these areas, and performances are held in the town's churches, theaters, and public buildings. Musicians who have performed here in recent years include Mauricio Kagel, the Ensemble Musique XX, Claude Helffer, Jean Michel Fischer, and Anna Prucnal.
The Festival also sponsors a contemporary piano music competition.
Director: Dr. Georges Sabatier
Accommodations: For information about accommodations, contact Service Hebergement, RIAC, 11 rue Chef de Ville, 17000 La Rochelle, France
Ticket information: Some performances have free admission; otherwise, tickets range in price from 10 to 25 francs. They can be bought at the Maison de la Culture in La Rochelle (tel. 46-413779). They can also be ordered by mail from the Hotel de Ville.
How to get there: There are train connections to La Rochelle from many French cities.

Rencontres Internationales de Musique Contemporaine (International Meeting of Contemporary Music)
Hotel de Ville, F-57000 Metz, France (tel. 87-751488)

CONDUCTOR JANOS FERENCSIK AT HUNGARY'S BUDAPEST MUSIC FESTIVAL.

Contemporary
Third week of November (4 days)
This international meeting of contemporary music takes place for 4 days each November. There are usually 4 different events each day, including lectures, seminars, rehearsals, and concerts. These events are held indoors in the Muicipal Theater, The Sports Palace, and the School of Fine Arts. In recent years this event has been host to the Symphony Orchestra of Nancy, the Groupe Electronique d'Itineraire, the Orchestra of Liege, Herbert Henck, and sopranos Sigune von Osten and Marie-Claude Vallin.
Director: Claude Lefebvre
Sponsors: Cultural Ministry of Paris and the town of Metz
Accommodations: Information about accommodations can be obtained by writing to Syndicat d'Initiative, Porte Serpenoise, 57000 Metz, France (tel. 87-756521)
Ticket information: Admission ranges from 10 to 50 francs. The box office of the Hôtel de Ville will open 45 minutes before each performance; also, to order tickets in advance, contact the Hôtel de Ville (they must be picked up in person).
How to get there: The French Railway Company gives a 20 % reduction, on a return trip, to the participants of the Festival, upon presentation of a "fichet SNCF", which can be obtained by writing to the Hôtel de Ville in Metz. There is free transport between the railroad station and some faraway concert places.

Samedis Musicaux de Chartres (Musical Saturdays of Chartres)
Chartres, France
Chamber Music
Saturdays in September and October
This annual chamber music festival was founded in 1950, and it features French classical artists such as Jeremy Menuhin, Jean-Claude Pennetier, and Henriette Gremy-Chauliac. Concerts are held every Saturday during September and October in 3 different historical monuments in the French cathedral town of Chartres. The Festival also sponsors free concerts each Sunday afternoon from July 1 to September 16; they are held in the Cathedral of Chartres.

Sponsor: Chartres Tourist Office
Accommodations: For information about accommodations, write to Tourist Office, 7, Cloître Notre Dame, 28000 Chartres, France. There is a municipal camping site in the area.
Ticket information: Tickets range in price from 20 to 40 francs and may be obtained by writing to the Tourist Office of Chartres; they may also be purchased at the door

Soirées Musicales au Château de Villeieille
c/o Mairie de Villevieille, F-30800 Villevieille, France
Classical
End of July through mid-August
Previous performers include Maurice André, Régine Crespin, Michel Corboz, Jean-Pierre Rampal, Jean-Francois Paillard, and Victoria de los Angeles
Director: Michel Garcin, Artistic Director
Accommodations/other items of interest in area: Camping and picnicking facilities are available.
Villeieille is an especially attractive region of France.
Ticket information: Tickets for various events range from 30 to 80 francs. Write to the Festival, c/o Mr. Sauveplane, F-30860 Salinelles, France; or Michel Garcin, Erato Records, 60 rue de la Chausee d'Antin, F-75009 Paris, France.

GREECE

Athens Festival
1 Voukourestiou St., Athens 133,
Greece
Classical (ballet and theater)
July to September
Performances take place outdoors; thea-
ter seats 5,000
Director: John Liakopoulos
Sponsor: National Tourist Organization
of Greece

HUNGARY

Budapest Festival
POB 80, Vörösmarty tér 1, H-1366
Budapest, Hungary
Classical, opera
Open-air performances from early July
through mid-August; music competition from mid- to late September;
Budapest Music Weeks from late September through late October
This annual, 3-month-long classical
music festival, founded in 1956, consists
of 3 types of events. The first is a series
of open-air concerts held on Margaret's
Island, from the beginning of July
through the middle of August, at a facility which accommodate 3,500. Then
there is an international music competition held for 2 weeks from the middle
through the end of September. And
finally, the Budapest Music Weeks, held
for 4 weeks each year from the end of
September through the end of October.
The latter 2 events are held in 2 indoor
halls, with a combined seating capacity
of 3,400.
In addition to the Hungarian State
Philharmonic and the Budapest Symphony Orchestra, guest performers at
the Festival are an international lot. In
recent years they have included the
Cleveland Symphony Orchestra, the
Prague Madrigal Choir, the Berlin Symphony Orchestra, and Stuttgart's
Schola Cantorum.
Accommodations: For information re-
garding accommodations (including
camping), write to Travel Agency
IBUSZ, V. Felszabadulás tér 1, Budapest,
Hungary
Ticket information: Ticket prices for
individual concerts run from 60 to 120
forints and may be ordered in advance
by writing to Travel Agency IBUSZ,
V. Felszabadulás tér 1, Budapest,
Hungary

**Esztergom International Guitar Festival
and Seminar**
Esztergom, Hungary
Classical
Early to mid-August
The Municipal Council of Esztergom
organized the 1st International Guitar
Festival and Seminar in 1973, in connec-
tion with the 1,000th anniversary cele-

bration of the town of Esztergom. The biannually organized festival of 2 weeks duration now attracts as many as 400 guitar teachers and artists.
Performances include concerts of invited guest artists in the Esztergom Cultural Centre and at other Hungarian towns, the playing of the Balint Bakfark Guitar Orchestra, and a joint gala concert in the Esztergom Basilica. A guitar competition is also held, as well as numerous lectures and seminars.
Director: Laszlo Szendrey-Karper
Sponsor: Municipal Council of Esztergom
Accommodations: For information, write to Festival Secretariate, Esztergom Municipal Council, H-2501 Esztergom, Hungary
Ticket information: For ticket information, write to Festival Secretariate

IRELAND

Dublin Festival of Twentieth Century Music
Music Association of Ireland Ltd., 11 Suffolk Street, Dublin 2, Ireland
Classical (contemporary)
Early January (1 week)
Held for 1 week each year, the primary purpose of this festival, which is in its 9th year, is to present a broad spectrum of solo, chamber, and orchestral music of the twentieth century. Special attention is given to works by Irish composers, and a number of new works are performed each year. Concerts are held in various halls around Dublin each evening, and the Festival also features lunchtime recitals. Past artists have included Fires of London, Panufnik, Lutoslawski, and Yvonne Loriod.
Director: P. G. Power
Sponsor: The Music Association of Ireland
Accommodations: For information, contact Dublin Tourism, Dawson Street, Dublin 2, Ireland
Ticket information: Single tickets cost £1.50, season tickets range from £6 to £10

Waterford International Festival of Light Opera
Theatre Royal, Waterford, Ireland
Light opera
Mid-September
The 16-day Waterford International Festival of Light Opera, which began in 1959, presents competitions among amateur operatic societies. Over the years societies from England, Scotland, Wales, Northern Ireland, the Republic of Ireland and the U.S. have competed for the many awards, and participation in the Festival is now regarded by many societies as the pinnacle of achievement in the world of light opera. Performances are in the evening at Theatre Royal, a 3-tiered theater built in 1788 which seats about 680.
Director: James Hassey
Sponsor: Irish Tourist Board, Waterford Glass, and others
Accommodations/other items of interest in area: Hotel accommodations are available in Waterford. For information and reservations, contact Southeast

Tourism, 41 The Quay, Waterford, Ireland (tel. 051-75823).
Waterford, a southeast Irish seaport, offers visitors fishing, river cruising, singing pubs, tours of the Waterford glass factory, and many sports.
Ticket information: Season tickets for stalls are £40. Single tickets range from £.60 to £2.50. All booking inquiries should be made to the Booking Office at the Festival, or call 051-74402 after the 1st week in August.

Wexford Festival Opera
Theatre Royal, High St., Wexford, Ireland
Opera
Late October to early November
This 12-day festival, founded in 1951, features productions of both well-known and rare operas, recitals, choral concerts, along with art, craft, and literature exhibitions. Performers who have participated include Janet Baker, Ugo Benelli, Mani Mekler, and Lajos Miller. Performances take place in the 450-seat Georgian Theater.
Director: Adrian Slack
Sponsors: Arts Council of Ireland, Guinness Ireland, others
Accommodations/other items of interest in area: White's Hotel and Talbot Hotel in Wexford can provide accommodations. No camping.
There are castles, abbeys, and other interesting antiquities nearby.
Ticket information: Opera tickets are £8 and up, recitals are £2.50 and up

ISRAEL

ISCM World Music Days
P.O. Box 11180, 73 Nordau Boulevard, Tel Aviv, Israel
Contemporary-classical
June 29 to July 5, 1980
Each year the International Society of Contemporary Music holds a World Music Days Festival and competition in a different country; in 1980, this event will be held for 6 days in Isreal. The Festival will consist of one symphony orchestra concert, several chamber orchestra concerts, an electronic music concert, and one evening of multimedia and concert music; the program of compositions will be chosen from among those works submitted by each National Section of the ISCM, works that have been composed in the last 10 years. Choices are made by an international jury.
A special project of the 1980 festival is the invitation extended to 3 composers to stay in the country for 4 months prior to the Festival, in order to write a new instrumental chamber music piece to be performed at the Festival. In addition, the Festival will sponsor sight-seeing tours and lecture-demonstrations of Israeli ethnic music.
The Jerusalem Symphony Orchestra, the Kibbutz Chamber Orchestra, international chamber music groups, and Stuttgart's Schola Cantorum Choir will be among the featured performers. Concerts will be held in the Jerusalem Theatre and the Tel Aviv Museum.
Director: Tzvi Avri
Sponsors: Israel Composers' League and Israeli Ministry of Culture and Education
Accommodations: There are many hotels in Tel Aviv. All information regarding registration should be addressed to the Israel Composers' League.
Ticket information: Ticket prices have not yet been determined; however, information can be obtained by writing to Secretariat, Israel Composers' League, P.O. Box 11180, 73 Nordau Boulevard, Tel Aviv, Israel

The Israel Festival at Ein-Gev
Kibbutz Ein-Gev, P.O. Ein-Gev, Israel
14 940
Classical (opera, dance)
April
Since 1943, a Passover week festival has
been held on the shores of the Sea of
Galilee at Ein-Gev Kibbutz. As well as
first rate Israeli orchestras, ensembles,
dance companies and soloists, guest
artists such as Rubinstein, Rostropo-
vitch, Krips, the Budapest String Quartet,
and the Martha Graham Dance Company
have performed at Ein-Gev. One concert
of each festival is devoted to music from
the kibbutzim.
Concerts are held at Kinneroth, Esco
Music Center, which is similar to the
Tanglewood Shed, but enclosed all
around. There is seating for 2,400.
Director: Yaakov Steinberger
Sponsors: Ministry of Education and
Culture and Ministry of Tourism
Accommodations: Lodging is available
at all Tiberias Hotels and Ein-Gev Motel.
There are camp grounds about 1 mile
S. of the kibbutz. Bungalows and mobile
homes are available for $3 to $12.
Trailers are welcome. There are picnic
spots both at the campgrounds and near
the Music Center.
Ticket information: Admission ranges
from $3 to $8. Tickets can be ordered
from Kinneroth Esco Music Centre,
Post Ein Gev 14 940, Israel.
Directions: For directions and more
information about the area contact
Israel Government Tourist Office

ITALY

Autunno Musicale di Como
Villa Olmo, 22100 Como, Italy
Classical
September to October
Directors: Gisella Bergeri and Italo
Gomez, Artistic Directors
Accommodations: Write to Azienda
Autonoma di Soggiorno e Tourismo,
1-22100 Como, Italy

Festival Autunnale dell'Opera Lirica "Teatro delle Novita"
Teatro Gaetano Donizetti, Piazza
Cavour, I-26100 Bergamo, Italy
Classical
October to December
The Festival presents operas, ballets, and
concerts
Director: Riccardo Allorto

Festival Internazionale di Clavicembalo
Associazione Musicale Romana, Via dei
Banchi Vecchi 61, I-00186 Rome, Italy
(tel. 65-68441)
Classical
May to June
Past participants include Gustav
Leonhardt, Alan Curtis, Nigel Rogers,
and Kenneth Gilbert
Director: Annamaria Romagnoli
Ticket information: Tickets are 3,000
lire, 2,000 lire for students

Festival delle Nazioni di Musica da Camera
c/o Azienda Soggiorno e Tourismo,
Piazza Garibaldi, 2, 06012 Citta di
Castello, Italy
Classical (chamber music)
August to September
Director: Gabriele Gandini
Ticket information: Tickets are free

Opera Barga
Casa Baldi, Via della Fornacetta 11,
I-55051 Barga, Italy
Classical
July to August
Director: Gillian Armitage Hunt,
General Director; Bruno Rigacci, Musical
Director
Ticket information: Tickets cost 1,000
to 4,000 lire

Rome Festival of Contemporary Music
Via Proba Petronia 82, I-00136, Rome,
Italy
Classical (20th century)
October (even-numbered years)
The Festival began in 1968. Perform-
ances take place in concert halls in and
around Rome, but the majority of per-
formances are in the Sala Accademica
of the Santa Cecilia Academy in the
center of Rome.
Director: Gian Paolo Chiti

Sagra Musicale Malatestiano
Azienda Autonoma di Soggiorno,
I-47037 Rimini, Italy
Classical
May to September
Concerts take place in 3 halls: the
Malatesta Temple seats 1,000; the
Novelli Theater, 800; and the S.
Agostino Church, 200
Other items of interest in area: Rimini
is a seaside resort and a popular tourist
area
Ticket information: Prices: 2,000 to
3,000 lire

Stagione Lirica, Arena Sferisterio
Arena Sferisterio, I-62100 Macerata,
Italy
Classical (opera and ballet)
July to August
Singers who have participated include
Placido Domingo, Giuseppe Giacomini,
Cornell MacNeil, and Fiorenza Cossotto.
In 1979 the Festival gave performances
of *Tosca, Romeo and Juliet* (Prokofiev),
Norma, and *Carmen*. Symphony con-
certs and ballet are also presented.
The open air arena seats 6,000.
Director: Carlo Perucci

**Stresa Musical Weeks—International
Festival**
I-28049 Stresa, Via R. Bonghi 4, Italy
Classical
Mid-August through mid-September
During the last month of summer, sym-
phony concerts, recitals, and chamber
music concerts are held in and around
Stresa. The Beaux Arts Trio, Wilhelm
Kempff, Isaac Stern, and many more
renowned artists have appeared at this
festival. The Festival also includes per-
formances by young winners of inter-
national contests.

The settings for many of the concerts
are spectacular.
Director: Avv. Italo Trentinaglia de
Daverio
Accommodations/other items of interest
in area: Contact the Festival for information on lodging. There is camping.
Stresa is on the shores of Lake Maggiore;
it is a green amphitheater, flooded with
sunshine and the blues of skies and
lakes. Everywhere you look you see
flowers.
Ticket information: Series tickets for
from 2 to 4 concerts range from 5,000
to 16,000 lire; series tickets for 17 concerts are about 90,000 lire, and a subscription for all concerts, with seating
preference, is about 13,000 lire. There
is an additional charge for tickets
ordered by mail.

**Giuseppe Tartini International Violin
Festival**
Piazzale Pontecorvo 6, Padua, Italy
Classical
May to June
Leonid Kogan, Nathan Milstein, Salva-
tore Accardo, Isaac Stern and Gidon
Kremer are among the violinists who
have appeared at the Giuseppe Tartini
Festival. I Solisti Veneti, under the
direction of Claudio Scimone, are
regular participants.
Director: Claudio Scimone
Ticket information: Tickets are avail-
able on the day of each performance

NETHER-LANDS

NEW ZEALAND

International Gaudeamus Competition for Interpreters of Contemporary Music

Gaudeamus Foundation, P.O. Box 30,
3720 AA Bilthoven, Netherlands
Classical (contemporary)
Mid-April
At this week-long competition performers from many nations must play only works composed after 1920, and at least some composed after 1955. This competition is unique in that it is not restricted to a special instrument or voice. All instrumentalists and vocalists may participate, including ensembles up to a maximum of 9 performers. The contestants, who must be age 35 or younger, choose the works which they perform.
All concerts are held in Rotterdam.
Sponsors: Gaudeamus Foundation and the Rotterdam Arts Foundation

International Gaudeamus Music Week

Gaudeamus Foundation. P.O. Box 30,
3720 AA Bilthoven, Netherlands
Classical (contemporary)
Early to mid-September
The aim of the International Gaudeamus Music Week is the promotion of new music by young composers from many nations. The best of the original works submitted each year are selected by a committee of 4 well-known composers, and performed by first-class Dutch chamber groups, soloists and orchestra. Electronic works are also performed. Additional events include a daily Analysis Course which focuses on the works presented, and workshops.
The concerts and other events are not concentrated in one city, but take place throughout the Netherlands.
Sponsor: Gaudeamus Foundation

Auckland Festival

P.O. Box 1411, Auckland, New Zealand
Classical and other
March (even-numbered years only)
This is the largest and oldest festival in New Zealand. It was established in 1948 as a music festival, and broadened to include all the arts in 1954. The musical program is varied, with a strong emphasis on classical.
Events take place throughout Auckland. Main concerts are held at Town Hall, which can accommodate 1,800.
Director: Elaine Beadle
Sponsor: Air New Zealand
Accommodations: Lodging in Auckland. is available at the Intercontinental, South Pacific, and Travelodge. There is no camping. Picnicking is allowed in the parks.
Ticket information: Admission ranges from 2 to 10 New Zealand dollars

Christchurch Arts Festival

P.O. Box 13203 Armagh, Christchurch, New Zealand
Orchestral music, recitals, theater, opera, ballet, modern dance, choral music, popular music
March (in even-numbered years)
The Festival began as a community enterprise in 1965 and is now a National Arts Festival with a comprehensive program not only of music, but of arts, crafts, and film as well.
Past years have seen performers such as Charles Rosen, the New Zealand Symphony Orchestra, Pascal Rogé, and Michael Ponti.
Concerts and performances take place in the Town Hall Auditorium, which seats 2,000; in the James Hay Theatre, with a 1,000 seat capacity; in 3 smaller theaters; and outdoors at the 20,000 seat Queen Elizabeth II Park.
Director: Helen Holmes
Sponsors: Queen Elizabeth II Arts Council of New Zealand and Christchurch Metropolitan Local Bodies
Ticket information: Ticket prices range from 1 to 8 New Zealand dollars. For tickets, write to Christchurch Arts

Festival, Town Hall Booking Office,
P.O. Box 13144, Christchurch, New
Zealand

NORWAY

Bergen International Festival
Postbox 183, N-5001 Bergen, Norway
Classical, opera (also drama, folklore,
ballet, art exhibitions)
Late May to early June (2 weeks)
This festival was begun in 1953, when it
was built around the music of Edvard
Grieg, who was born and lived most of
his life in Bergen. Today, the Festival
takes place for a 2-week period each
year, and although there is still at least 1
event per day devoted to Grieg's music,
the Festival itself has grown in scope to
include all the performing arts. A typical day at this festival starts at 11:30
A.M. and ends with a performance at
8 P.M.; each day there are no less than
6 events, including concerts, recitals,
plays, folklore shows, and ballets. Shows
are held in various churches and concert
halls in the city.
Recent performers and presentations
at the Festival include Mstislav
Rostropovich, the Wilanow Quartet,
the Oslo Philharmonic Orchestra, Peter
Ustinov, Tom Stoppard, and André
Previn's coproduction of *Every Good
Boy Deserves Favour.*
Director: Sverre Bergh
Sponsors: Norwegian government and
local authorities
Accommodations: There are many
hotels in Bergen. For information, contact Bergen Tourist Office, Bergen,
Norway.
Ticket information: Tickets cost any-
where from $1 to $20 for individual
events. Tickets may be booked through
travel agents or directly from the Festi-
val Office, Bergen International Festival,
P.O. Box 183, 5001 Bergen, Norway.

POLAND

Chamber Music Days
Artur Malawski, c/o State Philharmonic
Orchestra, Chopina 30, 35-055 Rzeszow,
Poland (Festival site is Lancut)
Classical
One week in May
Lancut is 18 kilometers from Rzeszow.
The concerts take place in the Baroque
Palace Museum.
Seating is for 306.
Director: Andrzej Rozmarynowicz

**Days of Organ Music (Dni Muzyki
Organowej)**
Philharmonia, Zwierzyniecka 1, 31-103
Cracow, Poland
Classical
Late April
Cracow's week-long festival of organ
music has been held each spring since
1966. Performers include Polish and
foreign organists, choirs, chamber en-
sembles, and symphony orchestras.
Concerts are held in Cracow's Philhar-
monic Hall.
Director: Jerzy Katlewicz
Sponsor: High Music School, Cracow
Accommodations: Accommodations
include the Orbis hotels in Cracovia and
Francuski and the Holiday Inn in
Francuski
Ticket information: Tickets are avail-
able at Philharmonic Hall box office.
Prices range from 10 to 30 zlotys

Divertimento of Naleczow
Festival site: Malachowskich Palace,
Nalaczow, Poland
Mailing address: Panstwowa Filharmon-
ica, Lublin, ul. Osterwy 7, Poland
Vocal and instrumental forms of chamber music
Mid-May (5 days)
This annual chamber music divertimento
is in its 7th year. The aim of this event
is to present a broad historical panorama, with both old and contemporary
music; 5 different concerts are given by
5 different Polish chamber groups. Concerts are held in the ballroom of the
Malachowske Family Palace, which can
accommodate 200 people. Those performing at the 1979 Festival were the
Kasia Danczowska Chamber Orchestra,
the Wilkomirska Trio, soloists of the

Grand Theatre, and pianist Janusz
Olejniczak.
Director: Adam Natanek
Sponsors: Culture Department of the
People's Provincial Council and Nalez-
cow Health Resort
Accommodations: The Przepiorka
Motel is in Nalaeczow; there are campgrounds in Nazimierz and Pulawy, and
the cost ranges from 30 to 80 zlotys
per night
Ticket information: Tickets for individual performances cost 20 zlotys;
they can be obtained at the Palace box
office or by writing

**International Festival of Contemporary
Music: "Warsaw Autumn"**
Rynek Starego Miasta 27, 00-272
Warsaw, Poland
Mostly contemporary and avant-garde;
also all types of classical
Starts 1st Friday after September 15
(10 days)
This festival got under way in 1956 and
has been held annually for a 10-day
period ever since. The aim of the Festival
is to make it a representative panorama
of all idioms of modern musical expres-
sion—from the classics to the latest
avant-garde experiments. In recent years
the Fires of London, the Finnish Radio
Symphony Orchestra, Stuttgart's Wur-
temberg State Theater, the Polish Radio
National Philharmonic Orchestra, K.
Andrzej Kulka, and Wande Wilkomirska
have performed at the Festival.
Performances take place in the Concert
Hall of the National Philharmonic in
Warsaw and in Warsaw's theaters and
clubs.
Director: Jozef Patkowski
Sponsor: Polish Composers Union
Accommodations: The hotels Orbis,
Europejski, and Bristol are among the
many in Warsaw
Ticket information: A ticket book,
which covers all events, costs 1,000
zlotys

**International Oratorio Festival
"Wratislavia Cantans"**
Swierczewskiego 19, 50044 Wroclaw
Poland
Classical
September
Director: Tadeusz Strugala
Sponsor: State Philharmonic of
Wroclaw

AN EVENING TATTOO AT THE EDINBURGH FESTIVAL.

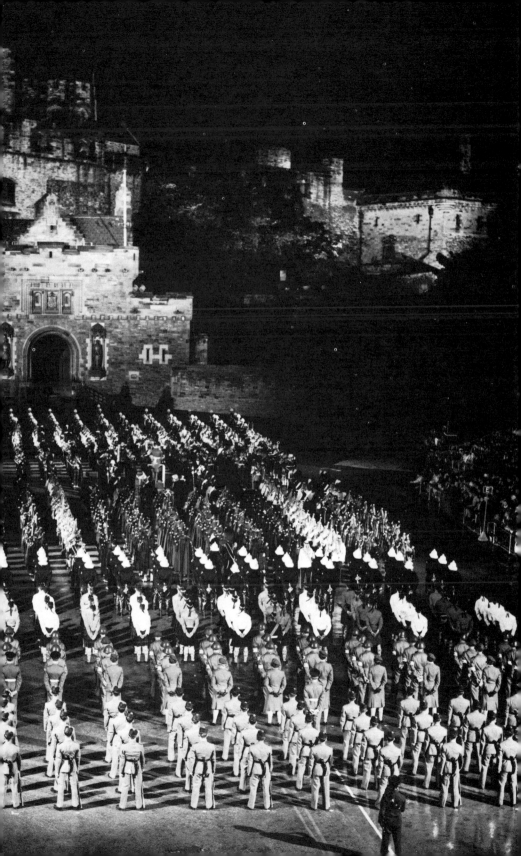

Accommodations/other items of interest in area: Some of the hotels in the city are the Panorama, the Novotel, the Odra, and the Monopol.

There are many churches and museums worth visiting, including the Gothic-Style Museum of Architecture.

Ticket information: Write to Festival Office, State Philharmonic, ul. Swierczewskiego str. 19, Pl-50044 Wroclaw, Poland

SCOTLAND

Edinburgh International Festival
21 Market Street, Edinburgh EH1 1BW, Scotland
Classical, opera, orchestral, ballet, other
Mid-August through early September
During this 3-week festival approximately 15 operas, 20 ballet and dance performances, 15 symphony concerts, 15 chamber music concerts, and numerous recitals are presented. There are also about 50 theater performances, 15 poetry readings, jazz concerts, late night shows, lectures and numerous other events. Participants have included the BBC Orchestra, the London and Boston Symphony Orchestras, Kent Opera, Scottish Opera, and the National Ballet of Cuba, to mention only a few, as well as accomplished chamber groups and guest artists from around the world. Performances are held in concert halls and theaters throughout Edinburgh; there are also some outdoor events.
Sponsor: Edinburgh Festival Society Ltd.
Accommodations/other items of interest in area: For reservations in hotels, guest houses, or private houses apply to the Tourist Accommodation Service, 9 Cockburn St., Edinburgh EH1 1BR, Scotland, with £.25 reservation fee. For reservations in University Halls of Residence apply to Deputy Steward, Pollock Halls of Residence, 18 Holyrood Park Road, Edinburgh EH16 5AV, Scotland.
An International Film Festival, a TV Festival and numerous theater and musical events are held in Edinburgh at the same time as the Festival.
Ticket information: Ticket prices range from £1 to £8.50

SWITZERLAND

Festival Tibor Varga
P.O. Box 3374, CH-1951 Sion,
Switzerland (tel. 027-226652)
Classical (orchestral and chamber music)
Mid-July to mid-September
This event, founded in 1964 by the
Hungarian violinist Tibor Varga, takes
place each year in Sion, Switzerland, a
small medieval city nestled at the foot
of the Alps. The Festival sponsors a
series of 12 orchestral and chamber
music concerts over a 2-month period,
and over the course of its history it has
been host to such artists as Antal Dorati,
Jakob Gimpel, Gyorgy Cziffra, Erick
Friedman, and Valery Klimov. During
the Festival season, the Sion Academy
of Music offers courses of instruction,
and the Festival also features an annual
international competition for violinists.
Concerts are held indoors in a facility
which seats 1,000.
Director: Joseph Pellegrini, Admini-
strator
Sponsor: Association du Festival Tibor
Varga
Accommodations: For information
about accommodations in the area,
contact the Office du Tourisme, CH
1950, Sion, Switzerland. Camping is permitted in the area.
For information regarding both courses
of instruction and the international
competition, write to the Festival.
Ticket information: Tickets for individual concerts cost from 6 to 25 francs.

International Festival of Music
Postfach 424, CH-6002 Lucerne,
Switzerland (tel. 041-233562)
Classical
August to September
Artists who have appeared at the
Lucerne Festival include Franco Gulli,
Enrica Cavallo, Salvatore Accardo, Kiril
Kondrashin, Krystian Zimerman, Michel
Corboz, Dietrich Fischer-Dieskau,
Svjatoslav Richter, the Quartetto
Italiano, and the Berlin Philharmonic
with Herbert von Karajan
Directors: Rudolf Baumgartner, Artistic
Director; Othmar Fries, Managing
Director
Ticket information: Prices for tickets
range from 10 to 90 francs

Menuhin Festival
Postfach 23, CH-3780 Gstaad,
Switzerland
Classical
August
Past participants have included Maurice
André, the Vegh Quartet, the Academy
of St. Martin-in-the-fields, Wilhelm
Kempff, Donald Gramm, Leonid Kogan,
and Ravi Shankar.
Performances are given in the Church
of Saanen (600 seats).
Director: Dr. R. Steiger
Accommodations/other items of interest
in area: Write to Verkehrsbureau,
CH-3780 Gstaad, Switzerland.
Gstaad is a beautiful alpine resort town.
Ticket information: Tickets range from
5 to 55 francs

Settimane Musicale di Ascona
c/o Ente turistico Ascona e Iosone,
CH-6612 Ascona, Switzerland
Classical
August to October
Performances take place in the Collegio
Papio Church (which seats 400) and the
San Francesco Locarno church (which
seats 800)
Director: Dino Invernizzi
Ticket information: Tickets cost from
5 to 40 francs

Zurich International June Festival
P.O. Box 8023 Zurich, Switzerland
Classical and theater
June
The tradition of the Zurich June Festi-
val goes back to 1909, when it was
largely devoted to the music of Wagner.
In its present day form the Festival
covers every sphere of cultural life in
Zurich with the emphasis continuing to
be on music. The Festival is proud of
its excellent, varied program; special
mention might be made of recent per-
formances of Arnold Schonberg's
Gurre-Lieder and a production by the
Zurich Opera House of Claudio Monte-
verdi's *Eighth Book of Madrigals*.
Concerts are held throughout Zurich.
Sponsor: City of Zurich
Accommodations: For information
about accommodations, contact the
Zurich Tourist Office, P.O. Box
CH-8023 Zurich, Switzerland
Ticket information: Admission varies

WALES

Cardiff Festival of 20th Century Music
P.O. Box 78, University Coll., Cardiff,
Wales
Classical
Winter
This 2-week festival presents modern
classical music, including first perform-
ances of works commissioned by the
Welsh Arts Council. Works of 18th and
19th century composers are also included
in the program. Past performers have
included Britton, Pears, John Lill,
Academy of St. Martin-in-the-fields,
Beaux Arts Trio, BBC Welsh Symphony
Orchestra and many fine soloists, choirs,
and chamber groups.
Concerts are held in New Hall, which
seats 400, and in other halls and theaters
in Cardiff.
Director: Alun Hoddinott
Sponsor: Welsh Arts Council
Accommodations/other items of interest
in area: Accommodations are available
at Angel Motel, Westgate Street, Cardiff.
The Welsh countryside is spectacular.
Ticket information: Admission ranges
from £1.50 to £5. For tickets write to
the Festival.

Fishguard Music Festival
Festival Office, Summerhill, Fishguard,
Pembrokeshire, Dyfed, Wales
Classical
Late July (1 week)
Founded in 1970, this annual week-long
festival is classed among the best festivals
in Wales and is noted for its choral concerts, presentations of new works, and
its friendly atmosphere. In addition
to evening classical concerts, the Festival
also sponsors poetry readings, morning
recitals, film showings, and art and
flower exhibitions. Concerts are held
in St. Davids Cathedral, which seats 800,
and various smaller halls. In recent years,
the Fishguard Music Festival has been
host to the Royal Liverpool Philharmonic Orchestra, the John Davies
Singers and Orchestra, the Dyfed Choir,
Helen Watts, and Swingle Singers II.
Director: John Davies
Sponsors: Welsh Arts Council, West
Wales Association for the Arts, Welsh
Amateur Music Federation
Accommodations/other items of interest

in area: The Fishguard Bay Hotel is
among the many hotels in the area.
Camping is allowed in designated areas,
as is picnicking.
Fishguard has a vacation environment,
with unspoiled sea and country areas.
Ticket information: Prices for individual
concerts range from £.50 to £4, and
they are half-price for students and
children

WEST GERMANY

Bach Week
Postfach 41, D-8800 Ansbach, West
Germany
Classical
July (odd years only)
Ticket information: Tickets are from
6 to 50 deutsche marks

Bad Hersfeld Festival Concerts
Arbeitskreis fur Musik e.V.,
Nachtigallenstrasse 9, D-6430 Bad
Hersfeld, West Germany
Classical
July to August
Director: Siegfried Heinrich
Ticket information: Tickets are 6 to 16
deutsche marks. Write to Kartenzen-
trale der Festspiele, Pavillon am Markt-
platz, D-6430 Bad Hersfeld, West
Germany

Bayreuth Festival
Festspielleitung Bayreuth, Festspielhaus,
D-8580 Bayreuth, West Germany
Classical
July to August
A small town in Bavaria, Bayreuth has
been the seat of the Richard Wagner
Festival since 1876. Together with the
conception of *Der Ring des Nibelungen*
Wagner formed the idea of building a
festival theater that should be devoted
solely to "ideal performances of master-
pieces of the German stage." In 1876
the theater was completed and the 1st
Bayreuth festival season took place.
The opening performance, *Das Rhein-
gold*, was attended by the German
Emperor, William I, King Ludwig II of
Bavaria, and a multitude of prominent
personalities of European cultural life,
such as Liszt, Grieg, Tchaikovsky,
Bruckner, Mahler, Saint-Saens,
Nietzsche, and the painters Franz
Lenbach and Adolf Menzel.
Director: Wolfgang Wagner
Ticket information: Tickets should be
purchased well in advance

Berlin Festival
Budapester Str. 48/50, 1 Berlin 30,
West Germany
Classical, opera, ballet, theater
Early September through early October
The Berlin Festival is a celebration of
music, opera, theater, dance, literature,
film, and visual arts—on the one hand
honoring the past and on the other pre-
senting contemporary trends. Past guest
performers have included, among others,
Peter Brook, George Tabori, Robert
Wilson, La Mama Theater, Comedie
Francaise, Giorgio Strehler, the Grand
Magic Circus, Thadeuz Kantor, and
Samuel Beckett.
Events are held in theaters and halls in
Berlin.
Director: Dr. Ulrich Eckhardt
Accommodations: Lodging is available
at Hotel Kempinski, Hotel am Zoo,
Savoy Hotel, Palace Hotel, Schweizer-
hof Hotel, and many more. There are
also small pensions near the Festival.
Ticket information: For information
and advance tickets contact the Festival

Corvey Music Festival
c/o Kulturamt der Stadt Höxter,
Berliner Platz 1, D-3470 Höxter 1, West
Germany
Classical
May to June

**Donaueschingen Festival of Contem-
porary Music**
Stadtisches Kultur und Verkehrsamt,
D-7710 Danaueschingen, West Germany
Classical
October
Director: Josef Häusler
Ticket information: Tickets are 3 to 25
deutsche marks

European Festival
c/o Europaische Wochen Passau e.V.
Nibelungenhalle, D-8390 Passau, West
Germany
Classical and dance
June to August
Director: Walter Hornsteiner

Gandersheimer Domfestspiele
Stadt Bad Gandersheim, Markt 10,
D-3353 Bad Gandersheim, West Germany
Classical
June to July
The 1979 festival included performances
of Orff's *Carmina Burana* in addition
to orchestral performances
Director: Walter Pohl, Artistic Director

Heidelberg Castle Festival
Theater, Friedrichstrasse 5, D-6900,
Heidelberg, West Germany
Opera
End of July to end of August
Heidelberg Castle provides a suitably
romantic setting for the performance
of classical German operas and redis-
coveries of baroque and pre-classical
operas. Operas are presented in German,
English, and Italian, depending on ori-
gin. More variety is provided by castle
concerts—like the Japanese Koto Ensemble from Kumamoto.
The Castle Courtyard provides uncovered concert space, while King's
Hall is the setting for the operas.
Director: Helmut Hein
Sponsor: City Theatre of Heidelberg
Accommodations: Tourist Information
can provide information about accommodations. Write to Tourist Information
am Schloss, Neue Schlossstrasse 54,
6900, Heidelberg, Germany
Ticket information: Tickets range in
price from $5.50 to $14. For tickets,
write to Tourist Information am Schloss.

International Organ Week
Bismarckstrasse 46, D-8500 Nuremberg,
West Germany
Classical (orchestra, vocal, instrumental,
organ)
Mid- to end of June
The Festival has performances of orches-
tral and vocal music with organ, as well
as organ recitals.
Director: Hanns-Helmut Mähner
Accommodations: Numerous hotels
and guest houses are available, as are
camping and picnicking facilities. Foul
weather clothing is recommended.
Ticket information: Write to Karten-
vorverkaufsstelle, Theatergasse 17,
D-8500 Nuremberg, West Germany
(tel. 0911-22988 or -204137

Kassel Music Festival
Heinrich-Schütz-Alle 33, D-3500 Kassel-
Wilhelmshöhe, West Germany
Classical
November (September in 1981)
Director: Dr. Wolfgang Rehm
Ticket information: Ticket prices range
from 10 to 30 deutsche marks

Konstanzer Internationale Musiktage
Postfach 1230 D-7750, Konstanz,
West Germany
Classical and romantic
Mid-June through mid-July
This festival of great classical music
was first held in 1949. It prides itself
on the quality of its performances by
world famous artists.
Concerts take place in and around Con-
stance, a picturesque medieval town on
the shores of Lake Constance.
Director: Eduard Fendel, Manager,
Tamas Sulyok, Art Director
Accommodations/other items of interest
in area: Information on lodging can be
obtained from Tourist Information
Konstanz, Postfach 1230, D-7750
Konstanz, Federal Republic of Germany.
Camping is allowed.
Constance offers spectacular mountain
scenery and fine museums, theater,
restaurants, and sports facilities.
Ticket information: Admission is 10 to
30 deutsche marks. For tickets, write to
Geschaftsstelle der Konstanzer Inter-
national Musiktage, Bahnhofplatz 6,
D-7750 Konstanz, Federal Republic
of Germany.

**Leitheimer Schloss Konzerte
(Leitheimer Castle Concerts)**
Baron von Tucher, D-8851 Leitheim,
Donauwörth, West Germany (tel.
09007-231)
Classical (chamber music)
Early May to mid-October
This chamber music concert series was
founded in 1960 by Baron Albrecht
Freiherr von Tucher, and it is held in
his residence, Leitheimer Castle. Concerts are held each weekend evening for
the period from the beginning of May
until the middle of October, and they
are given by candlelight in the Rococo
Festival Room, which was finished in
1751. Mozart played in this room in
1778. In recent years Frankfurt's Clari-
net Trio, Munich's Sonnleitner Quartet,
Peter Schmalfuss, Buffalo's Rowe String
Quartet, and the Israel Baroque Players
were featured performers in the concert
series.
Since the Festival Room seats a maximum of 150 people, tickets should be
ordered in advance.
Director/Sponsor: Baron Albrecht
Freiherr von Tucher

Accommodations: The Baron allows camping on the grounds of his estate
Ticket information: Admission is 18 deutsche marks for adults, 12 for children. Tickets can be ordered in advance only from the Baron, 8851 Schloss Leitheim/Donau, West Germany (tel. 09007-231).

Ludwigsburg Castle Festival
Elmar-Doch Strasse 40, D-7140 Ludwigsburg, West Germany
Classical
May to October
Director: Prof. Wolfgang Gönnenwein

Music in the 20th Century
Saarländischer Rundfunk, P.O. Box 1050, D-6600 Saarbrücken, West Germany
Classical (20th century)
July
This fesitval was founded in 1969 and has been presented yearly since then
Director: Prof. (Dr.) Hubert Rohde
Ticket information: Write to SR-Pressestelle, P.O. Box 1050, D-6600 Saarbrücken, West Germany

Musiktage
c/o Schloss Elmau, D-8101 Klais Oberbayern, West Germany (tel.08823-1021)
Classical
June
Peter Schreier, Konrad Ragossnig, Leon Lishner, Denes Zsigmondy, Anneliese Nissen, and the Bartok Quartet have performed at the Festival in past years
Director: Sieglinde Mesirca
Ticket information: Tickets cost from 15 to 25 deutsche marks

Nymphenburg Castle Summer Festival
c/o Freunde der Residenz, Zuccalistrasse 21, D-8000 Munich 19, West Germany
Classical
June to July
Performances take place in the "Steinerner Sall" in Nymphenburg Castle, which seats 380
Director: Eva Walz
Ticket information: Tickets range from 15 to 30 deutsche marks

Schäftlarner Cloister Concerts
D-8026 Schäftlarn, West Germany
Classical
May to October
Maurice André, Ingrid Haebler and Walter Klein are among the musicians who have performed at the Schäftlarner Cloister Concerts
Director: Benno Forster
Ticket information: Tickets are 10 to 25 deutsche marks
How to get there: Schäftlarner is 20 kilometers S. of Munich

Schwetzinger Festspiele
During the Festival: Schwetzingen Castle, D-6830 Schwetzingen, West Germany
Other times: Postfach 837, Neckarstrasse 230, D-7000 Stuttgart 1, West Germany
May
The Festival presents opera, ballet, plays, and classical music, including music of the 20th century
Director: Dr. Peter Kehm
Ticket information: Tickets cost from 8 to 45 deutsche marks for opera, ballet, and plays; 12 to 38 deutsche marks for concerts

Summer Academy of Collegium Musicum Schloss Pommersfelden
Schützenstrasse 54, 8600, Bamberg, West Germany (tel. 0951-27234)
Classical works for orchestra and chamber music
Mid-July through mid-August
For the past 21 years, the Collegium Musicum Schloss Pommersfelden has conducted a summer program of study for talented young musicians. Orchestral work and chamber music study form the basis of the program at the summer academy, and orchestral concerts and chamber music evenings are offered to the public in the Marble Hall of Pommersfelden Castle. The participants are young musicians who have almost completed their musical studies or who are on the threshold of professional musical careers.
Director: Richard Englebrecht
Ticket information: Tickets cost 12, 14, and 16 deutsche marks. Write to Schlossverwaltung Pommersfelden, D-8602 Pommersfelden, Germany (tel. 09548-203).

Witten Festival of Contemporary Chamber Music
c/o Kulturamt der Stadt Witten, Bergerstrasse 25, D-5810 Witten, West Germany
Classical
April
The Witten Festival features contemporary chamber music

Würzburg Bach Festival
c/o Bachchor der St. Johanniskirche, Hofstallstrasse 5, D-8700 Würzburg, West Germany
Classical
November to December
Artists who have performed in the past include Alexis Weissenberg, Jean-Pierre Rampal, and Elizabeth Speiser. Concerts take place in the St. Johannis Church, which seats 800.
Director: Christian Kabitz

YUGOSLAVIA

Dubrovnik Summer Festival
OD Sigurate 1, 50000 Dubrovnik, Yugoslavia
Opera, ballet, symphonic, theater, folklore
July through August
Begun in 1949, this festival has a long tradition in Yugoslavia, and is known world-wide for the ambience of its performances, which take place on 42 outdoor stages in Dubrovnik. Concerts feature orchestras and artists from as far away as England, the U.S., Russia, and Australia, as well as from Yugoslavia. The rich musical season includes opera, ballet, chamber music, recitals, and midnight serenades as well as orchestra and choral performances. Not to be missed are performances of folk song and dance by groups from all areas of Yugoslavia.
Director: Prof. Niko Napica
Accommodations/other items of interest in area: For information on lodging, contact Tourist Information Center, Placa, 50 000 Dubrovnik, Yugoslavia. Camping is allowed at a cost of about $2. Camping facilities are near the beach. Trailers are allowed at an additional charge of $1.50. There is picnicking. Dubrovnik is an historical old town with fine museums and beaches. One-day and half-day coach and boat tours are available.
Ticket information: Admission ranges from $3 to $12. Tickets can be ordered in advance or purchased daily in Dubrovnik.

International Summer Festival Ljubljana
Festival Ljubljana, 61000 Ljubljana, Trg francoske rev 1, Yugoslavia
Classical, opera, folklore, dance, theater
Mid-June to late August
This annual event has gone through many changes since its inception in 1952, when it was only 1 week long and included Yugoslavian cultural, economic, touristic, folklore, and sporting events. After 2 years it was decided to feature only cultural events, and the response to this change was so great that the Festival expanded to its current summer-long duration, featuring all of the performing arts. In 1955, an old monastery

of the crusaders was converted into the Festival site, and the monastery's garden, which seats 1,500, is where all large performances are held today. Smaller chamber concerts are held in the court-yard of an 18th century church. Along with the expansion of the Festival, it also became international; recent per-formers have included the Royal Liver-pool Philharmonic Orchestra, the Lenin-grad Philharmonic Orchestra, the Sydney String Quartet, Duo Mandel from the U. S., and Vienna's Anton Dermonta. All in all, this festival spon-sors over 70 events.
Director: Dr. Henrik Neubauer
Accommodations: There are many hotels in Ljubljana
Ticket information: Admission ranges in price from 40 to 160 dinars. For infor-mation on how to obtain advance tickets, write to the Festival.
How to get there: There are train con-nections to Ljubljana from nearly every European city

Music Evenings in St. Donat's
Narodno Kazaliste, I. L. Ribara 8, 57000 Zadar, Yugoslavia
Classical (early music)
Late July through mid-August
This 3-week festival presents pre-baroque European music in thematic blocks of concerts. A recent theme has been early music of the Mediterranean countries. Early music ensembles from throughout Europe perform. Concerts are held in St. Donat's, a 9th century church which is a characteristic example of old Croatian architecture, and in other his-torical buildings in Zadar.
Director: Dr. Marijan Grgic
Sponsors: City of Zadar, RTV Zagreb
Accommodations: Accommodations in Zadar are available at Turisthotel, Borik Hotel, Jadera Hotel, and Sunturist Agency. There is camping at a cost of about $1 per person per night. Facilities include shops, restaurants, and lava-tories. Trailers are welcome.
The ancient town of Zadar offers many historic and artistic monuments, excur-sions, galleries, museums, swimming,and entertainment.
Ticket information: Tickets range from $1 to $3. They can be reserved by writ-ing to the Festival (they go on sale one hour before the concerts).

Varazdinske Barokne Veceri (Varazdin Baroque Festival)
Zajednica Kulture, 42000 Varazdin, Yugoslavia
Classical (baroque)
Late September to early October
Founded in 1971, this annual autumn event features baroque music of the 17th and 18th centuries, paying special attention to Croatian composers. The performers are all Yugoslavian and in past years have included Ruza Pospis-Baladani, Karl Richter, Lovro Macic, and Milan Horvat. Concerts are given in various small halls in the town of Varazdin. It is suggested that patrons bring foul-weather clothing.
Director: Prof. Vladimir Kranjcevic
Sponsor: Zajednica Kulture (Varazdin)
Accommodations: In Varazdin there is the Hotel Turist, and campsites are avail-able in the area
Ticket information: Tickets for indi-vidual concerts cost up to $10
How to get there: Varazdin is approxi-mately 2 hours from Zagreb, and there are bus connections

Zagreb Biennial Music Festival
Trnjanska b.b., YU 41000 Zagreb, Yugoslavia
Contemporary
Mid-May (1 week); biennially
This festival of contemporary music has been held for 1 week every 2 years since 1961. Festival sponsors bill the event as a cultural link between the East and West, and the appearance in recent years of soloists from the Bolshoi Theater, Meredith Monk, the Cologne Opera, and various Yugoslavian avant-garde composers seems to bear this out. Concerts are held indoors either in a large hall with a seating capacity of 2,000 or at a more intimate setting, a club with 380 seats.
Director: Niksa Gligo
Sponsor: Zagreb Municipal Assembly
Accommodations: There are many hotels and pensions in Zagreb. For in-formation, write to Generalturist, Congres Department Zrinjevac 18, 41000 Zagreb, Yugoslavia.
Ticket information: Individual concert ticket prices run from 40 to 180 dinars and may be ordered in advance

JAZZ

BELGIUM

International Jazz Festival at Dendermonde
Honky Tonk Jazz Club, Leopold II
baan, Dendermonde, Belgium
Jazz (New Orleans, blues, swing)
First Friday and Saturday in September
This annual 2-day jazz festival, which
began in 1971, focuses primarily on New
Orleans, blues , and swing. Held at an
uncovered playground, where 2,000
people can be accommodated, the event
has had 16,000 spectators in its 9-year
history. Audiences have come to hear
performers such as Memphis Slim, Rhoda
Scott, the New Orleans Legends, and
Papa Blue. In addition to this special
event, weekly concerts are held at the
Honky Tonk Jazz Club throughout the
year.
Patrons are advised to bring foul-weather
clothing.
Director: Piet Henvinck
Sponsors: Sabena, Festival van Klaan-
deren, Coca Cola, Kredietbank
Accommodations: Campgrounds with
full facilities are available, and they are
free; there is also a hotel in Dender-
monde: Hotel Wets
Ticket information: Tickets cost 300
Belgian francs for the entire 2-day event.
They may be obtained in advance by
writing to the Honky Tonk Jazz Club.
How to get there: Dendermonde is in
the countryside, close to Ghent,
Brussels, and Antwerp

Jazz Bilzen
Bilzen, Belgium
Rock, jazz, folk
Mid-August
This is the oldest rock and jazz continen-
tal festival; it was started in 1965. It
features 4 days of outdoor concerts. Performers such as Rod Stewart, the Kinks,
Blondie, James Brown, Lou Reed, Ike
and Tina Turner, and many more provide entertainment.
Director: Theo Boelen
Accommodations/other items of interest
in area: Lodging is available in Bilzen at
the Liege, the Maastricht, and the
Aachen. Camping, with complete facilities, costs about $1. Trailers are not
allowed and there is no picnicking.

There are many castles and historic cities
in the area.
Ticket information: Admission is about
$10. Tickets go on sale throughout
Belgium.
How to get there: Bilzen is in East
Belgium

DENMARK

Copenhagen Jazz Festival
Copenhagen, Denmark
Jazz
First week in July
The intention is to make this new festival the European answer to the Newport Jazz Festival across the Atlantic. All kinds of jazz, from New Orleans to jazz-rock, are presented during the Festival, played by international stars as well as by the best Danish musicians. The event is opened by a street parade and every day there is an outdoor jazz concert followed by performances in the city's jazz clubs at night.
Other festival activities include showings of jazz-related films and visual art.
Director: Poul Bjørnholt
Sponsors: Ministry of Cultural Affairs, the Copenhagen Council, Tuborg Breweries
Accommodations/other items of interest in area: There are many hotels in Copenhagen, among them the d'Angleterre, Kongens Nytorv 34, DK-1050 København K, Denmark; the Scandinavia, Amager Boulevard 70, DK-2300 København S, Denmark; and the Sheraton-Copenhagen, Vester Søgade 6, DK-1601 København V, Denmark.
Copenhagen has many sites of interest, including the Latin Quarter, the Royal Palace, and many museums.
Ticket information: Tickets are free. For festival information, write to Poul Bjørnholt, Københavns City Center, Pilestrade 4, 2. sal. 1112 København K, Denmark.

Femø Jazz Festival
Femø, Denmark
Jazz
First weekend in August
The Festival began in 1969 and until 1977 took place at the Femø Inn. Success and larger crowds led to its site shifting to Femø's campground where performances take place in a large tent.
Sponsor: Femø Jazz Foundation
Accommodations/other items of interest in area: For information about accommodations, write to Tourist Office, Axeltorv, DK 4900 Nakskov, Denmark. St. Nikolaj, a late Gothic medieval church, is a point of interest in Nakskov.
Ticket information: Tickets are about 120 Danish kroner. For tickets write to Femø Jazz Foundation, Erantisvej 28, 4900 Nakskov, Denmark.

Holstebro Jazz Festival
Holstebro-Hallen, DK-7500 Holstebro, Denmark
Jazz and Folk
End of Spetember
Local amateur and professional musicians take part in this weekend festival. Stan Getz, Ceder Walton, and Yusef Lateef are among recent participants.
Sponsor: The Club Jass
Ticket information: Write to Holstebro Tourist Office, Brostraede 1, DK-7500 Holstebro, Denmark

Sorø Jazz Festival
c/o Sorø Tourist Office, Torvet, DK-4180 Sorø, Denmark (tel. 03-630269)
Jazz
August
Concerts are held both outdoors and indoors
Director: Peruna Jazzclub

FINLAND

Pori International Jazz Festival
Luvianpuistokatu 2D, 28100 Pori 10,
Finland
Jazz
Second weekend in July
In the Finnish coastal city of Pori, interest in jazz dates back to the end of World War II. In 1966, with the opening of the Pori International Jazz Festival, the jazz lovers' dreams came true; that year the event sponsored 2 concerts and 1 jam session. Today, this annual event begins on the afternoon of the 2nd Thursday in July, and by the time it is over Sunday night, there will have been 30 different sessions. The concerts are held on Kirjurinlluoto Island, in an open-air facility with unlimited seating capacity; the rest of the program consists of jam sessions held in restaurants and nightclubs in Pori. The Festival also sponsors ballet performances, film shows, and lectures. In addition to Ted Curson, who has played at all Pori festivals, Ornette Coleman, Max Roach, Freddie Hubbard, Sonny Rollins, B. B. King, and Australia's Brian Brown Quartet have been among those who have performed in recent years.
The Festival also gives special attention to young Finnish jazz musicians.
Directors: Ilkka Karumo and Matti Poijarvi
Sponsors: State of Finland, City of Pori, commercial advertisers
Accommodations/other items of interest in area: In addition to camping facilities, which cost about $1 per night, there are many hotels and motels in Pori. For information, contact Municipal Tourist Office, Antinkatu 5, Pori, Finland.
The Yytéri sands is among the many sights in the vicinity of Pori; there are many opportunities for outdoor activities.
Ticket information: Concert prices range up to $10; jam sessions range from $5 to $15, the more expensive ones including a meal. Tickets can be ordered by mail by writing to Pori International Jazz Festival, Luvianpuistok 2D, 28100 Pori 10, Finland (tel. 939-12124). In addition, there are advance sales of tickets at different music stores in Finland.
How to get there: There are 3 round-trip express trains a day from Helsinki via Tampere, several express buses, and 2 round-trip flights directly from Helsinki

NORWAY

Kongsberg Jazz Festival

P.O. Box 91, 3601 Kongsberg, Norway
(tel. 034-33166)
Jazz
Late June (1 week)
In 1979, the 15th annual Kongsberg
Jazz Festival took place. This week-long
event features jazz musicians from all
over the world, most recently Sonny
Rollins, Gil Evans, and Ron Carter.
Concerts are given in a hall which seats
600 and in 5 different small clubs in the
town of Kongsberg.
The Festival also sponsors seminars during the week of the event.
Director: Jon Eidsbraten
Accommodations: The Grand Hotel is
in Kongsberg; in addition, there are
camping facilities in the area
Ticket information: Admission at all
concerts is 35 Norwegian kroner; tickets
can be obtained in advance by contacting the Festival

Molde International Jazz Festival

P.O. Box 261, N-6400, Molde, Norway
(tel. 072-53779)
Jazz
Late July (1 week); in 1980, July 28 to
August 2
First held in 1961 as a 3-day event featuring Norwegian artists, this festival has
grown to international proportions and
now runs for one week each year. The
Festival also features poetry readings,
folk music, and art exhibitions, but the
emphasis is on jazz—contemporary, be-
bop, and traditional. Past performers
include Keith Jarrett, Jean Luc Ponty,
Muddy Waters Blues Band, Max Roach
Quartet, and McCoy Tyner. The Festival
always introduces up-and-coming groups.
Although concerts are held indoors (in
the Molde Cinema, which holds 500
people, and in 4 smaller clubs, each with
a maximum capacity of 200), Molde is
situated on the northern coast of Norway, which is subject to changeable
weather conditions, and patrons are advised to bring warm clothing.
Director: Otto Christian Saettem, Jr.
Accommodations/other items of interest
in area: Hotels in the area include:
Alexandra Hotel, N-6400; Hotel Nobel,

N-6400; and Romsdalsheimen Hotel,
N-6400; all in Molde, Norway. Camping is permitted (5 Norwegian kroner
per person per night).
Molde, a town of only 16,000 inhabitants, is surrounded by mountains,
fjords, and islands; it is suited to many
outdoor activities.
Ticket information: Tickets must be
ordered by mail or phone. Write to
P.O. Box 261, N-6400, Molde, Norway;
or call 072-53779. Tickets range in
price from 20 to 45 Norwegian kroner.

POLAND

International Festival of Jazz Music
Polish Jazz Society, Rutkowskiego 20,
00-020 Warsaw, Poland
Jazz
Late October (4 days)
This 4-day event, the biggest jazz festival in Eastern Europe, has been held annually since 1958. Although most of the concerts are held in Warsaw's Congresowa Hall, which seats 3,000, the Polish Jazz Society also sponsors jam sessions and small-club concerts both in other Warsaw locations and other Polish cities during the Festival. In its 21-year history, this event has featured musicians from 6 continents.
Director: Stanislaw Cejrowski
Sponsors: Polish Jazz Society and Polish Ministry of Art and Culture
Accommodations/other items of interest in area: The Victoria Hotel, the Forum Hotel, and the Solec Hotel are among the many available accommodations in central Warsaw.
Warsaw's Old City and the King's Palace are among the many places to be visited in this ancient capital.
Ticket information: Tickets may be purchased by writing to General Board, Polish Jazz Society, Rutkowskiego 20, 00-020, Warsaw. The price of admission is 1,250 zlotys and covers entry to 5 concerts.

Old Jazz Meeting
Polish Traditional Jazz Club, Betorege 10, 00612 Warsaw, Poland
Jazz (traditional)
February
"Traditional jazz" comprises all kinds of old jazz styles from blues, gospel, and spirituals through dixieland and Chicago to big band jazz of the swing era. For the last few years this festival has presented all these styles performed by bands and soloists from Europe and the U.S. The nucleus of the Festival, which reflects its early character in the 1960s, is the Golden Washboard Contest for Polish traditional jazz bands (mainly dixieland). Events in this 4-day festival are held in Congress Hall in Warsaw's Palace of Culture and Science, which seats 3,000, and in Stodola Hall, which seats 800. Winter clothing is recommended.

Director: Jerzy Bojanowski
Sponsors: Polish Students Union, Polish Jazz Society, Polish Radio and Television
Accommodations/other items of interest in area: Hotel accommodations are available in Warsaw. Reservations can be made through the Polish Travel Bureau, Orbis. Camping and picnicking are allowed, but the weather will be cold.
Festival goers might be interested in the Akwarium Jazz Club, open daily, at Emilii Plater 49. There are many places of interest in Warsaw.
Ticket information: Sets of tickets to all the Festival events are 300 to 400 zlotys. Tickets can be ordered from the Polish Jazz Society, Rutkowskiego 20, 00 020 Warsaw, Poland.

SWITZERLAND YUGOSLAVIA

Montreux International Jazz Festival
Montreux Tourist Office, Case Postale
97, CH-1820, Switzerland (tel. 021-
613384)
Jazz, rock, blues
Early to late July (2 weeks)
Founded in 1967, this event takes place
each year for 2 weeks in July. In its 13-
year history the Festival has been host to
nearly every jazz great in the world; in
recent years those who have performed
include Ray Charles, Clark Terry, Mary
Lou Williams, Oscar Peterson and Count
Basie, and Dizzy Gillespie. During the
past few years, the Festival has also
offered country rock and a jazz-rock
summit. In addition to the regular program, there are free afternoon concerts
and the annual Swiss Jazz Contest. Concerts are held in the Montreux Casino
Hall, which can accommodate 3,000
spectators, and in the uncovered garden
of the casino, which has flexible seating
arrangements.
Director: Claude Nobs
Accommodations/other items of interest
in area: In addition to the many hotels
in Montreux, the Festival also offers
free camping; for information, contact
Montreux Tourist Office, Case Postale
97, CH-1820 Montreux, Switzerland;
tel. 021-613384.
Montreux is situated on Lake Geneva,
which offers many sports activities.
Also, there is a casino in Montreux.
Ticket information: Tickets range in
price from 15 to 45 Swiss francs;
there are also festival passes for 3, 5, or
7 days of concerts; for information,
contact the Montreux Tourist Office

International Jazz Festival of Ljubljana
Mladen Mazur, Program Director, 41000
Zagreb, Ilica 48, Yugoslavia
Jazz
Mid-June (3 days)
This event began as a Yugoslavian national festival in 1960, in the former
health-resort town of Bled, in northwestern Yugoslavia. By 1962, the Festival became international, and the site
was moved to the urban center of
Ljubljana in 1967. The event extends
over a 3-day period each year, and con-
certs are held in the courtyard of an
old monastery; it is a covered outdoor
theater and can accommodate 1,800.
All styles of jazz are featured here, and
past performers have included Elvin
Jones Jazz Machine, McCoy Tyner,
Gary Burton, and the Yugoslav Radio
Big Bands, as well as many of the best
known jazz artists of Europe.
Director: Mladen Mazur
Sponsor: Fund of the Republic of
Slovenia, City of Ljubljana
Accommodations/other items of interest
in area: There are many hotels in Ljubl-
jana, including Union, Lev, the Holiday
Inn, and Turist.
Items of interest to tourists include the
Old Town of Ljubljana, the Postojna
Caves, and the town of Bled.
Ticket information: Tickets are priced
from 50 to 80 dinars; they may be pur-
chased in advance by writing to Mladen
Mazur, 41000 Zagreb, Ilica 48,
Yugoslavia

FOLK

DENMARK

Skagen Folk Festival

c/o Tourist Office of Skagen, Sct.
Laurentii Vej 18, DK-9990 Skagen,
Denmark (tel. 08-441377)
Folk
June
Begun in 1971 with a few musicians
and fewer listeners, the Festival has been
growing ever since. Concerts take place
in various halls in Skagen and outdoors.
The outdoor concerts are free.
Director: Gerd Parkholt (Tourist Office
address), tel. 08-445116
Ticket information: Write or call the
Skagen tourist office

ENGLAND

Berkshire Midsummer Folk Festival

Whitehouse Farm, Spencer's Wood near
Reading, Berkshire, England
Folk
Last full weekend in June
This festival of folk dance, music, and
song, now in its 7th season, has become
a popular, deliberately small festival,
where the artists mix with the audience.
Renowned for its organization, it is
mainly aimed at the folk-music enthu-
siast and consequently participation
and enthusiasm are high. Events include
concerts, ceilidhs, singarounds, and
children's activities. In addition there
is a craft marquee, featuring craft workshops and demonstrations, as well as
items for sale.
There are tickets for approximately
500 people. Events are held outdoors
and in the farm barn.
Director: Brian Jones
Sponsor: English Folk Dance and Song
Society
Accommodations/other items of interest
in area: Information on accommodations is available from the Festival sponsors. Camping facilities are available in
the area. Other items of interest in the
area are Windsor Castle and Oxford.
Ticket information: Tickets are available for the weekend and by the day
and individual event. Admission for the
entire weekend is £5.25. For tickets,
write to 53 Beechwood Ave., Woodley,
Reading, RG5 3DF, Berkshire, England.
How to get there: Leave MH Motorway
at Junction 11; take A33 toward Basing-
stoke and look for signposts

Billingham International Folklore Festival

Festival Office, Municipal Buildings,
Town Center, Billingham, Cleveland,
England
Folk
Mid-August
The Billingham International Festival
of folk music, song, and dance has
featured folklore ensembles from every
continent. This lively festival includes
outdoor concerts (in an uncovered
theater which seats 3,000 in the Town
Center), parades, and processions, as well
as indoor concerts.

The town library presents a daily children's program of story-telling and exhibition song and dance. There is nightly jazz and Carribean steel band music at the Billingham Forum, which also hosts a major arts and crafts exhibition and demonstrations of English crafts. The Festival presents films depicting life in the countries represented at the Festival, and an international barn dance for all.
Director: Philip T. Conroy, M. B. E.
Sponsor: Stockton Borough Council
Accommodations: Accommodations are available at the Billingham Arms Hotel, Town Center, Billingham, England. There are also nearby sites for Caravans, etc.
Ticket information: Ticket prices range from £.30 to £2.50. For tickets and a programme summary write or telephone Stockton 0642-552141.

The Black Horse Gathering
The Black Horse, Great Linford, Milton Keynes, England
Folk Dance and Song
Late August
This 1-day gathering for folk dance and song features local and national singers and dancers, including a French dance group. Now in its 8th season, it is a good family occasion and fun for all to see local performers. Most of the festivities are held outdoors, but the singing takes place in the local bars, which are open from 11:00 A.M. to 11:30 P.M.
Director: David Hall
Sponsors: The Black Horse and Mine Hosts
Accommodations: The Newport Pagrell Service Station Motel is in the area
Ticket information: There is no charge for admission, and tickets are not required. A collection is taken.
How to get there: The Festival is on AA22 road, between Newport Pagrell and Wolverton or Grand Union Canal

Broadstairs Folk Week
Hon Secretary: Pam Porritt, 88 South Wood Road, Ramsgate, Kent CT11 0AW, England
Folk
First full week of August
Musicians, singers, dancers, and other folk groups come to Broadstairs Folk Week not only from around England but also from Ireland and Europe. Entertainment includes Shows, barn dances,

singarounds, torchlight processions, ceilidhs, busking tours, dancers' dances, night spots, a craft fair, a pig roast, and children's events. There are numerous workshops on, for example, dancing (clog, Morris, Kentish, North Country, etc.), food, wine making, costumes, and crafts.
The Festival takes place indoors and outdoors. The Grand Ballroom, used for some evening events, seats 350; other smaller halls are also used for indoor events. The Open Air Show can accommodate 1,000. The weather is usually good, but raincoats may be advisable.
Director: Jack Hamilton
Sponsors: Local businessmen and Thanet District Council
Accommodations/other items of interest in area: Accommodations are available at Dundonald Hotel and Hanson Hotel, Belvedere Road, Broadstairs. Camping amenities are available to season ticket holders for a charge of approximately £8. There are also facilities for trailers. Broadstairs is 16 miles from Canterbury, with its fine old cathedral; there are many other old villages and towns in the area. Orchards, known as the "Garden of England," are nearby. Broadstairs is 80 miles from London and, by Hovercraft, 30 minutes from France.
Ticket information: A season ticket for the entire week-long festival is approximately £12. Weekend and day tickets are also available. Information and booking forms can be obtained from the Festival.

Bromyard Folk Festival
Bromyard, Herefordshire, England
Folk
Mid-September
The entire town of Bromyard participates in this 3-day folk festival. Many well-known British folk singers and musicians perform. There are over 50 events, including ceilidhs, dances, concerts, singarounds, ballad shops, music hall, shanty sessions, Punch and Judy, massed Morris, processions, and children's dances. There are many workshops in Morris dancing, clogging, and more, including children's workshops. Events are held under 3 large canopies, each of which can accommodate several hundred people, and in halls in town. There are also various outdoor displays.
Director: Dave Jones

Accommodations/other items of interest in area: Lodging in Bromyard is available at Hop Pole Hotel, Falcon Hotel, and Barneby.

Camping and picnicking are allowed. The cost of complete camping facilities is included in the price of the Festival ticket. Trailers cannot be accommodated on the Festival site, but there are good caravan sites nearby. Campers are advised to be prepared for cold weather.

Of interest in the area are the cathedral towns of Hereford and Worcester and historic Malvern.

Ticket information: Admission is about £6 in advance or £8 on the day of the Festival, if available. Tickets can be obtained in advance from Doug Isles, 15, Mile End Road, Coleford, Gloucester, England.

How to get there: Bromyard is midway between Worcester and Leominster, 123 miles from London, 60 miles from Bristol, and 36 miles from Birmingham

Cornwall Folk Festival
Wadebridge, Cornwall, England
Folk
Late August
This small 3-day festival focuses on traditional English music. Many of England's fine folk performers are sure to be there. Events include concerts, musicarounds, songswaps, ceilidhs, workshops, dance displays, craft displays, barn dances, and more.

Concerts and other events take place in Town Hall and in hotels and inns throughout Wadebridge. The Festival enjoys strong community support.
Director: L. Cann
Accommodations/other items of interest in area: A fine camp site is available to patrons of the Festival, with water and electricity provided for £1. Sites must be booked in advance.

The Cornish country and seaside are well worth seeing.

Ticket information: Only 350 tickets are sold. A season ticket is about £6.50, and day tickets are about £3. For information and tickets write to Roger Hancock, Ref. EM, Tollgate, Treningle Hill, Bodmin, Cornwall, England, or phone Lanivet 373. Please include a self-addressed envelope.

Crewe and Nantwich Folk Festival
15 Park Road, Haslington, Crewe,
Cheshire CW1 1TQ, England
Folk
Next to last weekend in July
This festival is held in the town of Nantwich, based at the town's Civic Hall, which seats 800, but also using other halls and pubs in the town. The program includes concerts, ceilidhs, singarounds, music hall, workshops, dance displays, craft stalls, and free reed. Many English folk groups come to Nantwich to perform at the Festival.
Director: Derek Schofield
Sponsor: Crewe and Nantwich Borough Council
Accommodations/other items of interest in area: Camping facilities, only minutes walk from the Festival, are free for patrons of the Festival. For information on hotel accommodations write to Information Office, Civic Hall, Nantwich, Cheshire, England.

South Cheshire is an area of architectural and historic interest. Nantwich dates to pre-Elizabethan times.

Ticket information: A weekend ticket is approximately £5 and can be obtained by writing to the Festival (day tickets are also available)

How to get there: The Festival is in South Cheshire

Durham City Folk Festival
Durham, England
Folk
Early August
Durham City Folk Festival, begun in 1972, has become one of the leading events of its kind in Britain. It features folk bands, singers, musicians, and dance groups. It presents workshops on songs and song-writing, Morris and clog dancing, and Northumbrian pipes, to name but a few. There are also singarounds, shanty sessions, instrumental sessions, and a clog dancing championship. For the children there are playgroups and special events. Fresh food will be available.

Events are held in Durham House, which can accommodate 600, and in Town Hall, which can accommodate 300. Guests are advised to bring foul-weather clothing in case of inclement weather.
Director: Ian McCulloch
Accommodations: For information on lodging contact the Durham Tourist

Information Office.
There is camping, with no charge to festival ticket holders.
Ticket information: Tickets are about £5.50. After July 1 the price goes up slightly. They can be ordered from Ian McCulloch, 8 Cedar Close, Gilesgate Moor, Durham, England.

Eastbourne International Folk Festival
Eastbourne, England
Folk dance
Early May (1 weekend)
This is a participatory festival, not a concert type, although dancers and bands do perform to the general public. It is intended for groups of dancers to meet each other, perform for each other, and learn from each other. The main emphasis is folk dance, though some singing is included. There are workshops in many aspects of English and Europeon dance, ancient and modern. All workshops take place under one roof, with the maximum attendance about 250, "to keep the Festival friendly." Additional events include barn dances, procession, folk shows, and concerts.
Director: Peter J. Mayes
Sponsor: English Folk Dance and Song Society
Accommodations: The Festival is based in a beautiful seaside resort with 5,000 beds, from the 5-star Grand Hotel to small bed-and-breakfast guest houses. Camping is also available.
Ticket information: For the weekend, including admission to all events, £8. Half-board accommodations are £20 (Friday evening to Monday breakfast). For tickets, write to Festival Office, 8 The Sanctuary, Eastbourne BN20 8TA, England.
How to get there: Directions to the Festival are sent to all ticket purchasers and inquirers

Folk Nights at Michelham Priory
Upper Dicker, Hailsham, East Sussex, England
Folk
The weekend nearest the longest day of the year
This festival has built up from a barn dance 12 years ago to what is now probably the best event of its kind in England. Events include folk dance,
song, ritual dance and drama, street theater, and a folk and craft fair. Maximum attendance is 1,000. There is full bar and supper service provided on the Festival site.
Director: Peter J. Mayes
Sponsor: English Folk Dance and Song Society
Accommodations: There are hundreds of hotels, motels, inns, and guest houses within 10 miles. Contact the Tourist Information Center in Eastbourne for information. There are campsites nearby.
Ticket information: Tickets for this festival are normally sold out several weeks in advance. Admission is £.90 to £1.75. For tickets, write to Folk Tickets, 8 The Sanctuary, Eastbourne BN20 8TA, England.
How to get there: Michelham Priory is off the A22 (London/Eastbourne Road) about 6 miles out of Eastbourne

Folk Under Aries
Romsey, Hampshire, England
Folk
Early April
Sponsored by 14 folk clubs from counties around Portsmouth, Southampton, and Salisbury, the Festival aims to stimulate interest in the local folk scene. Its standards are high, and it has thrived since it began in 1973. The Festival presents concerts, ceilidhs, workshops, mumming, and more.
Events are held in and around Romsey. Abbey Hall, seating 250, Abbey Hotel, seating 350, and Crossfield Hall, which seats 500, are all put to use by the Festival.
Sponsor: Southern Counties Folk Federation (SCFF)
Accommodations/other items of interest in area: Accommodations are available at Abbey Hotel and White Horse (Trust House) in Romsey. Camping facilities are planned for the future.
Romsey, a designated conservation area, presents an attractive townscape, rich in antiquity and historic value.
Other items of interest in the area are Lord Mountbatten's Estate, New Forest, Southampton, and Portsmouth.
Ticket information: Tickets are priced at £1.50. They can be obtained by mail from Fairhaven, High Street, East Meon, Hampshire, England.

How to get there: Romsey is on A31 due N. of Southampton

Lacock and Chippenham Folk Festival
Chippenham, Wiltshire SN14 OPN, England
Folk
Last weekend in May
Begun in 1972, the Festival provides mostly English traditional dance and song by virtually everyone in the British folk scene. Over 100 events happen during 4 days: ceilidhs, barn dances, shanty sessions, pub sing songs, busking, parades, and more. Besides taking place in several halls (average capacity about 300) there is the Monday outdoor village event with room for up to 10,000 people. Performers such as Ossian, Wayfarers, Yorkshire Relish, Leon Rosselson, and Tony Rose, to name only a few, have been participants.
Director: Bill Bush
Sponsor: English Folk Dance and Song Society
Accommodations/other items of interest in area: Angel Motel, Bear Hotel, and Oxford Hotel, all in Chippenham, can provide accommodations. Camping and trailer facilities are available.
The Lacock Abbey and Village and the Fox Talbot Museum of Photography are 3 miles S. of Chippenham.
Ticket information: Season tickets are £7. Write to Festival Booking Office, 7 Carnarvon Close, Chippenham, Wilts., England.

Morpeth Northumbrian Gathering
Chairman, Westgate House, Dogger Bank, Morpeth, Northumberland NE61 1RF, England
Folk
April
Founded by the Morpeth Antiquarian Society over 13 years ago, the Gathering is a 5-day grass-roots event which relies on amateur rather than professional musicians. The Gathering's concern is to strengthen the traditions of Northumberland, the heartland of the ancient Kingdom of Northumbria, by presenting a profile of traditional arts, crafts, other activities, local history, architecture, etc. These include a strong musical tradition. Musical events include singarounds, barn dancing, singing and playing competitions, dancing competitions, and dialect recitals.
Indoor events take place in halls in Morpeth, which can accommodate from about 200 to 400 people.
Director: Roland Bibby
Accommodations/other items of interest in area: Lodging in Morpeth is available at Queen's Head, Black Bull, Waterford Lodge, and George and Dragon.
It is too cold in April for camping. There is picnicking.
Within a 3-mile radius of the small town of Morpeth are 3 castles, 3 churches, 1 bridge-chapel, 1 manor house of the medieval period, and charming river and woodland scenery.
How to get there: Morpeth is on the Al highway from London to Edinburgh, 15 miles N. of Newcastle upon Tyne, It is on the main railway between London and Edinburgh, and is served by Newcastle Airport, which is 12 miles away.

Poynton Folk Festival
Folk Centre, Park Lane, Poynton near Stockport, Cheshire, England
Folk
Easter Weekend
This festival arose out of the folk activities that take place throughout the year in the Folk Centre. It rapidly grew until it achieved recognition as a national event, but it still claims to be the smallest and most intimate folk festival in the United Kingdom. The Festival takes place almost entirely within a large, rambling building—it includes a concert hall and about a dozen rooms. Total capacity is 500. Events include concerts, ceilidh, Morris and clog dancing, singarounds, and jug bands and jam sessions. Food is available throughout the day in the Centre at very little cost.
Director: Eric Brock
Accommodations: A list of hotels will be provided on request. There is a fully equipped campsite nearby. Most visitors to the Festival camp nearby or sleep in their own sleeping bags on the premises.
Ticket information: Admission is £1 for Friday evening; £2 for Saturday or Sunday; £4.50 for the full weekend. For tickets, enclose check and stamped, self-addressed envelope.
How to get there: Poynton is on the A523 between Stockport and Macclesfield

ALAN STIVELL, HOLDING A CELTIC HARP, AND PETE SEEGER (PHOTO PREVIOUS PAGE)

South Petherton Folk and Craft Festival
The Square House, Palmer Street, South
Petherton, Somerset TA13 5DB, England
Folk
Late June or early July
This weekend folk and craft festival is
a modern revival of a 15th century
annual fair honoring the nativity of St.
John the Baptist. It guarantees visitors
a rich and varied range of music, dance,
song, children's events, craft exhibitions—
a cross section of the multifarious traditions of English life. This is a small folk
festival which prides itself on its friend-
liness.
Events are held in locations all around
the village. In case of rain, all events
can be under cover.
Director: David Close
Sponsors: South West Arts, Yeovil
District Council, Somerset County
Council, Taunton Cider Co., others
Accommodations: A list of hotel accommodations is available on request; send
a stamped, self-addressed envelope with
your inquiry to 24 Compton Road,
South Petherton, Somerset, UK. Camping is allowed; facilities are free with a
season ticket to the Festival. Trailers
are allowed in principle, but extremely
long ones might have difficulty.
There are many points of historical
interest in the area.
Ticket information: Season tickets are
£5; day and single event tickets are available. Write to John Johnson, 24 Compton Road, South Petherton, Somerset,
UK. Enclose a self-addressed, stamped
envelope or 3 International Reply
Coupons.
How to get there: South Petherton lies
just N. of A303 between Ilchester and
Ilminster; during the Festival all major
local road-junctions will be signposted

Stainsby Folk Festival
Brunts Farm, Stainsby, Derbyshire,
England
Folk
August
For the last 12 years this 3-day festival
in the Derbyshire countryside has featured many fine folk singers and musicians and folk dance teams. Local farm-
ing families all attend the Festival and
help with the arrangements. Events,
which take place outdoors or in large
field tents, include concerts, ceilidhs,

singarounds, craft, dance and musicians'
workshops, competitions, folk theater,
and dancing.
Patrons are encouraged to bring foul-
weather clothing and sensible shoes.
They are also urged to sample the "real
ale" which will be available.
Director: Mr. Ken Blankley, Festival
Chairman
Sponsor: Stainsby Folk Group
Accommodations/other items of interest
in area: There is free camping; facilities
include flush toilets, water, catering, and
bar. Hotel accommodations are avail-
able at Portland, Station and Clifton
Hotels in Chesterfield, and Fernleaf
Hotel in Mansfield.
Hardwick Hall is very close by the Festi-
val, as is plenty of Derbyshire country-
side.
Ticket information: Weekend tickets
are £6 in advance. For tickets write to
Mrs. B. Whitmore, 67 Strettea Lane,
Old Higham, Derbyshire, England; or
Mrs. M. Blankley, 11 Durley Chine Drive,
Hasland, Chesterfield, Derbyshire,
England.
How to get there: Stainsby is a very
small Derbyshire village, but lies only
a mile away from exit 29 of the M1
motorway. Brunts farm lies centrally
in the village.

Towersey Village Festival
Towersey Village, Oxon, England
Folk
Late August
This folk festival and village fete and
fair, held on the August Bank Holiday
Weekend, started over 15 years ago, and
has increased both in size and quality.
Scheduled events include concerts and
shows by a variety of English folk
groups, ceilidhs, craft exhibitions, torchlight processions, puppet shows, story
telling, workshops, and more. There
are music and drama workshops for children at which the children help devise
a musical drama for presentation at the
Monday luncheon concert.
Events take place under canopies with
capacities of from 100 to 1,000 people.
All profits from this festival go to
charity.
Director: Steve Heap
Accommodations: Hotel accommodations are available 2 miles from Towersey in Thame at the Spread Eagle, Black
Horse, or Jolly Sailor. Camping is per-

mitted, and the cost of facilities is included in the season ticket. There are also facilities for trailers. Picnicking is allowed.

Ticket information: A season ticket is £7. Tickets for individual concerts begin at £1, and full day tickets are £2.50. For tickets and inquiries write to The Festival Secretary, 127 Chinnor Road, Thame, OXON OX93LP, England.

How to get there: Towersey is 2 miles southeast of Thame in Oxfordshire

FINLAND

Folk Music Festival
Festivalbyran, SF-69600 Kaustinen, Finland
Folk
July
The 1st Kaustinen Folk Music Festival took place in 1968. It is an international festival with around 2,000 performers and more than 70,000 visitors annually. Kaustinen is a small Finnish rural commune. Many of its 3,600 inhabitants take part in the Festival.
Concerts are given in 5 indoor halls (seating from 100 to 350), one concert hall (seating for 1,200), and outdoors (with room for 7,000).
Director: Mr. Viljo S. Maattala
Accommodations: In addition to hotel accommodations in the area, camping facilities are available
Ticket information: Tickets are 10 to 25 Finnish marks
How to get there: Kaustinen is situated in the central part of Finland, in Central Ostrobothnia (500 km form Helsinki). The nearest towns are Kokkolo (48 km), Pietarsaari (60 km), and Vaasa (130 km). One can travel by train and airplane to Kokkola, and to Pietarsaari and Vaasa by ship from Sweden.

Pispalan Sottiisi (International Folklore Festival)
Tampere, Finland
Folk
First weekend in June in even-numbered years
The Pispalan Sottiisi is organized by the Suomen Nuorison Liitto (the Youth Association of Finland) and has been held every 2nd year beginning in 1970, with the exception of the 1979 festival to commemorate the 200th anniversary of the city of Tampere.
The Festival consists of folk music and dance from Finland and other countries —each year there are up to 1,500 Finnish participants and 4 to 6 groups of foreign participants amounting to about 200. As many as 60,000 people come to see and hear the festivities, comprised of various dancing events in the street, folk dance concerts in theaters, and the main festival usually held in the 10,000 seat hockey arena.

In addition there are competitions in the pair dance and in folk-music composition as well as seminars and classes in folk dance and music.

Director: Suomen Nuorison Liitto

Accommodations: There are many hotels in all price ranges in Tampere. Camping is available.

Ticket information: Ticket costs range from 10 to 25 Finnish marks. For tickets, write to Suomen Nuorison Liitto, Simonkatu 12 A, SF-00100 Helsinki 10.

ISRAEL

Oriental Song Festival
The National Hall, Jerusalem, Israel
Middle-Eastern folk
December 25

Founded in 1969, this annual 1-day festival is held in Jerusalem's National Hall, which has a seating capacity of 3,000. Created with the goal of developing Oriental and Middle-Eastern folk music, the event also includes folk dances and popular music, and it is broadcast live on Israeli TV and radio. Singers Enrico Macias and Manos Hajidakis have performed in the past.

Director: Joseph Ben-Israel

Ticket information: Admission is from 50 to 100 pounds. Tickets are available only at the box office.

WALES

The National Eisteddfod of Wales
31A Gorwydd Road, Gowerton, North
Swansea SA4 3AG, South Wales
Traditional Welsh folk festival
Early August (one week)
This folk festival is a tradition of the
Welsh people, and it dates back to the
12th century when the *eisteddfod*
changed from a meeting of the bards to
discuss matters pertaining to their craft
into the competitive event it remains
today. In 1176, there were 2 main contests: one was poetic—to test the skills
of the bards in the traditional Welsh
meters; the other was musical—open to
minstrels and pipers of all nations. The
contemporary *eisteddfod* is in much the
same vein, although choral competitions
have been added to the program as well.
In addition, this annual week-long festival has grown into a national event; it
is patronized by 20,000 people each
year, who all share a love for poetry,
literature, music, drama, and arts and
crafts.
The Festival site alternates yearly between North and South Wales; performances and competitions are held outdoors in a pavilion which seats 5,000.
Other concerts and recitals are held in
2 smaller halls, with a combined capacity of 600.
Director: J. Emyr Jenkins
Accommodations: For information
about accommodations in the area,
write to Accommodations Secretary,
31A Gorwynd Road, Gowerton, Swansea, South Wales. There are campsites in
the area, and they have trailer facilities.
Ticket information: In 1978, ticket
prices ranged as follows: daily, from
£1 to £2; weekly, £13.50 to £18

YUGOSLAVIA

Balkan Festival of Folk Song and Dance
Dimitar Vlahov, 8, Ohrid, Yugoslavia
Folk
July
This 6-day folk festival reflects the com-
plex authenticity of the folk traditions
of Yugoslavia and the surrounding areas.
Groups from all the republics in Yugoslavia, and especially from Macedonia,
perform. In addition, folk groups from
most of the surrounding nations appear.
The Festival also sponsors symposia and
exhibitions. Events are held outdoors.
Director: Milorad Dusanic
Accommodations: Contact the Festival
for information on accommodations
in Ohrid.
There is camping and picnicking.
Ticket information: Admission is 30 to
50 dinars. Tickets can be reserved and
purchased during the Festival.

MISCELLANEOUS

AUSTRALIA

Adelaide Festival of Arts

Adelaide Festival Centre, King William
Road, Adelaide 5000 S.A., Australia
All performing arts: classical music,
jazz, pop music, theater, dance, mime,
mask, marionette, art exhibitions
Late February to mid-March (3 weeks,
every other year)
This 3-week event, held every other year
since 1960, is a celebration of all the
performing arts. During the Festival,
the Australian city of Adelaide turns
over all of its facilities (5 theaters and
halls, with a combined capactiy of
3,000) to international performers of
classical, jazz, and pop music, theater,
dance, and mime. All together, the
Festival program offers more than 300
performances of over 100 different
productions, concerts, recitals, and
special events. In addition, there are
many free outdoor activities planned for
family groups. Major art exhibitions
fill the city's galleries, and the Festival
also sponsors a Writers' Week.
Past performers include the Israel Philharmonic with Zubin Mehta, Les Per-
cussions de Strasbourg, Frans Brüggen,
Lucia Popp, Oscar Peterson, Peter
Schumann's Bread and Puppet Theater,
the Polish Mime Ballet Theater, and
many native Australian artists.
Director: Christopher Hunt
Accommodations/other items of interest
in area: Among the hotels in Adelaide
are the Gateway Hotel, Oberoi Hotel,
and Travelodge.
The area around Adelaide is a major
wine-producing region in Australia.
Ticket information: Tickets for individual events range in price from 3 to
15 Australian dollars
How to get there: There are flights to
Adlelaide from Sydney, Melbourne,
and Perth

Festival of Perth

University of Western Australia,
Nedlands, Western Australia 6009,
Australia
Classical, opera, jazz, folk, rock, and all
performing and visual arts
Mid-February through mid-March
The Festival of Perth is the oldest and
largest in the Southern Hemisphere. The
1980 Festival will be the 28th annual
event and will consist of over 500 performances in a 4-week period. On a
typical day there are up to 5 concerts—
classical, jazz, rock—several club performances, 2 film showings, a stage production, and a poetry reading. There are
many indoor facilities, with seating capacities from 200 to 8,000, and the outdoor Supreme Court Garden, which can
accommodate up to 30,000 people. In
recent years the Festival has been host
to a wide range of performers and artists,
including the Royal Shakespeare Company, Tom Stoppard, Count Basie,
Oscar Peterson, the Israel Philharmonic
Orchestra, Sir Michael Tippett, Rod
Stewart, and the Netherlands Wind
Ensemble.
Director: David Blenkinsop
Sponsors: Federal, state and local
governments, commercial sponsors
Accommodations/other items of interest
in area: In central Perth there are the
Parmelia Hilton Hotel, the Sheraton
Hotel, and the New Esplanade Hotel,
among others.
There are many sporting facilities and
beaches; temperatures in the summer
range from 25 to 35° Celsius.
Ticket information: Tickets for indi-
vidual events range from 3 to 12
Australian dollars. They may be bought
at or ordered by mail from the Festival
Box Office, Perth Concert Hall, 5 St.
George's Terrace, Perth 6000, Australia.
How to get there: Perth is the capital
of Australia's largest state, Western
Australia, and it has an international
airport

The Festival of Sydney

Box Q44, QVB Post Office, York Street,
Sydney, N.S.W., Australia 2000
Jazz, classical, rock, folk
New Year's Eve to the end of January
The Festival of Sydney was founded in
1977 for the purpose of promoting the
city and stimulating its artistic, cultural,
and commercial life. Each year it presents approximately 200 bands, theater
groups, ethnic dancing groups and soloists. The month-long festival caters to
all musical tastes, with indoor and outdoor concerts of jazz, rock, classical, and
folk music, as well as dance.
The settings for indoor concerts include
Sydney Opera House, Seymour Centre,
and other city theaters (capacities range

from 600 to 2,000). Outdoor settings
include the Forecourt of Sydney Opera
House (capacity of 100,000), Hyde Park,
and central city.
Director: Mr. Stephan Hall
Sponsors: N.S.W. Government, Sydney
City Council, private sponsors
Accommodations: For information on
hotels and motels, contact the Australian
Tourist Commission and Quantas
Ticket information: Ticket prices range
from 2.50 to 8.50 Australian dollars, but
many events are privately sponsored
and thus are free to the public. Tickets
are available through local booking
agencies.

BELGIUM

Festival Van Vlaanderen
BRT, Omroepcentrum, A. Reyerslaan
52, B-1040, Brussels, Belgium
Classical, folk, jazz, dance
April through October
This festival boasts a varied program,
but the emphasis is on classical music.
Guest performers include important
European and American orchestras,
European Opera Houses, American,
Japanese, and European ballets, and soloists and chamber ensembles from around
the world. Concerts are held at several
concert halls, churches, abbeys, and
town halls, with accommodations for
from 200 to 5,000 people.
Director: Prof. Dr. Jan Briers
Accommodations/other items of interest
in area: For information on accommodations, write to the Festival. There is
camping.
Flanders and its Medieval cities are of
great interest. For more information
write to the Festival at the address
above.
Ticket information: Admission ranges
from $2 to $ 33. For information and
tickets write to the Festival at the above
address.

DENMARK

Aarhus Festival Week
Aarhus, Denmark
Theater, ballet, opera, rock
One week beginning with the 1st
Saturday in September
This festival features sports and exhibitions in addition to theater, ballet, and opera performances. In past years the Paris Orchestra with Daniel Barenboim, the Israeli Philharmonic with Zubin Mehta, and the Rolling Stones have been featured.
Activities now take place at various halls in Aarhus, although in 1981 a new concert hall with full facilities will be inaugerated.
Director: Paul Koch
Sponsor: Municipality of Aarhus
Accommodations: For information about accommodations in the Aarhus area, write to the Danish Tourist Board, at either 75 Rockefeller Plaza, New York, N.Y. 10019; or 3600 Wilshire Boulevard, Los Angeles, Calif. 90010. Also, the Aarhus Tourist Office, Town Hall, 8000 Aarhus C. Denmark.
Ticket information: For tickets and information, write to Aarhus Tourist Office, Town Hall, 8000 Aarhus C, Denmark (tel. 06-121600)

Copenhagen Youth Festival
Copenhagen, Denmark
Classical, folk
One week in mid-July (even-numbered years only)
The Festival is organized by a non-profit group, People to People, in order to bring together young people from all parts of the world to play, sing, and dance for themselves and the public. Festival participants may spend an extra week with private families in the Danish provinces before or after the Festival.
Orchestras, choirs, marching bands, brass bands, folk dance, and chamber music ensembles from more than 20 countries participate. Performances take place both indoors and outdoors.
Sponsor: People to People
Accommodations: Although there are many hotels in Copenhagen, they are usually heavily booked and reservations

are strongly recommended. The Scandinavia, Copenhagen Admiral, Copenhagen Penta, and Sheraton-Copenhagen are a few of the larger hotels.
Ticket information: Prices vary. For information, write to People to People, 9, Romersgade, DK-1362 Copenhagen K, Denmark

Roskilde Festival
Parkvej 5, 4000 Roskilde, Denmark
Contemporary, jazz, folk, popular, orchestral
Last weekend in June
Music of all kinds is offered copiously at this 3-day festival and is supplemented by additional features such as theater, circus, and films.
As many as 25,000 people from all over the world come for the event for which such groups as Kraan (West Germany), the Chieftains (Great Britain), Focus (Holland), and Dr. Hook (U.S.) have played in the years since the Festival's initiation in 1971.
Performances are staged in large tents which can hold up to 40,000 people.
Sponsor: Roskildefonden (a charity)
Accommodations/other items of interest in area: Information about accommodations can be obtained by writing Tourist Office, Fondens Bro by the Cathedral, DK-4000 Roskilde, Denmark.
A site of interest is the Roskilde Cathedral, built in the 1170s in Romanesque and Gothic styles.
Ticket information: Ticket prices are from 120 to 150 kroner. Tickets may be obtained up to 60 days in advance by writing Roskilde Festival, Parkvej 5, 4000 Roskilde, Denmark.

Tønder Folk and Jazz Festival
Sønderbyvej 38, DK-6270 Tønder, Denmark
Jazz and folk
August
Founded in 1975, the Tønder Festival's intention was to bring together both Scandinavian musicians and musicians from around the world.
Director: Carsten Panduro
Accommodations: Write to Tønder Tourist Office, Østergade 2A, DK-6270 Tønder, Denmark (tel. 04-721220)
Ticket information: For tickets, write to the Tønder Tourist Office

Vendsyssel (Jutland) Festival
Baudersvej 3, 9300 Saeby, Denmark
Classical (chamber and orchestral),
opera, jazz, folk
Mid-July through mid-August (6 weeks)
In its 8th season, the Vendsyssel Festival
presents a wide selection of musical
events covering recitals, orchestral concerts, chamber music, opera, jazz, and
folk music. Held every evening for a
6-week period in the summer, concert
sites alternate among 24 towns in the
Danish province of Jutland. Concerts
are held indoors in local churches and
concert halls. Performers are primarily
Scandinavian soloists and groups.
Director: Bodil Clausen
Accommodations/other items of interest
in area: There are many campsites and
picnic grounds in Jutland, which is
tourist-minded, and there are many
sightseeing possibilities for those interested in old churches and manor houses.
Ticket information: Tickets can only be
purchased just before each concert. For
a program, write to Bodil Clausen,
Baudersvej 3, 9300 Saeby, Denmark.
Tickets cost 20 kroner for adults (children are allowed free admission).

ENGLAND

Bath Festival
Linley House, 1 Pierrepont Place, Bath
BA1 1JY, Avon, England
Classical and other
Late spring
This 17-day festival in the elegant sur-
roundings of Bath was founded in 1947
as a children's festival. Since then, under
the leadership of Yehudi Menuhin, Sir
Thomas Beecham, and other notables,
it has become a major festival including
a full range of classical music, as well
as ballet, jazz, and theater. The current
director, Sir William Glock, aims to encourage people to try a wider range of
music than they otherwise would, to
"nudge them gently into the 2nd half
of the 20th century," as he once put it.
Concerts are held in a number of halls
and churches throughout Bath. Lectures, tours, demonstrations and social
events are also sponsored by the
Festival.
Director: Sir William Glock
Sponsor: John Fisher
Accommodations/other items of interest
in area: For information on hotels and
guest houses and a festival brochure,
write to the Festival, including return
postage. For information on camping
write to Department of Tourism and
Leisure Services, the Pump Room, Bath,
England.
Visitors to Bath may also be interested
in the Roman Baths and Georgian City.
Ticket information: Ticket prices range
from £.50 to £6

Brighton Festival
Brighton Festival Office, Marlborough
House, Old Steine, Brighton, BN1 1EQ,
England
Classical and other
May
The Brighton Festival ranges from large-
scale symphony concerts to a series of
chamber programs given by leading
specialist ensembles. The London Symphony Orchestra, BBC Symphony Orchestra, and Philharmonic Orchestra are
frequently featured at this festival. The
Festival also includes jazz concerts, art
and sculpture exhibitions, and theater
performances.
Concerts are held at Dome Brighton,

which seats 2,000; Brighton Center, which seats over 3,000; and at several Brighton churches.
Director: Mr. A. J. Hewlson
Sponsors: Brighton Borough Council and Arts Council of Great Britain
Accommodations/other items of interest in area: Hotel accommodations are available in Brighton.
Festival Fringe activities feature local talent and events for all the family, including sports. Brighton artists open their studios to the public.
Ticket information: Ticket prices range from £.80 to £5. Applications for festival tickets should be addressed to Dome Box Office, 29 New Road, Brighton, Sussex, BN1 1UG, England.

Bristol Festival
The Chequers, Hanham Mills, Bristol, England
Folk and jazz
Early to mid-June
This 3-day festival presents a balanced program including well-known artists and others less renowned, among the finest the British folk scene has to offer. In addition to folk and jazz concerts there is a music hall show, children's shows, theater, and folk dance displays. Events take place under large canopies but will be on outside stages if the weather is good.
Director: Reg Mann
Sponsor: Pilning Forge
Accommodations/other items of interest in area: Hotel accommodations are available in the center of Bristol. There is free camping, with all the amenities, near the Festival. Trailers are welcome. There is picnicking.
The Festival is on the very attractive banks of the Avon; boats are welcome. Information on the area can be obtained from Colston House, Bristol, England.
Ticket information: Day admission ranges from £2 to £3, weekend tickets are £6
How to get there: The Festival is on the outskirts of Bristol; it will be signposted

Camden Festival
St. Pancras Library, 100 Euston Road, London NW1 2AJ, England
Classical, jazz, modern dance, more
Last fortnight in March
The philosophy of Camden Festival programming is the presentation of un-

justifiably neglected works (especially to meet the ever-increasing interest in opera), to encourage the performance of contemporary compositions, and to give opportunities to the best of young talented musicians to appear before the public. A further aim in recent years has been the promotion of a wider range of events, including ethnic music and dance from other lands, jazz, and a week of musical and operetta films. The program also includes lunch-time recitals, choral concerts, puppet theater, and other events.
Events take place in various halls, theaters, and churches in the London Borough of Camden. Patrons are advised to bring winter clothing.
Director: Jack Henderson
Sponsor: London Borough of Camden
Accommodations: Accommodations are plentiful in London
Ticket information: Admission ranges from £.60 to £6

Cleveland Inter-TIE
27 Baker Street, Middlesbrough, Cleveland TS1 2LE, England
Classical and folk
Mid-July (even-numbered years)
Cleveland inter-TIE is an internationally known competitive music festival with classes ranging through the field of choral, vocal solo, instrumental solo and ensemble, folk song and dance. It includes both performances and competitions. Cleveland Inter-TIE was founded in 1966 as a biennial festival. Since 1976 it has been held in Middlesbrough Town Hall, which seats 1,200.
Director: Peter J. Shipp
Accommodations: For details on the program, tickets, and accommodations write to Peter J. Shipp (at the above address)

Harrogate International Festival
Royal Baths, Harrogate, North Yorkshire, England
Classical, jazz, dance, theater, film, literary, lectures
First 2 weeks in August
This annual international festival was founded in 1966 with the notion that it should include as many art forms as possible; and indeed, that is what has become of this event. For the first 2 weeks in August there are continuous performances of all the performing arts,

exhibitions of the visual arts, and lecture series. The event takes place in the Yorkshire town of Harrogate, and performances are held in varying indoor halls, with a combined seating capacity of 3,000. Performers who have taken part in the Festival in the past include Oscar Peterson, Pinchas Zukerman, the Young Vic Theatre Company, Shmuel Ashkenasi, Emanuel Hurwitz Chamber Orchestra, Itzhak Perlman, and Daniel Barenboim. The Festival also features current films.
Director: Clive Wilson
Sponsor: Harrogate Festival of Arts and Sciences Ltd.
Accommodations: For information regarding the many hotels in the area, write to Tourist Information Centre, Royal Baths Assembly Rooms, Crescent Road, Harrogate HG1 2RR, England; or call 65912 in Harrogate
Ticket information: Tickets for individual performances range in price from £.75 to £10. They may be bought at the box office or purchased in advance.

International Festival of Youth Orchestras and the Performing Arts
24 Cadogan Square, London SW1X OJP, England
Classical, dance, jazz
August
This 2-week festival brings to Scotland youth orchestras, dance groups, choirs and bands from around the world. These talented young people give performances of a quite varied repertoire. In addition, several first-rate professional groups perform.
Concerts are held in halls and theaters in Aberdeen, which seat from 200 to 1,500 and outdoors in Hazlehead Park, with a capacity of up to 10,000.
Director: Lionel W. Bryer
Sponsors: City of Aberdeen District Council and private firms
Accommodations/other items of interest in area: For information on accommodations write to Information Centre, St. Nicholas House, Aberdeen, Scotland. Aberdeen, an ancient university and cathedral town, is the 3rd largest fishing port in Britain and a leading Scottish holiday resort.
Ticket information: Admission ranges from £.25 to £5. There are several free concerts. For information and tickets write to IFYO Box Office, 61-65 Saint

Nicholas St., Aberdeen, Scotland.
How to get there: The Festival takes place in Aberdeen and throughout Scotland

Leeds College of Music Festival
C.L.C.M., Cookridge St., Leeds, England
Classical, jazz, opera
April
The purpose of this 9-day festival is to provide the general public with the opportunity to hear the range of music offered by students and staff of Leeds College of Music. The program includes classical music, jazz, and opera performed by ensembles, orchestras, choirs, and soloists from the College of Music. Visiting soloists are also featured. Concerts take place in Leeds Town Hall, Leeds Institute Gallery, and Kitson College Hall.
Director: Joseph Stones, A.R.M.C.M.
Sponsor: City of Leeds
Accommodations: Accommodations in Leeds are available at Queen's in City Square and Merrion Hotel in Merrion Centre. There is no camping.
Ticket information: Admission ranges from about £.50 to £2. Tickets can be obtained from the college by mail or in person.

Norfolk and Norwich Triennial Festival of Music and the Arts
Theatre Royal, Theater St., Norwich NR3 1AD, England
Classical, jazz, folk, dance, theater
Mid-October
The Festival made its debut in 1824 and over the years attracted musicians who are now legends—Verdi, Dvorak, Liszt, and Paganini. By 1961 it widened its scope to include theater, jazz, fireworks, and exhibitions. In recent years visual arts and other events such as folk music, revue, mime, and satire have become part of a 10-day celebration. Recent performers of note have included the Philharmonia Orchestra and the Festival Chorus, the BBC Concert Orchestra, the Royal Philharmonic Orchestra, the Philip Jones Brass and Wind Ensemble, the Amadeus Quartet, and the Parikian Trio.
Director: Norman Del Mar
Accommodations/other items of interest in area: Information about accommodations can be obtained from Incoming

Tourist Services, 26 Princes St., Norwich NR3 1AD, England.
The city of Norwich has many historic sites, including the Music House, the oldest house in Norwich, built in 1186.
Ticket information: Ticket prices for events range from £1.25 to £5.50

FINLAND

Helsinki Festival
Unioninkatu 28, SF 00100 Helsinki 10, Finland
Classical music, dance, pop-jazz, opera, ballet
Late August to early September
Hundreds of thousands of people, many from abroad, now attend this festival each year—a comeback from difficulties in the late '60s. It is the only Finnish institution with the means to invite the leading foreign orchestras, theater companies, and experimental dance and drama groups of Finland; because of this, the Festival acts as a showcase for the Finnish arts.
Participants in recent years include Svjatoslav Richter, Emil Gilels, New York Philharmonic Orchestra, Dance Theater of Harlem, Nacional Ballet de Cuba, Israel Philharmonic, Isaac Stern, Alvin Ailey Dance Theater, and Fortune's Fire, from London.
The main concert hall is Finlandia Hall—planned by Alvar Aalto—with a 1,718 seat capacity. Some concerts are held outdoors in Kaivopuisto Park.
Director: Seppo Kimanen
Sponsors: State of Finland and City of Helsinki
Accommodations: Information is available from the Helsinki Tourist Office
Ticket information: Ticket prices vary from 15 to 50 Finnish marks. Advance booking from Musiikki Fazer, Aleksanterinkatu 11 SF 00100 Helsinki 10, Finland, or Ticket Service, Mannerheimintie 5, SF 00100 Helsinki 10, Finland.

Kuopio Dance and Music Festival
Kuntokuja 4H, 70200 Kuopio 20, Finland
Dance and music
Early June (1 week)
This event, in its 10th year, has already become a dance and brass music happening in the country of Finland, where this festival starts off the series of cultural events that comprise the Finlandia Festivals. Although the Festival concentrates primarily on dance, featuring Finnish dance companies, famous international visitors, dance courses, lessons, seminars , and daily puppet shows for

children, the event also sponsors a
nationwide brass band contest, and both
brass band and organ concerts.
These events take place in an uncovered
facility which seats 4,000 to 5,000
people; it is suggested that patrons bring
foul-weather clothing.
Director: Anneli Patomaki
Sponsors: Town of Kuopio, Ministry
of Education
Accommodations: Camping is permitted
in the vicinity, and costs 20 Finnish
marks per night. For information about
all types of accommodations, write to
Kuopio Tourist Service, Haapaniemen-
katu 17, SF 70100 Kuipio 10, Finland
·(tel. (9)71-121411).
For information on competitions, contact Kuopio Dance and Music Festival,
Kuntokuja 4H, SF-70200 Kuopio 20,
Finland.
Ticket information: Tickets range in
price from 20 to 40 Finnish marks and
may be purchased in advance by contacting Kuopion Kaupunginteatteri, Niiraian-
katu 2, 70600 Kuopio 60, Finland (tel.
(9)71-220210)

Turku Music Festival
Sibeliuksenkatu 2 B, 20110 Turku 11,
Finland
Classical, rock, folk, jazz, opera
August
This 6-day festival on the beautiful west
coast of Finland was begun in 1960.
Every year it presents about 30 concerts
which are held in local concert halls, a
castle, museums, and parks. The program is varied, ranging from chamber
music concerts by renowned ensembles
such as the Kodaly Quartet or the Alban
Berg Quartet, to rock concerts in
Ruissalo National Park with audiences
of up to 30,000.
Director: Alarik Repo
Accommodations/other items of interest
in area: For information on accommodations in Turku write to Kaupungin
matkailutomisto, Kasityolaiskatu 4,
20100 Turku 10, Finland. There is
camping at a cost of 10 Finnish marks
per person or 20 Finnish marks per
family. Facilities include cafe, cooking
stall, sauna, etc. Hook-ups are available
for 100 trailers.
Turku, on Finland's west coast, has
several museums, a Medieval cathedral,
and a 13th century castle.
Ticket information: Admission ranges
from about 12 to 30 Finnish marks, depending on the event. For information
and tickets write to Music Fazer, Human-
listonkatu 5, 20100 Turku 10, Finland.

FRANCE

Choregies d'Orange
B.P. A-Z, Place Freres Mounet, F-84100
Orange, France
Opera, classical, jazz
Classical: Early August (7 days)
Jazz: Early July (4 days)
This annual festival consists of 2 parts—
the 4-day series of jazz concerts in early
July, and the 7-day series of classical
music concerts and operas in August.
All concerts are given in the uncovered,
ancient Roman amphitheatre of Orange,
which seats 8,000 spectators. Among
the jazz musicians who have appeared
here in recent years are B. B. King and
Lionel Hampton. The Festival has also
been host to the Philharmonic Choir
of London, the Orchestra and Choir
of the Munich Opera, and vocalist Teresa
Zylis-Gara.
Director: Max Ferri
Accommodations: For information
about hotel and campground accommodations in the area, contact Syndicat
d'Initiative, Cours A. Briand, F-84100
Orange, France (tel. 340600)
Ticket information: Tickets to individual
events cost from 15 to 250 francs. They
can be obtained in advance by writing.

Festival de Bellac
1 bis rue Louis Jouvet, 87300 Bellac,
France
Classical, jazz, dance, theater
June and July
Director: Andre Cluzeau, President of
Les Amis du Festival de Bellac
Ticket information: Write to Pavillon
du Festival, 1 bis rue Louis Jouvet,
87300 Bellac, France

Festival of Carpentras
Hotel de Ville, 84200, Carpentras,
France
Popular, jazz, classical, theater, ballet,
folklore
Mid-July to mid-August
This performing arts festival takes place
each year in the French town of Carpentras, located approximately 60 miles
N. of Marseilles. The event consists of
a series of 25 concerts—both classical
and popular—operas, plays, recitals, and
ballet performances, held during a 1-

month period. Past performers at the
event have included Nureyev, Pink
Floyd, the National Ballet of Brazil, and
Michel Polnareff.
Performances are held outdoors, at a
facility which seats 1,700.
Director: Dr. Pierre Girard
Accommodations: Among the many
hotels in Carpentras are the Bureau de
Théâtre, Hôtel du Cours, Hôtel du
Fiacre, and Hôtel de France. Reserva-
tions may be made through the hotel
office in nearby Avignon (tel. 816380).
Ticket information: Tickets can be
ordered by mail, starting on July 1, by
writing to Service de Relations Publiques,
Festival, Hôtel de Ville, 84200, Carpen-
tras, France; or by calling 90-630089

Festival de Marais-Paris
68 rue Francois-Miron, 75004, Paris,
France (tel. 887-7431)
Classical, jazz, popular, folk, theater
Mid-June to mid-July
The month-long Festival de Marais celebrated its 16th anniversary in 1979.
The Festival site is Paris' 4th district,
and performances are held in churches,
concert halls, courtyards, and gardens
of that area. This is a performing arts
festival which offers chamber music,
theater, jazz, poetry recitals, café theater, puppet theater for children, expositions, and a yearly colloquium on
musicology. Those who have performed
here in recent years include Tamás
Vásáry, Strasbourg's Collegium Musicum, the Nas Ensemble, the French
Vocal Quartet, and the Trio Risler. The
event also sponsors outdoor folklore
exhibitions, mime, and commedia dell'
arte, all of which take place in the streets
of Marais.
Director: Michel Raude
Ticket information: Admission ranges
from 8 to 50 francs; box offices open a
half hour before each performance;
advance tickets can be purchased in
various locations in Paris; they can also
be obtained by writing or calling Centre
d'Information du Festival de Marais,
68 rue Francois-Miron, Paris, France
(tel. 887-7431)
How to get there: The different festival sites are all in Paris' 4th district;
the Metro stops in that area are
Rambuteau, Hôtel de Ville, Pont Marie,
Saint Paul le Marais, and Bastille

OUTDOOR PERFORMANCE AT THE VERSAILLES (PHOTO PREVIOUS PAGE)

Festival d'Occitanie
30, rue de la Banque, F-82000
Montauban, France
Classical, theater, folk, jazz
End of June to early July

HONG KONG

Festival of Asian Arts
City Hall, 5th floor, High Block, Edinburgh Place, Hong Kong
Various performing and visual arts
October to November
The Festival consists of Asian cultural presentations covering both the performing and visual arts
Director: G. N. Richardson
Sponsor: Urban Council, Hong Kong
Accommodations: Write to Hong Kong Tourist Association, P.O. Box 2597, G.P.O. Hong Kong. No camping is allowed.
Ticket information: Maximum price is about $6.50. Tickets may be obtained by writing or in person at Hong Kong City Hall.

HUNGARY

Szeged Open-Air Festival
Festival site: Dom Square, Szeged
Mailing address: Attila u. 11, Szeged,
H-6722, Hungary
Opera, chamber music, drama, ballet,
folk
Mid-July to mid-August
The inspiration for the Szeged Open-Air
Festival came from the construction of
the Szeged Cathedral in 1929. In 1931,
the Budapest National Theater went to
Szeged to perform a Hungarian passion
play in the square in front of the cathedral, and the Festival grew into an international event by 1935, when Pietro
Mascagni conducted his *Cavalleria
Rusticana* at the event. In 1939, World
War II wiped out this festival, and it
took 20 years for the reopening of the
event. Since that reopening, it has grown
into a month-long event which concentrates primarily on opera, but also offers
a diverse program of chamber music,
drama, folk dance, and pop concerts,
called the Szeged Youth Festival. Performers here have included Hungarian
artists, the Belgrade Opera, the Bologne
Opera, the Bolshoi, and the Moisyev
Ensemble.
Large performances are held in the
Cathedral Square, an uncovered facility
which can accommodate 6,200 spectators; recitals are held in small indoor
halls.
Director: Mihály Horváth
Accommodations/other items of interest
in area: Hotel Hungaria, Hotel Royal,
and Hotel Tisza are in Szeged. In addition, there is one campground, with no
trailer facilities, in the city; the cost is
60 to 75 forints per night.
There are several historic churches in
the city; Szeged is also near the Tisza
River, which has many beaches.
Ticket information: Ticket prices range
from 20 to 90 forints; they can be obtained in the Central Booking Office in
Budapest and at IBUSZ travel agencies
throughout Hungary

ICELAND

Reykjavik Arts Festival
Gimli, P.O. Box 623, Reykjavik, Iceland
Classical, jazz, pop, folk, dance, theater
Late May through mid-June (even-num-
bered years)
This 2-to-3-week festival, held biannu-
ally, sponsors as many as 24 major concerts. Festival guest artists have included
Vladimir Ashkenazy, who is also an ad-
visor to the Festival, Victoria de los
Angeles, Yehudi Menuhin, Renata
Tebaldi, Daniel Barenboim, Andre
Previn, Itzhak Perlman, Pinchas Zucker-
man, and John Williams and the London
Symphony Orchestra. In addition to
classical music there are folk, jazz, and
pop concerts. Regional musicians, poets,
and singers hold numerous minor con-
certs.
The Festival also includes art exhibits
and drama. In fact, for the duration, all
Reykjavik is given over to the celebra-
tion! Events are held in halls throughout
Reykjavik.
Director: Ornolfur Arnason
Sponsors: Icelandic Government, City
of Reykjavik, Associations of Icelandic
Artists, all major cultural institutions in
Iceland

IRELAND

Belfast Festival at Queen's
Festival House, 8 Malone Road, Belfast
9, Northern Ireland
Classical, folk, jazz, theater, others
November
This 2-week festival presents more than
100 events in over 10 halls, theaters, and
studios throughout Belfast, from Whitla
Hall which seats 1,200, to smaller set-
tings such as Hays Folk Club or Guinness
Spot. The Festival tries to strike a good
balance between something new each
year, and the return of old favorites.
There are many 1st-rate performances.
The wide range of events includes
classical and folk music concerts, jazz,
theater, puppet shows, lectures, poetry,
films, and exhibitions. Children's programs are also scheduled.
Director: Michael Barnes
Sponsors: Arts Council of Northern
Ireland, Queens Univ., Guiness, others
Accommodations: Accommodations are
available at Wellington Part Hotel,
Malone Road, Belfast, and at Europa
Hotel, Great Victoria St., Belfast.
Ticket information: Admission ranges
from £.50 to £4

ITALY

**Rome Festival Orchestra—Festivale
Estata**
Vicola del Piomba, 7 00187 Roma,
Italia or Via del Babuino, 79 00187
Rome, Italy
Classical and jazz
End of June to 3rd week of July
Festivale Estata is a major festival begun
in 1969 which provides concerts in
various Basilicas with excellent acoustics
in central Rome. The Basilicas usually
seat less than 1,000.
Performers in recent years have included
James Stagliano, Conrad Klemm, George
Zazofsky, Betty Oberacker, and Jean-
nette Ferrell.
Director: Fritz Maraffi
Sponsors: Rome Festival Orchestra,
Ltd., and Societa Rome Festival
Orchestra
Accommodations: Write to the Festival
before June for hotel recommendations.
After June 1, phone 678-1268 in Rome.
Ticket information: Tickets cost under
$5. Write (prior to June 1) to Via del
Babuino, 79 00187 Roma, Italia, or
170 Broadway, Suite 201, New York,
N. Y. 10038.

JAPAN

World Popular Song Festival
3-24-22 Shimo-Meguro, Meguro-ku,
Tokyo 153, Japan
Popular Music
Early November
Since its inception in 1970, the World
Popular Song Festival has grown fast.
Performers are selected from applica-
tions which come in from all over the
world. Such notables as Elton John and
Glen Campbell from the U.S. have per-
formed at this unique Asian song
festival.
The Festival is a 3-day contest with
prizes, and, sometimes, fame for the
winners.
The event is held in mammoth Nippon
Budokan Hall, an arena with a capacity
for 13,000.
Sponsor: Yamaha Music Foundation
Accommodations: The Festival site is
in central Tokyo; many hotels can be
found in the area
Ticket information: Starting in September, tickets will be sold at ticket bureaus
in Tokyo

LUXEMBOURG

Festival International Echternach
Luxconcert 9, route de Luxembourg,
Dalheim, Luxembourg
Classical and jazz
June to July
Many of the world's well-known musi-
cians have appeared at the Echternach
Festival. Among these are Isaac Stern,
Gidon Kremer, Christa Ludwig, Jean-
Pierre Rampal, Elisabeth Schwarzkopf,
Alexis Weissenberg, Vladimir Ashkenazy,
the Melos Quartet, Lazar Berman, and
Montserrat Caballe.
There are 1,500 seats in Echternach
Basilica and 1,000 other seats in
churches in the area where festival
events take place.
Director: Arthur Wildanger
Accommodations/other items of interest
in area: Hotels in the Echternach area
include the Bel-Air, des Ardennes, du
Parc, and La Petie Marquise. Camping
is allowed.
Echternach is a medieval town with
many attractions nearby.
Ticket information: Prices range between 150 to 480 francs

MARTINIQUE

Martinique Carrefour Mondial de la Guitare (Martinique World's Crossroads' Festival of Guitar)
Avenue Frantz Fanon, Bellevue, 97200
Fort de France, Martinique FWI
Classical and jazz guitar
December
This international classical and jazz guitar festival takes place each December on the island of Martinique, and in addition to concert offerings, holds an international competition of guitar interpretations. Past performers have included Harlem Jazz Guitar, Paco Pena, Fredy Reyna, Alberto Ponce, Alirio Diaz, John Williams, Leo Brouwer, and Michael Lorimer.
Performances are held in a hall which seats 680.
Director: Fanny Auguiac
Accommodations: For information about accommodations, write to C.F.P.A., Pointe de Jaham, 97200 Scheolcher, Martinique FWI
Ticket information: Tickets may be ordered in advance by writing to C.M.A.C., Avenue Frantz Fanon, Bellevue, 97200 Fort de France, Martinique FWI. Tickets cost 30 or 40 French francs.

NETHER-LANDS

Holland Festival
Willemsparkweg 52, 1071 HJ
Amsterdam, Holland (tel. 020-722245)
Performing arts (music: classical, chamber, opera, jazz, folk)
First 3 weeks in June
The Holland Festival of the performing arts has been the yearly cultural highlight in the Netherlands ever since it was created shortly after World War II, in 1947. The parent cities of Amsterdam, the Hague, and Rotterdam are the sponsors of this event, which takes place over a 3-week period each June. During this time, there are daily performances of classical music—symphonic and chamber—opera, theater, dance, puppet theater, contemporary theater music, folk music, jazz, and poetry.
In recent years the Festival has been host to an assortment of Dutch and international performers and artists, including the Netherlands Opera, the Fires of London, the Alban Berg Quartet, the John Alldis Choir, the Kuyken Ensemble, Merce Cunningham and Dance Company, the Netherlands Dance Theater, and the Tandarica Theatre of Bucharest.
Performances are held in the theaters and concert halls of Amsterdam, the Hague, and Rotterdam.
Director: Frans de Ruiter
Sponsors: Dutch government and the cities of Amsterdam, the Hague, and Rotterdam
Accommodations/other items of interest in area: Information about accommodations in the Netherlands can be obtained through the Netherlands National Tourist Office in Europe and the United States (New York and San Francisco). Holland is very rich in museums; in Amsterdam alone there are the Rijksmuseum, the Rembrant House, the Van Gogh Museum, and the Museum of Modern Art.
Ticket information: Tickets can be acquired starting on May 30 at various theater box offices in Amsterdam, the Hague, and Rotterdam. Brochures and tickets can be ordered by mail by contacting Holland Festival Booking Office,

14 Haarlemsestraat, Scheveningen, the Netherlands. Prices range from 2.50 to 25 guilders.
How to get there: Information concerning travel arrangements in the Netherlands can be obtained by writing to the Netherlands National Tourist Office in Europe and the U. S.

Vondelpark-Openluchttheater
Jeugdzaken-Z.I.A., Singel 158, Amsterdam, Netherlands
Classical, folk, jazz, dance, pop
June through August
The Open Air Theater in the beautiful Vondelpark in the center of Amsterdam offers a varied summer program. On Wednesdays there are classical lunchtime concerts, on Thursdays, folk or jazz concerts; there is dance on Fridays and Saturdays and various programs on Saturdays and Sundays.
The Open Air Theater has a covered stage, bench seating for 600 people, and space for a total of 3,000 people.
Director: Rene Penders
Sponsor: City of Amsterdam
Accommodations: Lodging is readily available in the center of Amsterdam. There are several camp sites in Amsterdam, but not in the Vondelpark.
Ticket information: Admission is free
How to get there: Vondelpark is in the center of Amsterdam

POLAND

Intervision Festival in Sopot
Intervision Festival, Polskie Radio i Telewizja, ul. Woronicza 17, 00-950, Warsaw, Poland
Popular
Late August (3 days)
Founded in 1961, this international pop music festival has been host to Joan Baez, Manolo Escobar, Nancy Wilson, Jean Claude Pascal, Samantha Jones, and all the leading Polish musicians. The event is held for 3 days each August in the open-air Opera Lesna in Sopot, Poland, in a covered facility with a seating capacity of 5,000. Sponsored by the Polish Committee for Radio and Television, the programs are broadcast over both media; it has been reported that in the Soviet Union alone, over 40 million television viewers see the event each year.
Director: Lech B. Sikorski
Sponsor: Polish Radio and Television
Accommodations/other items of interest in area: Hotel Orbis-Grand is at ul. Powstánców Warszawy 8/12, in Sopot, Poland. For information about camping, write to the Tourist Office Orbis, Gdánsk, Poland.
The Old City of nearby Gdánsk is recommended for sightseers.
Ticket information: The cost is 1,000 zlotys for 4 concerts; for tickets, write to the Tourist Office Orbis, Gdánsk, Poland

TOM PAXTON.

SCOTLAND

Edinburgh Festival Fringe
Fringe Office, 170 High Street, Edinburgh, Scotland
Recitals, dance, plays, classical, folk, popular music
Mid-August to early September
The Fringe began in a small way in 1947, at the same time as the official Edinburgh International Festival. Eight theater companies decided to offer shows in addition to the 1st festival program. They performed in small halls around Edinburgh, doing work of their own choice and at their own financial risk. The groups attracted audiences and each year after 1947 more companies turned up uninvited and unheralded to do shows. In 1959 the groups came together to form the Festival Fringe Society, in effect an artists' cooperative.
Now more than 300 groups perform plays, recitals, dance pieces, revues, mime, films, exhibitions, concerts—over 5,000 performances crammed into 3 weeks, played in 107 halls, theaters, schools, churches in Edinburgh—in what amounts to the largest arts festival in the world. As many as 300,000 tickets are sold each year.
Director: Alistair Moffat
Sponsor: Festival Fringe Society
Accommodations/other items of interest in area: For information about accommodations, write to Fringe Office, 170 High St., Edinburgh, Scotland.
The Edinburgh International Festival and the Edinburgh International Film Festival also take place at this time.
Ticket information: Tickets cost from £.50 to £2. For tickets, write to Box YQ, Festival Fringe Society, 170 High St., Edinburgh, Scotland.

Edinburgh International Festival
21, Market Street, Edinburgh EH1 1BW, Scotland
Classical, opera, jazz, dance, folk, theater
Mid-August through early September
When the Edinburgh Festival began in 1947 it was a gesture of cultural defiance in a world made weary by war, misery and destruction, and quite a number of the citizens of Edinburgh thought that the city fathers were quite mad to get themselves involved in the expense and complexity of producing what has become the world's most comprehensive arts festival. At present, the Festival offers about 200 performances by first-rate orchestras, chamber ensembles, opera, dance, and jazz companies, and by individual performers of both classical and folk music. There is also theater, poetry, film, and exhibitions. Events take place throughout Edinburgh.
Director: John Drummond
Sponsors: Edinburgh City and District Council, Scottish Arts Council, others
Accommodations/other items of interest in area: For information on lodging and camping write to Edinburgh Tourist Accommodation Service, 9, Cockburn Street, Edinburgh EH1 1BR, Scotland. Enclose 25p reservation fee.
Edinburgh is the capital of Scotland, full of buildings of historical and architectural interest, one of the most beautiful cities in the world and the gateway to the glorious scenery of the Scottish Highlands and borders.
Ticket information: Admission ranges from 75p to £12.50. Tickets can be obtained by mail.

SWITZERLAND TURKEY

International Festival of Lausanne

Théâtre Municipal de Lausanne, case postale 3972, 1003 Lausanne, Switzerland
Classical, jazz, ballet, opera
Approximately 30 programs in May and June
This international festival was founded in 1956 with the goal of offering its audience a diverse artistic program; the founder placed equal emphasis on classical and jazz concerts, opera, and ballet, and the result is that during the Festival's annual 2-month run, 40,000 people attend the various offerings. All performances are held in the Beaulieu Theater, which seats 1,980. Past guest artists have included Maurice Béjart's 20th-Century Ballet, Memphis Slim, the Kirov Opera, and the Royal Philharmonic Orchestra of London.
Director: Manuel Roth
Accommodations: There are many hotels in Lausanne
Ticket information: Tickets for individual concerts range in price from 10 to 60 francs, and may be bought, starting in March, at any booking office in Switzerland, or by writing.

Istanbul International Festival

Inönü Caddesi, 92-94 Mithatpasa, Apt. d3, Gümüssuyu-Taksim, Istanbul, Turkey (tel. 45-1912)
Classical (orchestral and chamber), opera, traditional, ballet, theater, folk-dancing, art exhibitions
Mid-June to mid-July
This international festival was founded in 1973, the year that the Turkish Republic celebrated its 50th anniversary. Since that time, it has taken place every year, over a 1-month period. The central aim of the Festival is the presentation of both traditional and modern works of music, ballet, and theater from all over the world, and the list of artists and presentations at this event in past years bears this out. Among them are the Leningrad Philharmonic Orchestra, the Sofia State Opera Choir, the Munich State Opera Ballet, Peter Shaffer's *Equus*, Yehudi Menuhin, and Jean-Pierre Rampal.
Concerts and other performances are held in Istanbul's historical palaces, chateaux, and fortresses; in addition, there is an open-air facility which seats 4,000.
Director: Mr. Aydin Gün
Sponsors: Turkish Republic and private enterprises
Accommodations: There are many hotels in Istanbul
Ticket information: Tickets range in price from 50 to 200 lire for individual events

WALES

Llangollen International Musical Eisteddfod

Eisteddfod Office, Llangollen, Clwyd, Wales
Choral and folk
July
This international festival of competitions, 1st held in 1947, developed from the wish to make a contribution to world peace following World War II. Each year since then some 200 choirs from 30 to 40 countries have performed works from the chief European schools of composition. Folk singers and dancers from the same countries have been judged on the authenticity and vitality of their performances. Each year many thousands come to North Wales to experience this cosmopolitan musical event. Performances are held under a canopy with a capacity of 10,000. Patrons are advised to bring a raincoat and strong shoes.
Director: J. N. Bowen, Chairman; Arwel Hughes, Music Director
Accommodations/other items of interest in area: For information on accommodations and food one may write to Hon. Secretary, Hospitality Committee, at the Festival address. There are sites for camping and caravans.
North Wales is a beautiful area to visit, with many items of historical interest.
Ticket information: For tickets write to Hon. Secretary, Tickets Committee, at the Festival address. Season tickets are from £10 to £15, while reserved tickets for individual performances are £1.20 and £1.60. Unreserved seats or ground admission, not available in advance, are £.50 for adults and £.30 for children under 15.

WEST GERMANY

International May Festival

c/o Hessisches Staatstheater, Postfach 3247, D-6200 Wiesbaden, West Germany
Classical (opera), jazz, drama, ballet
End of April to end of May
Director: Christoph Groszer

Musicher Herbst

Theater in Pfalzbau, Berliner Str. 30, 6700 Ludwigshafen am Rhein, West Germany
Dance, opera, jazz, theater
September to October
This series of concerts has featured such guest artists as the Vienna State Opera, Thorlanerchor Leipzig, the National Ballet of Amsterdam, the State Opera of Stutgart, the State Opera of Sofia, and the Peking Opera. Events are held in a theater which can seat 1,200, and in a chamber theater seating 400.
Director: Dr. Rainer Antoine
Accommodations/other items of interest in area: Accommodations in Ludwigshafen are available at City-Hotel Europa, Ludwigsplatz 5-6; Pfalz-Hotel Excelsior, Lorientallee; and Hotel Ramada, Pasadena-Allee 4. There is no camping or picnicking.
Of interest in the area are Heidelberg, Rococo Theater Schwetzingen, the Rhine area, BASF Center of Capital Industry, and the city of Manheim.
Ticket information: Tickets are 6 to 75 deutsche marks. They are available at the box office of the theater.

YUGOSLAVIA

Days of Yugoslav Light Music (Dani Jugoslavenske Zabavne Muzike)
c/o "Mozaik", 51410 Opatija, M. Tita 8, Yugoslavia
Light music (instrumental, chansons, and rock)
Mid-March
This 4-day music festival presents a variety of light music, including Yugoslav big bands, singers, and rock groups.
The Festival, held annually since 1958, presents seminars and lectures on light music for radio producers, in addition to its concerts.
The concerts are held indoors, and seating capacity is 1,000.
Director: Marijana Oppenheim
Sponsors: Yugoslav Radio Television and the city of Opatija
Accommodations: Opatija is a holiday resort with 25 hotels
Ticket information: Admission ranges from 80 to 100 dinars; tickets are available at the door

Festival Vojnih Orkestara
Skupstina Grade Sarajevo, Mis Irzina 1, 71000 Sarajevo, Yugoslavia
Military band festival
First week of June
This annual week-long military band festival is in its 12th year and features 26 international bands in addition to domestic ones. The program consists of a parade of all the bands through the streets of Sarajevo, and in addition, each participating band holds an individual concert in City Hall, which can accommodate 5,000 spectators. There is also a competition is which the best march is chosen by the European Radio and Television Union of Geneva.
Director: Borislav Lilkac
Sponsor: City Assembly of Sarajevo
Accommodations: There are many hotels in Sarajevo, among them the Hotel Europa and Hotel Bristol
Ticket information: Admission is free

International Slovene Song Festival
c/o Radiotelevision Ljubljana, Tavcarjeva 17, 61000 Ljubljana, Yugoslavia
Pop and other
Second week of October
This event has developed into an international event through the cooperative effort of various European radio stations, which send artists to perform each year in Ljubljana. There they join Yugoslavian performers in a series of concerts held in an indoor hall which seats 3,500. Samantha Sang, Linda Lewis, Vince Hall, the Rubettes, Gianni Nazzaro, and Les Troubadors are among those who have performed at the Festival in recent years.
Sponsors: Radiotelevision Ljubljana, RTV Ljubljana Records
Accommodations: Hotel Union and the Holiday Inn are among the many hotels in Ljubljana
Ticket information: Tickets may be purchased by writing to Organizing Committee, International Slovene Song Festival, c/o Radiotelevision Ljubljana, Tavcarjeva 17, 61000 Ljubljana, Yugoslavia. Tickets cost 100 dinars.

FOREIGN CURRENCY CONVERSION TABLE

Ticket-price information for countries outside the U.S.

Ticket prices are usually given in the currency of the country in which the festival is held. Thus, if a concert is held in Belgium, for example, and the ticket price is "10 francs," it should be assumed that the monetary unit referred to is the Belgian franc, not the French franc. The exception to this is for countries that use dollars as monetary units; the particular country is named for clarification: "10 Australian dollars." (When the dollar symbol [$] is used, it always refers to U.S. dollars.)

The rates of exchange given in the table below are as of March 1980. Since rates fluctuate widely, it is advisable to obtain current information at the time of your trip abroad.

Units of Foreign Currency per U.S. $

Australia (dollar) .91
Austria (schilling) 12.83
Belgium (franc) 29.13
Britain, (England, Scotland,
    Wales) (pound) .45
Canada (dollar) 1.16
Denmark (krone) 5.60
East Germany (mark) 6.00
Finland (Finnish mark) 3.79
France (franc) 4.20
Hungary (forint) 20.35
Ireland (pound) .49
Israel (pound) 39.22
Italy (lira) 833.00
Japan (yen) 248.05
Luxembourg (franc) 30.00
Netherlands (guilder) 1.97
New Zealand (dollar) 1.03
Norway (krone) 4.99
Poland (zloty) 31.79
Switzerland (franc) 1.71
Turkey (lira) 70.00
West Germany (deutsche mark) 1.85
Yugoslavia (dinar) 19.50

INDEX

Photo Credits:
Photographs are by Herbert Wise unless
otherwise indicated.
Pages 4-5 courtesy of the Aspen Music Festival.
Pages 14-15 courtesy of the Aspen Music Festival.
Page 27 courtesy of the Carmel Bach Festival.
Page 35 courtesy of the Victoria Symphony
Summer Festival.
Pages 44-45 courtesy of the New Orleans Jazz
and Heritage Festival.
Pages 140-141 courtesy of the Caramoor Festival.
Page 149 courtesy of the Carmel Bach Festival.
Pages 162-163 courtesy of the German
Information Center.
Page 169 courtesy of the Round Top Festival.
Page 187 courtesy of the British Tourist
Authority.
Pages 226-227 courtesy of the French Embassy
Press and Information Center.